Biblical Meditations
for Ordinary Time
Weeks 23-34

by
Carroll Stuhlmueller, C.P.

PAULIST PRESS
New York/Ramsey

Library of Congress
Catalog Card Number: 84-60390

ISBN: 0-8091-2648-6

Published by Paulist Press
545 Island Road, Ramsey, N.J. 07446

Printed and bound in the
United States of America

Contents

PART THREE—Feasts and Solemnities of Ordinary Time
(Weeks 23-34)

Dedicated
to
Emma Stuhlmueller
Albert H. Stuhlmueller
Ferd and Patty Stuhlmueller

Seasonal Table of Principal Celebrations of the Liturgical Year

Year	Sunday Cycle	Weekday Cycle	Ash Wednesday	Easter	Ascension	Pentecost	Weeks of Ordinary Time before Lent ending	in week no.	Weeks of Ordinary Time after Easter season beginning	in week no.	First Sunday of Advent
1981	A	I	4 March	19 April	28 May	7 June	3 March	8	8 June	10	29 Nov.
1982	B	II	24 Feb.	11 April	20 May	30 May	23 Feb.	7	31 May	9	28 Nov.
1983	C	I	16 Feb.	3 April	12 May	22 May	15 Feb.	6	23 May	8	27 Nov.
1984	A	II	7 March	22 April	31 May	10 June	6 March	9	11 June	10	2 Dec.
1985	B	I	20 Feb.	7 April	16 May	26 May	19 Feb.	6	27 May	8	1 Dec.
1986	C	II	12 Feb.	30 March	8 May	18 May	11 Feb.	5	19 May	7	30 Nov.
1987	A	I	4 March	19 April	28 May	7 June	3 March	8	8 June	10	29 Nov.
1988	B	II	17 Feb.	3 April	12 May	22 May	16 Feb.	6	23 May	8	27 Nov.
1989	C	I	8 Feb.	26 March	4 May	14 May	7 Feb.	5	15 May	6	3 Dec.
1990	A	II	28 Feb.	15 April	24 May	3 June	27 Feb.	8	4 June	9	2 Dec.
1991	B	I	13 Feb.	31 March	9 May	19 May	12 Feb.	5	20 May	7	1 Dec.
1992	C	II	4 March	19 April	28 May	7 June	3 March	8	8 June	10	29 Nov.
1993	A	I	24 Feb.	11 April	20 May	30 May	23 Feb.	7	31 May	9	28 Nov.
1994	B	II	16 Feb.	3 April	12 May	22 May	15 Feb.	6	23 May	8	27 Nov.
1995	C	I	1 March	16 April	25 May	4 June	28 Feb.	8	5 June	9	3 Dec.
1996	A	II	21 Feb.	7 April	16 May	26 May	20 Feb.	7	27 May	8	1 Dec.
1997	B	I	12 Feb.	30 March	8 May	18 May	11 Feb.	5	19 May	7	30 Nov.
1998	C	II	25 Feb.	12 April	21 May	31 May	24 Feb.	7	1 June	9	29 Nov.
1999	A	I	17 Feb.	4 April	13 May	23 May	16 Feb.	6	24 May	8	28 Nov.
2000	B	II	8 March	23 April	1 June	11 June	7 March	9	12 June	10	3 Dec.

a) The First Sunday of Advent indicates the beginning of the new liturgical year and belongs to the preceding civil year: i.e., the liturgical year of 1985 begins on 1 December 1984.

b) A few feasts of the Lord and solemnities of the saints take precedence over the ordinary Sunday mass. Please consult the parish calendar or bulletin for these changes.

Foreword

The story of these meditations seems as long and tortuous as the journey of Abraham and Sarah from Ur of the Chaldees to the Promised Land.

This book owes its origin to a suggestion several years ago from Robert Heyer of Paulist Press that I write a biblical meditation book for Lent. Upon the encouraging reception of that book, the project expanded to the other major liturgical seasons, *Biblical Meditations for the Easter Season* and *Biblical Meditations for Advent and the Christmas Season*. Quite a few persons wrote to me or they spoke with me at lectures or conventions, asking about the continuation of the series into Ordinary Time, the thirty-four weeks of the rest of the church year. A deacon and his wife even telephoned long distance about the matter.

The occasion to follow through came when my own life's journey took me to Korea, the Philippines and Japan for a five month stint of lecturing and preaching. For the most part deprived of books and personal files, my resources turned out to be most appropriate for composing a meditation book: my heart and memory along with stretches of silence and solitude in between assignments. These assets could have been empty and sterile, were it not for the inspiring presence of missionaries and local religious leaders, and, of course, the source of all inspiration and life for everyone, God's Holy Spirit.

The vitality of the church in these countries has contributed enormously to the insights and possibilities of these meditations. Day by day as I prayed with pen and paper or at other times with all sorts of typewriters, I may have been looking out my window upon the Korean mountains in the Green Belt around Seoul and hearing the gong of Buddhist drums, exorcising the demon; or beyond my window there may have stretched the lovely Japanese gardens at the Passionist retreat house near Osaka, Japan, and the way of the cross winding up the wooded mountainside; or I may have been lecturing at the energetic East Asian Pastoral Institute of Manila, an extraordinary school where students include capable religious leaders, catechists, bishops and a cardinal archbishop, from the Solomon Islands to Pakistan; or I may have been alone during the early morning hours, high in the mountainous area of the Tboli tribe where Fr. Rex Mansmann, C.P., is salvaging and ennobling the handcraft, folklore and customs of this most ancient people of the Philippines. These are only a few of the many stages along the way where these meditations took shape.

The journey from initial drafts to printed book followed another long path. Everyone who reads this book owes a fervent, grateful prayer to Paul I. Bechtold, C.P., long time friend and brother Passionist, founding president of the Catholic Theological Union at Chicago and a former professor of mine. During my preordination studies he had conducted a course on creative composition; this training has been most influential for the bits of clarity and insight in my writings. His editorial assistance appears particularly with the weekday meditations. At times an entire paragraph was added, sometimes just a word, but a word that turned darkness into light!

Through the long journey the pages of these meditations became tattered, strangely numbered, sometimes running backward. They were transformed into a readable script by the patient, expert typing of Sister Kay Sheskaitis, I.H.M., Sister Judy Hahn, O.P., and Sister Ann Maloney, O.P. To them I express special gratitude.

Others came to my aid in proofreading and in preparing the indices. I gratefully recognize the careful contribution of such good friends as Sister Julie Clare Greene, B.V.M., Sister Jeanette Flaherty, S.P., Sister Isabella Stokes, O.P., Sister Rosemary Dewey, R.S.C.J., Ms. Gerry Boberg and Ms. Mary Ellen Drake.

The three volumes of these meditations cover the liturgical period of Ordinary Time, the thirty-four weeks from mid-January till the end of November, exclusive of Lent and the Easter Season. During the *weekdays* of these thirty-four weeks the first reading from Scripture runs on a two year cycle while the gospel is on a one year tract. This fact presented its own problem and challenge. In these meditations the two weekday cycles are joined and generally find their key or unifying theme in the gospel. In this way a new, sometimes creative focus is beamed upon each of the two first readings of cycles I and II. Care has been taken to identify each cycle, so that a person can separate the two and remain with the proper one for the individual liturgical year.

The *Sundays* proceed on a three year cycle, designated A, B and C. Each Sunday has its own set of readings, generally from the Old Testament, the Epistles and the Gospel of the year. Because of the prominent place of Sundays in the liturgical year, a separate meditation is proposed for each of these clusters of biblical readings. At times the "Ordinary" Sunday mass is displaced by a solemnity (the highest ranking type of liturgical celebration) or by a festival honoring Jesus Christ. Each of these has a special meditation, located in the final section of the volume.

A calendar is provided as a road map through the intricacies of the liturgical year. As a friendly piece of advice, we note that the liturgical year begins with the first Sunday of Advent, not with the first of January.

At the beginning of each meditation there is a two to four line summary of each biblical selection. These are not meant to replace the reading of the entire passage from one's Bible or lectionary. The summary highlights the principal motif for meditation. Ideally, one will first read the entire passage from the Bible, then the summary and meditation in this book, again the passage from the Bible, and finally remain silent before God. The Holy Spirit will lead beyond words and even beyond thoughts into the mystery of the burning bush (Exod chap. 3) and ''the tiny whispering sound'' on Mount Horeb (1 Kgs 19:12–13). As another biblical writer concluded a major section of his book:

> More than this we need not add,
>   let the last word be, God is all in all!
> Let us praise him the more, since we cannot fathom
>   him,
>   for greater is God than all his works (Sir 43:28–29).

Like the three previous books in this series of *Biblical Meditations* these new volumes are not a substitute for prayer nor do they supply a homily for the occasion. If questions are raised and insights explored, they are intended to prompt the reader to stop and abide in God's presence:

> By waiting and by calm you shall be saved,
>   in quiet and in trust your strength lies . . . .
> The Lord is waiting to show you favor . . . .
>   Blessed are all who wait for him! (Isa 30:13,18)

The purpose of these meditations, therefore, is not so much to settle upon an answer but to leave a person quietly, peacefully, in God's presence, enriched and strengthened for appreciating God's companionship in one's daily life. This life-setting is one that is shared with all men and women of faith. In this way we will pray with the larger family of God's people.

Prayer, not study, is the determining factor. Nonetheless, enough background is provided so that the reader feels at home with the biblical passages, but academic details are curtailed lest these books turn into a manual for study. On controversial issues only one position is presented, generally without proof or documentation. My own personal preference will be evident, yet these conclusions will hopefully command a respectable consensus among scholars.

These volumes are dedicated to my uncles and aunts. Some have already joined my parents in our eternal home with God; others like Emma, Albert, Ferd and Patty still grace our homeland in Hamilton, Ohio, even in their eighties and nineties keeping warm and loving homes for us. They have surrounded my life with love, concern and an exceptionally strong religious spirit.

PART ONE

Weekdays of Ordinary Time
Weeks 23–34

Monday, 23rd Week

Col 1:24–2:3. Paul rejoices to fill up what is lacking of the
  sufferings of Christ for his body, the Church. To Paul was
  entrusted the privilege of making human the mystery,
  hidden from generations past, Christ in you.
1 Cor 5:1–8. Paul excommunicates a man for an unlawful
  marriage. The Corinthians are to rid themselves of the old
  yeast of boasting and wickedness and celebrate the new
  Passover with the unleavened bread of sincerity and truth.
Luke 6:6–11. Jesus heals the man with a withered hand on
  the Sabbath, to the frenzied anger of his opponents.

There is a common tendency to put restrictions on the
love of Jesus. We try to limit Jesus' power of goodness and
exclude individuals or whole groups of people. Or we bind
the power of Jesus with a heavy load of rigid traditions.
Only the clever, the wealthy or the influential can keep their
head above water and not be pulled under by the dead
weight of legalism. So many facile, false reasons can be advanced: Sabbath, the wrong day of the week for a miracle;
fear to side with a poor, unemployed, disabled person; the
wrong race or nationality; inability to correct an influential
person, even for the scandal of marrying his own father's
wife. In the biblical readings people advance many reasons
why God should not act generously and miraculously.

Jesus did not enter the synagogue to stir up a quarrel
nor to prove his miraculous power. We read: "On a sabbath
Jesus came *to teach* in a synagogue." At once, however, he
sensed the hostility and even the trap to catch him in evil. A
disabled man was being "used"—how calloused we can get
towards the handicapped, to notice them only to *our own* advantage!—to gather evidence against Jesus. Jesus was
caught in a seemingly no-win situation: either he would vi-

olate the Sabbath by "working" a miracle, or he would deny his compassion for the poor out of fear or self-respect. Without a moment's delay, Jesus proceeds to act:

- he knew their thoughts
- he said to the man whose hand was withered, "Get up and stand here in front."
- he said to the opponents: "I ask you, is it lawful to do good on the sabbath—or evil? To preserve life—or destroy it?"

We sense a quick sequence here. Jesus lost no time and located the question where it belonged. It was not a matter of keeping the Sabbath or breaking it, but of doing good or evil, of preserving life or destroying it. The first law always is compassion. Out of concern for people enslaved in a foreign country God summoned Moses at the origins of Israel's religion; out of love for sinners, God sent his eternal Son to be born of a woman and to die on the cross.

Compassion then is the first way that God breaks down the barriers that we impose upon him. The second way to reveal the mystery of salvation comes to our attention in the letter to the Colossians (cycle I). The treasures of wisdom and love in Christ are to be *shared with everyone*. We read about "his word in its fullness . . . the glory beyond price which this mystery brings to the *Gentiles*." We can interpret "Gentiles" as outsiders whom we disqualify from receiving the faith and from participating in the joy of Christ. We read still further in today's selection:

we admonish *all* men and *all* women and teach them in the *full* measure of wisdom, hoping to make *every* man and *every* woman complete in Christ.

A third way of reunion in Christ plunges us into suffering and forces us to follow the way of the cross. Again we read:

> I find my joy in the suffering I endure for you. In my own flesh I fill up what is lacking in the sufferings of Christ for the sake of his body, the church.

The hope of being *one* body, Christ and all his members, cannot be accomplished any more easily than Christ's action of restoring the impaired hand and thereby stirring up the frenzied anger of his opponents.

Yet the suffering to reconcile all men and women brings great joy and satisfaction. Paul attributes to this ideal:

- my joy in suffering
- word in its fullness, once hidden from generations past and now revealed to the holy ones,
- Christ in you, your hope of glory,
- every treasury of wisdom and knowledge.

If this ideal is so glorious, then there is little surprise that Paul feels himself, in the midst of his "work and struggle," to be "impelled by that energy . . . so powerful a force within me." For Paul to deny this embrace of the outside world would be as self-destructive as for God to suppress his compassion for suffering people.

This ideal, moreover, cannot be bought by fear, privilege or clever reasoning; in that case it would be just as easily sold or compromised! In 1 Cor 5 (Cycle II) Paul would not tolerate a compromise in public morality, no matter how influential the person may be. He speaks of the "lewd conduct [of] a man living with his own father's wife.'' Most probably the father is deceased. Nonetheless, this type of marriage was seriously scandalous to the Jewish people and struck at the heart of their customs and moral fiber (Lev 20:11). Paul demands: ''Get rid of the old yeast,'' for just a little of it ''has its effects all through the dough.'' Paul then takes the occasion to speak of the sincerity and fidelity expected of Christ's followers. Although union with Christ is expected of *all*, regardless of race or nationality, still it is not union at any cost or compromise. To be one body in Christ, member for member (1 Cor 12:12,27) means that the purifying, strengthening blood of Jesus flows through all the members.

Prayer:

Lord, my soul is at rest in you. You are my refuge and stronghold. Yet I can enter this fortress of compassion, only if I myself am compassionate and open towards all others. Lead me in your justice, strengthen me to reject evil, then in your family, as one body in Christ, I will be glad and sing your praises.

Tuesday, 23rd Week

Col 2:6–15. In baptism you were buried with Christ and through God's power raised with Christ from the dead, so that we continue to live with him. Our sins are nailed to the cross.

1 Cor 6:1–11. Paul condemns lawsuits before pagan courts. Church members ought to act as judges and arbiters. You have been washed and consecrated in Jesus and in the Spirit.

Luke 6:12–19. Jesus spends the night in prayer and afterwards calls the twelve to be his disciples. Coming down the mountain, he taught a large crowd and healed the sick.

We notice a dramatic transition from death to life in Colossians (Cycle I), from serious, public wrangling to a new consecration in Jesus and the Spirit in 1 Corinthians (Cycle II); and in the Gospel from night-time to daybreak and new church life.

Night is the time of death and contention, as well as of rebirth and ecstatic prayer. Night is fearful in that we lose our healthy inhibitions and self-control. We can be swept into any number of evil actions or evil thoughts. If Paul lines up a devastating list of sins which excludes from God's kingdom, then we must conclude that sin was found in Corinth:

> fornicators, idolators, adulterers, sodomites, thieves, misers, drunkards, slanderers, robbers.

Some sins, like that of miserliness, may not be as serious as others on the list, and therefore all the sins have to be understood in the larger setting at Corinth. Altogether, however, sin was dividing and destroying the church. The worst sin, if we can speak in such a way, is located in disunity and in the pain of hurting one another: "You yourself injure and cheat your very own brother and sister." Paul then singles out the scandal of mistrust and deceit in the Corinthian church, so that members feel obliged to take their problems and disputes to secular law courts. Paul is so enflamed that he adds: "I say this in an attempt to shame you."

Night then is a time of sin and deceit. Consequently it is also a time of struggle against evil. Paul names these forces of evil as superhuman agents, "principalities and powers,'' over whom Christ triumphed, ''leading them off captive'' (cycle I). Locked in such superhuman struggle, we cannot survive, much less be victorious, without Jesus. If night-time pits us against devils, it also unites us closely with Jesus. We are advised in Colossians:

> Continue to live in Christ Jesus the Lord, in the spirit in which you received him. Be rooted in him and built up in him.

This union with Jesus is frequently compared to the union of parts or members in the human body. Normally, the one arm is not conscious of the other arm, nor are we aware of the heart or lungs, unless something is wrong with them. A certain type of silent, yet dynamic darkness surrounds the union of bodily members with one another.

Night, therefore, is a time of profound, silent prayer.

> Jesus went out to the mountain to pray, spending the night in communion with God.

Jesus' entire self is lost in the godhead of Father, Son and Spirit. What Paul writes becomes emphatically true of these nightly vigils:

> In Christ the fullness of the deity resides in bodily form.

Night is also a time of recovering lost resources, healing wounds and hurts, the sweet medicine for every ailment. As such, silent prayer of such intense surrender to God turns into a dynamic time of new life. We move from death to life. We read in Colossians:

Even when you were dead in sin . . . , God gave
you new life in company with Christ. In baptism
you were not only buried with him but also raised
to life with him because you believed in the power
of God who raised him from the dead.

New life in Christ results in new activity in Christ.
After being restored by the night of struggling with evil, of
intense union in Christ and of rising to new life, we go forth
energetically into the new day. Such was the case with Jesus:

At daybreak he called his disciples and selected
twelve of them to be his apostles . . . .Coming
down the mountain with them, he stopped at a
level stretch where there were many of his disciples [and] a large crowd of people with them.

Jesus proceeded to share his life by teaching and by healing.
''Power went out from him which cured all.''

Prayer:
Lord, we extol you. You are compassionate with all
your works. Renewed as we are by your life through baptism and prayer, we praise your name. From our nightly vigils, you adorn us, your lowly ones, with victory. This is the
glory of all your faithful ones.

Wednesday, 23rd Week

Col 3:1–11. You have been raised from the dead with
Christ. Therefore, set your heart where Christ is, at God's
right hand, and not on evil deeds. In Christ there is no

Greek or Jew, slave or free person. Christ is everything in all of you.

1 Cor 7:25–31. Christians are free to marry or to remain single, but all should live as though the world is passing away.

Luke 6:20–26. The Beatitudes, spoken on the plain to a large crowd.

Today we are seriously warned, as was stated in still another book of the Bible, that "here we have no lasting city; we are seeking one which is to come" (Heb 13:14). This latter statement from the Epistle to the Hebrews comes from the final period of New Testament writing. The three readings for this Wednesday span the other periods: First Corinthians from the early time before the fall of Jerusalem, the Gospel of Luke after the fall and the separation of Jesus' disciples from the synagogue, Colossians at the end of Paul's ministry. It is remarkable, then, that the understanding about the passing phase of earthly life is sustained.

The seriousness of Luke's Beatitudes becomes more apparent as we compare them with Matthew's which are somewhat theoretical and more general. Luke's are more simple and direct. Matthew's are addressed to the disciples who alone follow Jesus up the mountain, not to the crowd, and are phrased in the third person:

How blest are the *poor in spirit*;
　　the reign of God is *theirs* . . . .
Blest are they who hunger and thirst *for holiness;*
　　they shall have their fill (Matt 5:3,6).

Luke portrays Jesus' "coming down the mountain [to] a level stretch [and addressed] many of his disciples [and] a large crowd of people" (see yesterday's Gospel). Luke's

Beatitudes are closer to Jesus' original words, phrased in the second person:

> Blest you *you* poor; the reign of God is *yours*.
> Blest are *you* who hunger; you shall be filled.

Luke, therefore, is not writing a general, catechetical discourse but is specifically and immediately addressing "you poor" and "you who hunger."

As we carefully re-read Luke's Gospel, we also notice a frustrating, no-win circle of human life. The "hungry" are promised to be "filled"; then a woe is read upon "you who are full"!

> Blest are you who hunger; you shall be filled.
> Woe to you who are full; you shall go hungry.

This frustration should not paralyze us, only reinforce the seriousness that on earth we have "no lasting city" and we are to live as though "the world as we know it is passing away."

We are being told, in fact, rather bluntly, that God accomplishes more with our poverty than with our wealth, more with our faith than with our activity. Poverty and faith have nothing to lose and an almost infinite variety of choices before them. Wealth and specialization restrict a person's options and weigh that person down with anxieties. Yet, we feel the need of more direction, and for this we turn to the epistles.

In writing to the Corinthians (cycle II) Paul admits that "I have not received any commandment from the Lord" on the matters now to be discussed. He proceeds to give the results of his own reflection. The first direction then for us, as we face problems and questions is to place ourselves in God's presence and *to think*. The Scriptures may not always give the final answer, as difficulties arise that were not addressed by the writers of the Bible.

Paul then advises the Corinthians to arrive at a *careful decision*. They are not to rush into marriage nor are they to remain in the single state as the easy way out of responsibility. Once married, or settled in the single state whether it be within religious community or with secular careers, one is *not to be overly possessive*. Husbands and wives are not related as owners of property but are united in the Lord. Those who buy and sell should never overlook God's statement:

> The land shall not be sold in perpetuity; for the land is mine. And you are but aliens who have become my tenants (Lev 25:23).

We recall again the seemingly no-win circle of the Beatitudes whereby the hungry shall be filled, but woe is called down upon those who are full. In the light of Paul's letter to the Corinthians, we can interpret Jesus' words as a warning. We should recognize the signals that we have begun to have too much. There is a serious difference between receiving as a gift and being greedy for more. We are asked to recognize the danger of never having enough, no matter how much one possesses. The sage remarked in this connection: "Lust [whether for sex or for wealth] indulged starves the soul" (Prov 13:19), for it never has enough.

Still other directives for living in a world that is passing away came from today's reading (in cycle II) from the Epistle to the Colossians. *We are already living our heavenly existence*:

Since you have been raised up in company with Christ, set your heart on what pertains to higher realms where Christ is seated at God's right hand.

The following exhortation constitutes one of the finest, most stirring calls to living a heavenly existence upon earth:

- Be intent on things above
- you have died
- your life is hidden now with Christ in God
- put on the new person . . . formed anew in the image of the Creator

Paul is not afraid to translate these magnificent statements into practical language:

- put to death fornication, uncleanness, evil desires,
- put aside anger, quick temper, malice, insults, foul language.
- stop lying to one another.

With Paul the center point where all discussion stops always turns out to be unity, trust and charity. Here he states our new life in Christ where "there is no Greek or Jew, circumcised or uncircumcised, foreigners, Scythian, slave or free person." Paul's final directive here is engraven upon many banners and should be cut into the flesh of our heart: "Christ is everything in all of you."

Prayer:
Lord, you are compassionate towards all your creatures. Give me that same love and concern and let it direct my every decision. Then in all that I think, say or do, I am living now as though I am already accompanying you in

heavenly glory. Each moment I enter your palace with gladness, joy and peace.

Thursday, 23rd Week

Col 3:12–17. Because you are God's chosen ones, clothe
  yourselves with heartfelt mercy, with meekness and patience. As members of one body in Christ and with
  Christ's word dwelling in us, we are called to peace.
1 Cor 8:1–7, 11–13. Knowledge inflates if it injures a
  brother or sister. Love upbuilds. We should never wound
  the conscience of the weak by our liberty in Christ.
Luke 6:27–38. Be compassionate, as your Father is compassionate. Love your enemies. Give and it will be abundantly given to you, pressed down and running over.

The biblical goals of love, compassion, humility, forgiveness and generosity reach beyond our human ability, at
least beyond normal expectations, certainly beyond laws
and prohibitions. Yet, there is a tone about the scriptures
that leaves us little or no option. The Gospel repeats frequently the phrase to ''love your enemy.'' In writing to the
Corinthians Paul goes so far as to state that he will never
again eat meat, if meat is an occasion of sin to another. In
the Epistle to the Colossians the entire list of expectations
relies upon the opening statement of who we really are:
''Because you *are* God's chosen ones . . . .'' If that is who
we are, then there is no longer any liberty to act differently.
If *we are human* by birth, then we have no freedom to act in
any other way than humanly—unless we are willing to destroy ourselves.

The goals of love, then, are not beyond our nature as
created and blessed by God: ''You are God's chosen ones,

holy and beloved." God's choice has drawn us into the life of Jesus. We are chosen in Christ Jesus and form one body in Christ. In a sense we have no freedom but to be Christlike in our love, compassion, practice and meekness. When the Epistle to the Colossians (Cycle I) proceeds to exhort us to act as Christ would, it is also telling us *to be truly who we are* as already created in Christ Jesus.

- Forgive as the Lord has forgiven you;
- Christ's peace must reign in your heart;
- Let the word of Christ, rich as it is, dwell in you;
- Sing gratefully to God;
- Do all in the name of the Lord Jesus;
- Give thanks to God through him.

If we reflect on who we are as chosen in Christ Jesus, heroic charity will be second nature. But that fact does not make it any easier for us than it was for Jesus. He spontaneously sought to be who he truly was, the Word spoken by God the Father and the Son begotten by the Father, and therefore he would always and immediately be obedient. Yet we know how Jesus' sweat became like drops of blood from the tense fear and overwhelming repugnance to accept the cup of death on the cross (Luke 22:39–46). "He learned obedience from what he suffered" (Heb 5:8). The innate summons to heroic love is not any easier on the flesh because it is rooted in our natures as God's chosen ones. We are not free, not to be heroic—unless we opt to destroy our truest selves.

If we are all "members of the one body" (Cycle II), then Christ's inspiration and grace flow through us like blood. We breathe in Christ's responses to life like air through our nostrils. Before we act, Christ is already alive within us. His heart is the signal to regulate our heart; his breath or spirit purifies our lungs and blood. He is giving us health and strength. Moreover, as "members of one body," we all exist in an extraordinary bond of intimacy with one another. Our instinctive reaction to one another ought to be concern, kindness, patience, humility.

The Scriptures, we remind ourselves again, are not esoteric, gnostic, unearthly, unrealistic, isolationist documents. Along with heavenly goals to be followed instinctively on earth, we are reminded of the real world of our daily existence. Paul is conscious of grievances that people hold against each other. If we are asked to "forgive as the Lord has forgiven," then real sins surround us and exist in each of us. Furthermore, with the rich word of Christ dwelling in us and "in wisdom made perfect, [we are called to] instruct and admonish one another." Each one of us, no matter our position in life, no matter what be our maturity, needs to seek and receive advice, direction and admonition.

Writing First Corinthians Paul is all the more practical and specific! Knowledge inflates, so that we no longer act as a true flesh and blood person, but as an unrealistic speculator or as a bag of wind! We argue speculatively and forget the realistic fact of scandal. Some people can be so obsessed with theological correctness, that they have lost contact with reality. Part of the heroic dedication to Jesus is a refined sense of concern for people with weak consciences. Paul uses the example of meat dedicated to the gods. Because those "gods" are really "no-gods," we can eat all food. But if a brother or sister does not yet make these distinctions and their weak or under-developed consciences are scandalized and injured, then as Paul puts it bluntly:

you have sinned against a brother or sister
  for whom Christ died.
Therefore, you are sinning against Christ.

With this same supernatural practicability, we should re-read the Gospel and seek to understand Christ's expectations:

> bless those who curse you,
> turn the other cheek,
> if someone takes what is yours, do not
>   demand it back,
> love your enemy.

These statements reflect the supreme law of Christian life: all are God's chosen ones; you are members of one body; do not injure the weak brother or sister.

Prayer:
Lord, if we are all one in Christ and share in Christ's heavenly existence, then let everything that breathes praise you with timbrel and dance, with sounding cymbals. Since, Lord, you knit us all together as one body, we are fearfully, wonderfully made; in Christ Jesus, all the more wonderfully. Guide us, Lord, in his everlasting ways.

Friday, 23rd Week

1 Tim 1:1–2,12–14. Grace has been granted Paul in overflowing measure, along with faith and love in Christ Jesus.
1 Cor 9:16–19,22–27. Paul describes his apostolic ministry. It is under compulsion from God, adapted to the weak and the strong, with bodily discipline. He is the slave of all to win all for Christ.

Luke 6:39–42. Can the blind lead the blind? Why look at the
speck in the eye of a brother or sister and miss the plank
in one's own eye?

The biblical selections center mostly upon religious
leadership but their application reaches outward to all human relationships. Very positively too we are asked to interact with one another, not so much as superior to inferior
but as recognizing the unique gift of each person. It is because of diversity of strength and grace that problems arise
and helpful direction is necessary.

What Paul writes about himself in First Timothy (Cycle
I) is true of each one of us. We all act at times out of ignorance and misguided zeal and so we appear arrogant to others. We are also the recipient of "the grace of our Lord . . .
granted in overflowing measure, along with faith and love
which are in Christ Jesus." Such abundant grace solves
many problems, converting a persecutor like Saul of Tarsus
into a missionary like Paul who belongs to a world mission.
Yet this overflowing measure raises still other problems.
Each of us, like Paul in comparison with Peter on the question of Gentile conversions (*cf.*, Gal 2:14), can appear arrogant, demanding and a source of difficulty. The problem
is no longer our ignorance but now our brilliant insight that
others do not share!

The Scriptures ask us to respect, admire and learn from
the gifts of one another. Otherwise, in our ignorance we will
not only be arrogant but also "a blind person [who attempts
to] act as a guide to another blind person." Both will fall
into the pit, both teacher and student! Each of us needs the
wisdom of others to balance our own special insights and
strengths. We find this complementarity of gifts in regard to
Paul and Peter. We also notice the problems that arose from

the differences so pronounced in each one. We are told by Paul himself that the pillars of the church in Jerusalem recognized:

> that I had been entrusted with the Gospel for the uncircumcised [Gentiles] just as Peter was for the circumcised for he who worked through Peter as his apostle among the Jews had been at work in me for the Gentiles (Gal 2:7–8)

The greatest problems emerge when the gifts are the greatest and when these abundant gifts are spread around, only in diverse forms and emphases. It is extremely difficult for a learned, experienced person to receive advice from another learned, experienced person. We even find such confrontation in Scripture, not only between Paul and Peter, but also between two other saints, Paul and Barnabas, who disagreed over the presence of Mark. We are told:

> The disagreement which ensued was so sharp that the two separated. Barnabas took Mark along with him and sailed for Cyprus. Paul, for his part, chose Silas to accompany him on his journey (Acts 15:39–40).

Only when the Church reunites the works of all these missionaries in the New Testament and in later writings, can a proper balance be achieved. We too need the Church to keep all of our gifts united, at the service of all, lest the body of the Lord be misshapen or psychologically imbalanced.

By an ability to see the goodness in others, will we have the sight to recognize and correct the plank in our own eyes. After that, we are in a proper position to correct others for the speck in their eye. The sequence is important to observe: 1st) to see the good in others; 2nd) to correct one's own imbalance; 3rd) to remove the speck from the other's eye.

Again in that extraordinarily practical document, the First Epistle to the Corinthians (Cycle II), still further advice is offered to us. Each line deserves long reflection; some of the lines are masterpieces of eternal wisdom. Our memory nods in recognition as we read:

> I have made myself all things to all
>   men and women in order to save
>   at least some of them;
>
> I discipline my own body and master
>   it for fear that after having preached
>   to others I myself should be rejected.

Paul is certainly affirming our earlier reflection to learn from the goodness of others and to adapt to their needs and possibilities. "To the weak," he says, "I became a weak person with a view to winning the weak. . . . In fact, I do all that I do for the sake of the Gospel in the hope of having a share in its blessings." This Gospel, we know from elsewhere in Paul's writings, is more than words; it is the person of Jesus Christ, the living word. Therefore, by sharing and extending the effective presence of Jesus among others, Paul shares in their blessings through Jesus Christ.

Prayer:
   Lord, show me the path to life and bring me to the fullness of joys in your presence. Show me how to find your exceptional goodness in all my neighbors so that together we discover the fullness of your joys. Lord, I yearn and pine for

this, your holy presence. You withhold no good thing from those who walk humbly and sincerely.

Saturday, 23rd Week

1 Tim 1:15–17. Christ Jesus came into the world to save sinners and display his patience, especially in me, Paul says, an extreme case, an example to those who would later have faith.

1 Cor 10:14–22. The cup of blessing we bless is a sharing in the blood of Christ; the bread we break is a sharing in the body of Christ. Because the loaf is one, we, many though we are, are one body.

Luke 6:43–49. A good tree produces good fruit. Thus we know that we build our house securely on rocks, not on sand, and so it survives the flood.

A key which unlocks the Scriptures for our meditation today is found within First Timothy, Jesus Christ displays all his *patience* (Cycle I). Patience is the virtue of that person who has built on rock. When evil times hit, when disappointment and misunderstandings sweep everything else away, when the heavens collapse on earth with angry, uncontrollable floods, that house remains standing if it is built with deep foundations in the rocky subterrain.

"Rock" takes on any number of important symbolical meanings in the Bible, but all of them converge on strength, consistency, fidelity, and continuity.

In Num 20:11, the rock is struck by Moses' rod and produces sweet water.

In 1 Cor 10:4 this rock follows the Israelites through the desert as a continuous source of water. The rock, says Paul, is Christ. In Ps 81:17 it even produces honey.

In Isa 28:16 the rock supports the Jerusalem temple where God dwells among his people.

In Ps 95:1 God himself is acclaimed as ''the rock of our salvation.

In Matt 16:18 Peter is the rock or foundation of the church.

As these and many other passages are stitched together, rock indicates the steady assurance of God's grace, the presence of God in temple or church, the human representatives of God as Rock. Patience builds this kind of house.

Impatient persons build on sand and so are not dependable. They act or react impulsively. Anger takes control of them before they can think. Rash words are spoken that cannot be obliterated from people's memories. Within all this haste wisdom is lost. When difficulties come, this person is not dependable. ''When the torrent rushed upon it, it immediately fell in and was completely destroyed.''

It is little wonder that people are easily driven out of the church and out of their homes by the impatience of parents and religious leaders. Impatience easily leads to lies and deceit. The impatient person speaks and acts too quickly and then attempts to cover up by false explanations. Impatience is killer number one in church and family; deceit and lack of trust is killer number two.

In the Church today another symbol of presence and unity, of trust and strength is found in the Eucharist. Paul reiterates this Eucharistic grace on several occasions. Today he writes (Cycle II):

> Is not the cup of blessing we bless a sharing in the blood of Christ? And is not the bread we break a sharing in the body of Christ? Because the loaf of bread is one, we, many though we are, are one body, for we all partake of the one loaf.

Not only does the Eucharistic table stand as a pledge of our total unity in Christ, and therefore of strength and continuity, but the Eucharistic table also calls us to peace and patience. We can never enjoy a meal together, if we are angry or jealous, distrustful or deceitful. The eucharist is our pledge to one another to live honorably and honestly. We will not partake of the table of demons and be guilty of immoral deeds.

Yet, we are all weak and prone to sin. We make mistakes. If we return sorrowfully to the Lord, we will be forgiven and embraced anew with love. In the First Letter to Timothy (Cycle I), we are assured in the name of St. Paul:

> Christ Jesus came into the world to save sinners.
> Of these I myself am the worst.

Therefore, Jesus can display his patience all the more bounteously and Paul may become an example to those who would later have faith in him.

Patience builds the house on rock and assures us of God's presence, even when we are unsteady and disloyal. "To the King of ages . . . be honor and glory forever and ever! Amen!"

Prayer:

From the rising of the sun to its setting is the name of the Lord to be blessed. The Lord is always faithful, raising the lowly from the dust and dwelling always in our midst. To you, O Lord, we offer a sacrifice of praise. We call upon your name. Be patient and receive us.

Monday, 24th Week

1 Tim 2:1–8. Prayers are requested for civil authority that we might live tranquil lives in perfect piety. Christ died for all and wants all to be saved and to know the truth.

1 Cor 11:17–26,33. The Eucharistic meal is profaned by division and revelry. Paul then transmits the eucharistic tradition that he himself received.

Luke 7:1–10. The Roman centurion has greater faith than all Israel and receives from Jesus the cure of his servant.

While First Timothy (Cycle I) proclaims the missionary apostolate to the world, the Roman centurion in Luke's Gospel shows how well prepared the world can be and Paul's Letter to the Corinthians (Cycle II) how much the Gentile community stands in need of correction and warning. Many different sides of the Church's mission to outsiders are seen in today's reading. While foreigners and distant people will never hear of Christ unless missionaries be sent to them (Rom 10:14), the home church which sends the missionaries can be shamed by the fervent spirit and anticipatory faith of the mission country. While the home church provides the line of continuity from Old Testament times and Jesus to the contemporary movement and beyond, that line may not always be worth survival without the contribution of the new mission church.

The mission statements in First Timothy are clear and engaging:

- God wants *all men and all women* to be saved and to know the truth,
- Christ Jesus gave himself a ransom *for all*,
- I have been made a herald and apostle, the teacher *of the nations*,
- *in every place* prayer shall be offered.

Because God wants the salvation of everyone, then we must conclude that the bulk of the human race are being saved without the Gospel. God's wish cannot remain frustrated for centuries and for the majority of people. Christianity still does not count even fifty percent of the world's population. The preaching of the Gospel, therefore, does not make the difference between heaven and hell but rather distinguishes between the joy and strength of knowing Jesus and the difficulty and fear of living without Jesus.

Paul prays that not only all be saved but also that they "come to know the truth." Truth frees and envigorates, truth brings greater peace and self-respect. The truth, according to Paul, consists in this:

- *God is one*. Therefore all his children form one human family.
- the *mediator* between God and ourselves, *is also one*, the man Christ Jesus. Therefore our unity must include all the human factors of our life.
- Jesus died as a *ransom for all*. "Ransom" is to be interpreted as the bond of union, the blood which unites in a single body.

Salvation becomes easier and more joyful, more respectful of human dignity, more attractive and effective for good, because salvation in Christ Jesus unites all men and women as members of one family. The missionary apostolate is urgent and necessary.

A friend, and all the more so, a new child can enrich and even instruct the parents and older members of the family. New friends and new children bring new insights, new hopes and new questions. Those questions probe the depths of truth and love. In today's Gospel the new person, a Gentile centurion, shows up with even stronger faith than existed in Israel! If we transfer this biblical text into our contemporary world, the Buddhist or the Moslem in their faith can take the Christian by surprise. The Roman centurion shows an alertness, a gentle concern, a direct simplicity and a gracious style. He is alert to the needs of his slaves, probably a foreigner from Syria or Macedonia. He sends to Jesus for help, and as a member of the hated military presence of Rome he risked refusal. He shows gentle concern for Jesus:

> "Sir, do not trouble yourself, for I am not worthy
> to have you enter my house."

There is a direct simplicity. Open and honest, he does not beat around the bush and is not afraid to admit publicly his confidence in Jesus. He graciously sends a delegation of Jewish elders to intercede for him and his slave. All of these qualities produce the portrait of a consummate diplomat. These natural virtues, which engendered faith, also served to create a distinguished public servant.

Jesus turns to the crowd of Jews to praise the faith of this foreigner. Jesus' actions can be expressed in contemporary mission language today as "mission in reverse"!

Those who are proselytized are themselves "missionaries" to teach this parent church! For some inexplicable reason believers can become hardened to their faith, take it for granted, use it for their selfish benefit, and even lose their wholesome natural virtues of alertness, concern, simplicity and graciousness.

In fact, this sad situation of a bad spirit within Christianity already corroded a church founded by St. Paul (Cycle II). The Corinthians were not united charitably and peacefully in Christ but split apart according to the wealthy and the poor, according to their spiritual master, be this one Paul or Cephas or Apollos, or according to their selfish appetite for food and drink. All this was showing up at the time of the Eucharist!

In this context Paul repeats the ancient eucharistic tradition. The one body is that of Christ, the one blood is that of Christ. The Corinthians are united with Jesus' death and with Jesus' second coming. Together, they suffer and together they share hopes; together as human beings ransomed by the man Christ Jesus.

Prayer:

Lord, may our Eucharist manifest our unity, our peace and our love for one another. This is your will, may we always be as obedient as your son Jesus and say immediately, "Behold, I come!" In this obedience may we be drawn into our world family and be your instruments of reconciling everyone in Jesus.

Tuesday, 24th Week

1 Tim 3:1–13. The qualities of bishop, deacon and deaconess—even tempered, self-controlled, modest, hospitable,

gentle, respected, truthful, good managers of their own
family.

1 Cor 12:12–14,27–31. The body is one and has many members; so it is with Christ. Whether Jew or Greek, slave or
free, all are baptized into one body. God has set up many
gifts or offices in the church: apostles, prophets, teachers,
miracle workers, healers, etc.

Luke 7:11–17. Moved with compassion, Jesus raises to life
the dead son of a widowed mother at Naim. Fear seized
the people and they began to praise God.

If we follow today's scriptural selection in reverse, beginning with the Gospel, and then proceed to First Corinthians (Cycle II) and finally read First Timothy (Cycle I), we
can detect important stages of development within church
leadership. In the *Gospel*, Jesus acts spontaneously to work
a miracle at the sight of a dead man being carried to his
grave, the only son of a widowed mother. In *First Corinthians*, miracle worker is named fourth in line along with such
offices in the church like apostle, prophet, teacher, healer,
assistant administrator, and still others. In *First Timothy*
such offices as apostle or miracle worker are not mentioned
and the focus is now upon bishop, deacon, deaconess and
later in this epistle upon presbyter and widow.

As the church spread throughout the world, expanded
in number and was plunged into crises of internal leadership
and external persecution, there was even greater need of
careful organization. Perhaps we can see a parallel in human
life. Children and youth are filled with hope and seem willing to tackle giants and work miracles; as young adults, they
must choose a definite way of life yet they still bring new
spirit and creative innovation within the office or vocation;
finally, as mature men and women they settle down into
their role or job with caution, wisdom and strength.

In this natural evolution, the Scriptures ask us to be at peace. God who created human nature and through Jesus founded the church must be exercising a providential hand and must be blessing the development. Yet a series of important questions and observations come to mind as we meditate upon the Scriptures.

First, what is obvious, the development from the more charismatic to the more organizational is normal and necessary. If the more charismatic and freer type of leadership is closer to Jesus, chronologically, the later church is also called the body of Christ or simply Christ in the Sacred Scriptures. If we translate Paul's phrase literally in First Corinthians, he says:

> The body is one and has many members, but all the members, many though they are, are one body, *thus* [*is*] *Christ*.

The question, therefore, is not so much around the doctrinal question, which style is essentially the more perfect, but rather around the pastoral or practical question, which one is best adapted to the time and place of church life.

A second observation becomes apparent. The more charismatic types of leadership are fraught with more danger. Throughout the Bible miraculous feats were not always the sign of God's presence or God's approval. Some of Moses' miracles were matched by Pharaoh's magicians. We read: "The Egyptian magicians did the same by their magic art" (Exod 7:22; 8:3). Miracles can sweep people along in mad fervor. Religion becomes a cult, and the leader exercises absolute and often lucrative control. Yet, on the flip side of the coin, we must recognize the presence of the miraculous in biblical religion and in church history. We can also organize religion so completely that it runs as smoothly as a well oiled machine. This too is excessive, human control over the divine. Whether in the church or in our own personal lives, we must never lose faith in miracles nor forget the beautiful memories of Jesus, the compassionate miracle worker.

We are led to a third observation. Our compassion and concern for others should drive us to expend ourselves completely for the poor, the sick, the helpless, the needy. We will be amazed at the results; they might even be miraculous! Miracles too impart to each of us what children and youth give to society, a bustling spirit of hope and confidence. Perhaps one of the deadliest cancers in middle age and beyond, as in church life and civil administration, is to be found in the quiet acceptance of monotony, mediocrity and heavy passivity. To live happy normal lives we must always be ready for a miracle around the corner! This miracle testifies to a large hearted compassion.

This combination of human precaution and divine wonder induces a healthy spirit within church and within each human life. The virtues which are expected of bishop, deacon and deaconess are admirable indeed:

> irreproachable, married only once, of even temper, self-controlled, modest, hospitable, not addicted to drink, gentle, peaceful, not greedy, a good manager of one's own household, respected in the community, straightforward, truthful, holding fast to the divinely revealed faith with a clear conscience.

To hope for all these virtues must imply a belief in miracles. We ask God to begin the miracles in our personal lives of in-

tegrity, in our happy home life, in our peaceful neighborhood, in our church of humble service, hospitable love and
inspiring apostolate.

Prayer:
    Lord, work your first miracle in our hearts, that we
may always walk the way of integrity, faithfully and perseveringly. We are your people and we trust that you always
care for us with the same compassion that you returned a living son to the widow of Naim.

Wednesday, 24th Week

1 Tim 3:14–16. To the church, God's household, there has
    been entrusted the wonderful mystery of our salvation: Je-
    sus, God's word, manifested in the flesh, vindicated in
    the Spirit, believed in throughout the world.
1 Cor 12:13—13:13. A hymn to charity, the supreme virtue,
    which will outlast faith and hope into eternity.
Luke 7:31–35. Some people can be so self-centered that
    they are unable to dance when someone pipes a joyful
    tune or to mourn when someone sings a dirge.

    The key word upon which our meditation hangs is
household. We are each "a member of God's household" or
family. Like any family, God's household is the scene of a
wonderful enfolding of mystery. It treasures many wise sayings; it sings its traditional hymns. First Timothy quotes a
confession of faith, popular among his readers. The Gospel
cites a bit of ancient wisdom, which deserved a place in the
Book of Proverbs but was nonetheless repeated from parent
to child, rabbi to student. Paul most probably did not com-

pose the hymn to charity but drew upon a well-known hymnic statement of the early church.

A family needs and therefore possesses this diversity of tradition as the parents, children and grandchildren, the relatives and neighbors pass through the different phases of life, from birth to death, from innocent faith to tried and nature faith, from gifts that divide and instigate jealousy and suspicion to gifts that are now the source of enrichment and family pride.

First we see how God's own beloved son passed through all of these phases:

- eternally with Father and Spirit;
- *manifested in the flesh*, so as to experience birth, life's mission and sorrowful death;
- *vindicated in the Spirit*, when raised from the dead;
- *seen by angels*, as Jesus takes his place at God's right hand;
- *preached among the Gentiles and believed in throughout the world*, through the marvelous mission apostolate of the church;
- *taken up in glory*, at the end of time.

The wide range of every family's experience can be located somewhere in this Christian household's confession of faith. While each family finds its individual place within this early "creed," each family is united to all others throughout the world where the faith is preached. Each family, moreover, finds an integral unity in its own long experience. Its life is not a scattering of starts and stops, but a steady movement, always modeled on Jesus and within God's providence. It will be taken up to share in Jesus' final glory. When all seems lost, it will be "vindicated in the Spirit."

Families and religious communities, such as these, become the model for the church, while the church and its preaching apostolate interprets, explains and so clarifies what God is already accomplishing mysteriously and wonderfully in the family. The Epistle for Cycle I therefore speaks of being

> a member of God's household, the church of the living God, the pillar and bulwark of truth. Wonderful, indeed, is the mystery of faith.

A good family is never monotonous and its members are gifted in very many ways. In the reading from First Corinthians (Cycle II) Paul speaks of many of these talents:

> prophecy, full knowledge, comprehension of mysteries, confidence to move mountains, generosity in feeding the poor, willing to die heroically.

The greater diversity and intensity of these talents, the greater problems that will arise in the family and the church. Paul does not ask that any talent be suppressed. In fact, he speaks of growing up from child to adult and of passing from an imperfect condition to one still more perfect. Up till now, we see only dimly, as through a mirror; we will eventually see face to face, each gift in its fullness through the immediate presence of God in our midst.

Yet, those gifted children in a family or community can instigate much trouble. All of us sin, where we are gifted and alive; we commit our worst sins where we are most active, talented and confident! Paul calls some of these gifted people "a noisy gong," "a clanging cymbal." Such people, he states "put on airs" and become "snobbish." They can be "rude . . . self-seeking . . . prone to anger [and given to] brood over injuries.'' Paul, however, wants no gift suppressed, only that all gifts be united in love. The quality of this affection is such that:

> There is no limit to love's forebearance, to its trust, its hope, its power to endure. . . . There are in the end three things that last: faith, hope, and love, and the greatest of these is love.

True love within God's household not only unites all these magnificent gifts but is also compassionate and understanding. Perhaps these are its greatest assets. Genuine love dances with happy tunes and wails with mournful dirges. It enjoys the happiness of others who eat and drink; it can fast and abstain with those who mourn. It does not call such severe discipline ''madness'' nor does it criticize others as ''gluttons and drunkards.'' To love in such an outgoing, understanding way, the members of God's household cannot be privatized individuals. They are people who are thrust outward into the family, neighborhood and church. If there is strength in unity, these people inspire true confidence, hope and dignity.

Prayer:
Lord, how great are your works. In our household of family and church you make a remembrance of your abundant goodness. Great are your works, exquisite in all their delights. Happy are we, O Lord, that you have chosen us for your very own. We put our hope in you.

Thursday, 24th Week

1 Tim 4:12–16. The young, newly ordained Timothy is instructed how to conduct himself for his own salvation and

that of the church committed to him through prophecy and
the laying on of hands.

1 Cor 15:1–11. The Gospel which Paul preached is the one
that he himself received. By God's favor his ministry,
more energetic than all others, has not proved fruitless.

Luke 7:36–50. Parable of the generous money-lender. The
narrative of the once sinful woman, now holier by her
compunction for sin and her tender regard for Jesus than
the pure, proud, self-righteous and indignant host.

We are all called to minister to others, some of us as
priests and persons of pastoral care, others as teachers,
nurses and counselors, many others as parents, relatives and
neighbors. All of us know from experience that there is no
single way of responding to others, not even if these be children in the same family or adults in the identical social or
cultural bracket. Fortunately, the three biblical passages for
this Thursday call our attention to various aspects of serving
and helping one another.

First of all, as we find in First Corinthians (Cycle II),
we must be anchored in the Gospel. This announcement of
good news reaches back to Jesus and continues in the
church. Paul writes with a keen sense of tradition:

I remind you of the Gospel I preached to you . . .
and in which you stand firm. . . . I handed on to
you first of all what I myself received.

Paul summarizes this gospel of salvation:

- Christ died for our sins, was buried and rose again;
- Christ was seen by Cephas, the Twelve, many others
  and "last of all . . . by me . . . the least of the apostles."

Paul, in preaching the good news of Jesus Christ, is also conscious of the church and of those whom Jesus placed in leadership roles: first, Cephas or Peter, then the Twelve and a larger group of five hundred, afterwards James who led the Jewish Christians, and finally Paul himself. We are advised to minister to one another within the faith of Jesus' death and resurrection and within the visible bond of church unity. Faith and unity are both seen in a human, humble and hopeful way. Faith declares that Jesus died ''for our sins'' and unity is enclosed within Paul's humble attestation: ''I am the least of the apostles, . . . I do not deserve even the name.'' We minister to one another in the faith that Jesus died for the sins of each of us. We never lord it over others, we the least of all!

At other times we must encourage and support another person who may be ignored or may feel diffident, as Paul wrote to Timothy, ''because of your youth.'' The exhortation to Timothy (Cycle I) is a classic combination of strong support, self-confidence and avuncular advice! Youth stands in need of respect for its talents, appreciation of its ideals, assurance of its ability to teach and preach, acceptance of its genuine leadership gained by natural talent, training and divine call within the church. Along with this strong seconding of Timothy's role in the church, the young man is given a handy manual of good advice: continue in love, faith and purity; devote yourself to Scripture, preaching and teaching; do not neglect your gifts; attend to your duties; watch yourself and watch your teaching; persevere. Perhaps, the most practical counsel for the young: keep busy. Paul expresses it this way for Timothy: ''[As] you attend to your duties, *let them absorb you*, so that everyone may see your progress.''

Finally, we come to the sharp contrast of attitudes and

responses in the Gospel. Jesus can be stern with the pure and proud, tender and protective towards the humble and repentant. Jesus grounds his teaching in the parable of God's generous initiative in loving and forgiving. In fact, the person with heavier debts of sin seems to be loved more by God than the other person with lighter debts. God can seem unjust, until we remember that pride is a greater sin than sexual excess. At first, we may think that the woman, a public sinner in town, is the one who owes the five hundred gold pieces to God, and that the Pharisee has the small debt of only fifty gold pieces. There is still hope for the proud, if the woman can be forgiven this easily.

Jesus commends the woman for her love: "her many sins are forgiven, because of her great love." It is not correct to conclude, however, that Jesus' love is in response to the woman's. The preceding parable of the generous moneylender teaches that God first takes the initiative. The woman must have long observed the gentle ways of Jesus and so felt free to approach him in her own tender way.

The Gospel also provides one other, very important piece of advice for helping a brother or sister. We are urged to be as one of them. Jesus identifies himself in today's gospel with the most despised of all groups, prostitutes and moneylenders. Jesus allows himself to become ceremonially unclean, for being touched not only by a strange woman but also by a public sinner. Last of all, Jesus can be severe in his reaction to the Pharisee, not to belittle him but to draw him towards a confession of faith in the goodness of God.

We minister towards one another, within the Gospel and authority of the church, with encouragement and esteem for the young, with tenderness for the repentant, with stern dedication to God's love in the case of the proud and self-righteous.

Prayer:

Lord, you are faithful and just, reliable for ever and ever. Your covenant and Gospel are always directing our lives. Your mercy endures forever. Therefore, Lord, you will not let us die but live in your name. Our life proclaims how good you are.

Friday, 24th Week

1 Tim 6:2–12. Exhortation to sound doctrine, peace, integrity, disinterestedness about wealth, piety, gentleness, following through with one's profession of faith.

1 Cor 15:12–20. If there is no resurrection of the dead, Christ himself has not then been raised. If our hopes in Christ are limited to this life only, we are the most pitiable of all people.

Luke 8:1–3. Jesus journeyed with the twelve and the women, preaching the good news of the Kingdom of God.

We catch a somber heaviness within the reading from First Timothy (Cycle I), an argumentative tone about the resurrection in First Corinthians (Cycle II), and a tone of enthusiasm, hope and accomplishment within the short Gospel passage. Naturally, the Gospel appeals to us, but the two other selections have their necessary place in our lives. Sometimes we need to be sobered up from intense excitement!

Luke seems to breathe the first spring of Jesus' apostolate. He is journeying ''through towns and villages, preaching and proclaiming the good news of the kingdom of God. The twelve accompany him and also some women . . .

who are assisting them out of their means.'' The scene is idyllic. It seems that Jesus is on a glorious tour, winning everyone for the kingdom. The community of disciples around him, the twelve apostles, the women, ''and many others'' impress us with their serene way of life. Some of these people had been cured of serious illness or physical handicap. The phrase ''evil spirit'' or ''seven devils'' does not necessarily mean sinfulness, much less demonic posses- sion. Sickness and death were introduced into the world by sin and therefore reflect the reign of the evil one. They must be totally conquered and removed from the Kingdom of God. That final triumph is already anticipated by Luke. Luke, who wrote the ''Gospel of women,'' gives them a place of honor in this peaceful scene. Again, typical of Luke, the names of influential political figures are intro- duced, like ''Johanna, the wife of Herod's steward, Chuza,'' Somehow or other, the political and the spiritual Kingdom have come graciously together.

Moments like this exist in everyone's lives and in the history of the church. Let us be grateful and enjoy the rich tranquility and the quiet enthusiasm. These times are not just a concession on God's part, nor are they compromising the call to follow Jesus in his way of the cross. We are antici- pating already the purpose of the cross, which is complete redemption, body and spirit, men and women, friends and strangers, heaven and earth, all at once!

In a rather different tone in Second Corinthians Paul in- sists upon the full impact of the resurrection of Jesus:

> If Christ was not raised, your faith is worthless
> [and] we are the most pitiable of men and women.

Christ, moreover, is ''the first fruits of those who have fallen asleep.'' The first is always the assurance of more to

follow. If Paul sounds argumentative, in this reading for
Cycle II, then he cannot afford to give an inch right here. To
deny the resurrection is to deny the dignity of the human
body. For this reason the Corinthians succumbed to sexual
excesses which compromised the sacredness of themselves
as body and spirit. Neither Paul nor ourselves can afford to
let discouragement drive out hope or physical exhaustion
weaken one's stamina. The disregard of our body leads to
the corruption of the body. Its dignity through the physical
resurrection of Jesus saves it for life everlasting and enhances it with esteem and goodness in the hope of the resurrection.

If the human body and spirit are surrounded already
with the glory of Jesus' resurrection, then they are capable
of discipline and righteousness. Every honest person will
confess that he stands in need of such a reminder. At times
we cannot depend on enthusiasm and encouragement. We
need specific advice, straight from the shoulder, clear and
unmistaken. These are not the most exhilarating moments of
our life, neither are they even our better moments. These are
the grey days, the monotonous times, when we feel like giving up and not caring any more about anything or anyone.
The line is taut, nerves are tense, and we can barely stay on
the ''straight and narrow path.'' First Timothy was written
for those moments. It is clear and specific. We will not mistake the meaning and lose our way. We will not snap and
collapse. We pass through the trial and can again allow ourselves the privilege of enthusiasm and the free spirit of the
resurrection.

First Timothy (Cycle I) comes to our assistance in less
gloomy moments. After we have completed a stretch of joy,
peace and accomplishment, it may be time to settle down
and review the situation. We need to interrelate events and
achievements, to take stock where we have gone, to realize

the responsibility of what we have done. Perhaps, we need most of all a time of silence, prayer and settling in the Lord.

Prayer:

Lord, we believe that by sharing in your resurrection we can be happy and peaceful now. The Kingdom of God is already our possession. We do not fear evil days, for we have the strength and wisdom of your Scriptures. We believe that when your glory appears, we will see you and share in the fullness of your joy.

Saturday, 24th Week

1 Tim 6:13–16. We are to keep God's command without reproach until Our Lord Jesus Christ shall appear, an appearance brought to pass by God who dwells in unapproachable light, whom no one has ever seen.

1 Cor 15:25–37,42–49. What is sown as corruptible seed, rises incorruptible as new life. The spiritual will transform the natural or physical in us and we shall resemble the heavenly person, the risen Jesus.

Luke 8:4–15. The parable of the seed and the sower is not explained to the crowd, lest they see, hear and understand, but is made known to the apostles to whom the mysteries of God are revealed.

A divine mystery is simmering in the depths of each of us. Jesus and Paul compare it to a seed, buried in the ground. Looking at the seed before it is planted, one would never suspect the plant and its flower to develop out of it. The process by which the seed ''dies'' or disintegrates within the earth cannot be rushed. It needs not only time but also a *silent* waiting within the *dark, warm* earth *without light.*

The word, therefore, is mystery, hidden with God in unapproachable light (Cycle I), a heavenly person whose likeness we bear (Cycle II), the wonders of the reign of God in parables (Gospel). In one sense we cannot anticipate our mode or style of existence in heaven for all eternity, and in another sense we feel the stirrings of our future life already within us like a pregnant mother. In one way this mystery seems so fragile, even non-existent in its silent, gradual evolution; in another way it is the most delicately sensitive part of ourselves. We have the ability to ignore and suppress the mystery, yet tenaciously the seed preserves its life and by its very dissolution as a seed it grows into its new stage of life. How are we to react to this mystery?

First, as we read in First Timothy, to respect those secret stirrings of new life as *God's command.* Our truest self, not yet visible and certainly not understood by ourselves, is like a divine word or command. To know ourselves we must be exquisitely attuned to our hopes and desires. These are wonderful, even thrilling parts of each person. They impart such excited joy to the face of youth, such peaceful anticipation to the face of the aged. Hope can also drive a person to selfish extremes, even to open violation of other people's rights. Therefore, we are charged "to keep God's command without blame or reproach." The question arises: for how long? The answer is given quickly and simply, "until our Lord Jesus Christ shall appear." The waiting, therefore, can extend through the nameless, faceless years of the prophet Habakkuk:

> O Lord, I have heard your renown,
>   and feared, O Lord, your work.

> In the course of the years revive it,
>> in the course of the years make it known;
>> in your wrath remember compassion (Hab 3:1).

These are secret parts of ourselves which will outlast all trials and be the source of our new existence. We dare not deny or compromise this mystery which is ourself!

Another way of reflecting upon this mystery comes from Paul's letter to the Corinthians (Cycle II). *Part of ourself must die.* It "is subject to decay." It is not that this dying part is bad or useless. Actually it is the "kernel of wheat," something that once existed as a lovely flower or bloom. After the flower faded and fell away, the seed developed. Now the seed, once sown in the ground, must disintegrate. The whole process seems at first very frustrating, but on second consideration we notice that flowers impart joy and color to life even though they are intended to die! Parts of ourselves, which may seem the most conspicuous and active, are not intended to be our own future but to minister to others.

Our true self emerges in a form of life, certainly in direct continuity with our former self, as a new plant grows out of the seed, yet *surpassing the old* in unimaginable ways. The "old" begins to appear weak and even frustrated. The external expression of our inner talents and divine "command" begins to pale before the new and becomes incapable of bearing the weight of the future.

> Weakness is sown, and strength rises up.
> A natural body is put down, and a spiritual
>> body rises up.

Perhaps the most trying moment of our human existence comes when our best cannot support our hopes, our own actions even seem to betray our dreams. How seriously we need our faith that Jesus "made his noble profession before Pontius Pilate" (Cycle I), died and rose from the dead.

From Matthew's explanation of the parable of the sower, further pointers are given to us. God's word, the seed, can fall upon the footpaths which cut through fields and there be trampled upon. The mystery of our lives cannot be subjected to *every* person's advice and be easily subjected to anyone's opinion. Or else the seed is scattered on rocky ground where it cannot take root. It quickly grows and just as quickly dries up. We must allow God's inspiration to sink its roots deeply into our lives and become a part of ourselves. Seed can also be dispersed amid briers. This is the situation in our own lives when we go for instant pleasure, at times recklessly, and lose our taste for prayer, reflection and the self-denial which belongs to every mature person. Finally, seed falls on good ground and yields a plentiful harvest. Even though the mystery of our lives is breathed into us by God, nonetheless, it must become thoroughly ourselves. The harvest depends upon the quality of our lives over a long period of time.

Prayer:

Lord, when your glory appears in our lives, our joy will be full. We hope in you and ask you to shelter us, our hopes and mysterious personality in the shadow of your wings. As we proceed prayerfully through our lives, you are leading us into your heavenly sanctuary. Here the Lord Jesus will appear to us and we will experience his kindness forever.

Monday, 25th Week

Ezra 1:1–6. Cyrus decrees that the Jews return to their homeland in order to rebuild the temple. Like the exodus from Egypt, the neighbors will contribute to this noble cause.

Prov 3:27–34. Rules for dealing justly and honorably with one's neighbor.

Luke 8:16–18. We place a lamp on a lampstand, to enlighten the way for whoever comes in. Whoever has will be given more. Whoever has not, will lose even that little!

This short gospel selection prepares us for the two weeks in Cycle II from the sapiential literature of Israel. Jesus' statement about the lampstand is rather clear yet startles us in its implications; the next sentence, however, about having and getting more or not having and losing even that little is enigmatic and baffling like the best of the proverbs in the sapiential literature.

The readings in Cycle I for the next three weeks are drawn from the early postexilic literature of the Bible that centers upon the temple: Ezra and Nehemiah, the prophets Haggai, Zechariah, Baruch, Jonah, Malachi and Joel. What Cycles I and II have in common is the postexilic age, yet the sapiential literature pays but little attention to the temple, while the prophets, despite their diverse attitudes and responses, deal with the role of the temple in people's lives. Typically of the Bible with its long history and variety of human authors, the final answer depends upon prayer, prudence, guidance and a sincere desire to follow God's will. The Epistle to the Hebrews opens its magnificent theological statement about Jesus by referring to:

times past [when] God spoke *in fragmentary and varied ways* to our ancestors through the prophets (Heb 1:1).

Without further ado we can catch an insight into Jesus' cryptic statement in the Gospel:

> the one who has, will be given more
> the one who has not, will lose even that little!

This intriguing remark can be paraphrased: the one who has *time to pray and reflect* will be given more; the one who has not *taken the time to turn to God and friend for advice* will lose even the little wisdom that he or she possesses. The sapiential books in particular remind us that the Bible is not a child's answer book but an adult's prayerbook and reflection-book. The variety of postexilic prophets leads to the same conclusion.

Mature reflection must always take into consideration one's relation with one's neighbors. This is the topic of the short essay from Proverbs, Cycle II. Each line is as down to earth as sidewalks and working clothes.

> Say not to your neighbor, ''Go and come again,''
>   when you can give at once.
> Quarrel not with a person without cause
> Envy not the lawless person.

Typical of the sapiential literature, the responses are moderate and possible. The cardinal sin of the sapiential literature is extremism and radicalism. The sage even seems to permit ''quarrels'' or ''envy''—but not without cause nor with the lawless person!

The sapiential literature in Cycle II, like the narratives and prophets in Cycle I, comes from the postexilic age. We are introduced to this long, generally bleak and unexciting period from 539 B.C. onward by the Book of Ezra. The Israelites, dragged into exile in 597 and 587 B.C. when the Babylonians twice captured Jerusalem, are among many captive peoples freed by the benevolent despot, Cyrus the Great. Two years after his army entered Babylon without even a whisper of opposition, he permitted all exiles to return. The account here centers upon the southern tribes of Judah and Benjamin; the ten northern tribes, deported in 721 B.C. by Assyria, are lost to history. We also notice how the writer has a keen sense of history and models this return to the homeland upon the exodus out of Egypt. We read about the latter:

> The Egyptians urged the people on, to hasten their departure from the land. The people . . . asked the Egyptians for articles of silver and gold and for clothing. The Lord indeed had made the Egyptians so well disposed towards the people that they let them have whatever they asked for (Exod 12:33–36).

This account can be turned into a spiritual application, very probably intended by the inspired writers. We will always be greatly enriched, if we leave everything behind us for the Lord's sake! If we seek the Lord's will unreservedly, everything will be given to us. Whoever has *followed the Lord obediently and wholeheartedly* will be given more; whoever has not *obeyed the Lord's inspiration* will lose even that little *fearfully preserved in excessive caution*.

Israelites had to leave everything behind. We know from historical documentation that life in Babylon (now a province of Persia) had become pleasant and prosperous. The Jews who never returned eventually produced the famous Babylonian Talmud, still the book of regulations for devout Jews. To return to the homeland meant a drastic, dramatic decision for the Lord. This action will always remove the lamp from under a bushel basket or under a bed and place it on a lampstand. ''Whoever comes in will see it'' and walk in the beam of its courage and clear-sighted wisdom. Such decisive action separates the child from the adult in each of us, it reveals our truest self. ''There is nothing hidden that will not be exposed.'' When hidden aspects of our character or relationships are brought to light, they can either be explicitly rejected, if unworthy of God's will for us, or else be fully embraced if compatible or helpful.

These moments are heroic and demanding; they do not share the moderation of the sapiential literature. Evidently we need both parts of the Bible for the diverse needs and challenges of our life. There is a time to be ''pampered'' or quietly prodded by the sapiential style; there is another time to be shaken up by prophets. At times we leave behind our past, at other times we seek our future!

Prayer:

Lord, we are confident that you will bring us back rejoicing from our captivities—our bondage to sin and selfishness, our imprisonment from injustice and jealousy. We have sowed in tears; you enable us to reap rejoicing. Help us in our freedom to walk blamelessly in your sight, to think the truth in our heart and never to be disturbed again.

Tuesday, 25th Week

Ezra 6:7–8,12,14–20. At the command of God, the encouragement of the prophets, the decrees of Cyrus and Darius, and the financial help of the Persian empire, the Jews proceed to rebuild the temple.

Prov 21:1–6,10–13. This prudent advice for discreet self-control and moderation is drawn from the major collection of Solomon's proverbs.

Luke 8:19–21. My mother and my brother, says Jesus, are those who hear the word of God and act upon it.

As we glance over the first reading for Cycles I and II, we are impressed again, as we were yesterday, with the variety of ways that God's will is made known and accomplished. Chap. 6 of Ezra refers to imperial decrees from the Persian kings Cyrus and Darius, to the message of the prophets, Haggai and Zechariah (which we will begin to read on Thursday of this week), to financial help from Persian taxes, to the sanctuary liturgy and the functions of priests and levites. The Book of Proverbs draws upon advice from Solomon and the Jewish schools for noble youth.

On our part we must belong to the total world. We cannot isolate ourselves in a sanctuary or in the pages of the Bible. We must be a person interested in and profiting from politics, local, national and international, schools of higher learning, economics and finances, cautious scholars and threatening prophets. As we integrate and form decisions from this wide background, we are drawn into a world family. In such a setting we arrive at God's will for us. From this background we can gradually understand Jesus' statement in today's Gospel.

Within the Books of Ezra and Nehemiah we observe the foundation of Judaism as it will take shape and exist into the days of Jesus, even as it will survive the destruction of the second temple by the Romans in A.D. 66. Judaism secured a strength and identity by which the people maintain their identity even in our twentieth century. Religion was associated with every aspect of life, and life found its meaning and value within religious faith. Even though the reading of the Book of Ezra seems monotonous, foreign and impractical *to us*, the reason for our difficulty lies in the close interaction of this book with real life. We ourselves cannot duplicate the details nor form identical judgments, and we are being continuously challenged to unite our religion and our life just as intimately.

Perhaps we should review the sequence of events in chap. 6 of Ezra: 1) *political realism*. Even if the Persians did not grant the Jews full, national independence, still the Jews made the most of their subordination and restrictions. Reduced to a tiny principality, ten miles square around Jerusalem, they proceeded to find their "independence" in the full observance of the Torah. Only a Jew could do this. Outsiders were excluded. This religious restriction enabled a Jew to know his or her Jewish identity. 2) *temple*. External symbols are necessary for identity and survival. The Jews concentrated energy upon this project, so that they could celebrate their history and repeat their hopes and dreams. Within the temple their ancient traditions of Passover out of Egypt and covenant on Mount Sinai were kept alive and were relived in their new circumstances. 3) *unity*. The Jews at Jerusalem kept in close contact with those who remained in Babylon. Prayers and sacrifices were offered at the temple for *all* the people. 4) *religious leaders*. We read that "they set up the priests in their classes and the levites in their divisions for the service of God." Great care was exercised that each priestly and levitical family could trace ancestry back into the earlier times and that their behavior was totally in accord with what "is prescribed in the book of Moses."

If our world seems upset and rudderless, or if we as a people are divided and confused, we may learn from these important actions by which Israel reorganized and set a course clearly and energetically into the future.

A different type of organization is reflected in the Book of Proverbs (Cycle II). The wise sayings in this book cluster around the names of great sages: Solomon (10:1—22:16; chaps. 25–29), an Egyptian scribe, Amen-em-Ope (22:17—24:22), Agur (30:1–6), and Lemuel (31:1–9). These individuals may have conducted schools at Jerusalem, as we know to have been the case with another respected sage, "Jesus, son of Eleazar, son of Sirach" (Sir 50:27), commonly known as Sirach or from a later title, Ecclesiasticus. Around 190 B.C. Sirach wrote to the young men of his country:

> Come to me, you untutored,
> and take up lodging in the house of
>   instruction (Sir 51:23).

Most of the sapiential literature, certainly that within the Book of Proverbs, defers very little to temple and religious authority and concentrates upon common sense and ancient wisdom. What has succeeded for so many years, even centuries, has an exceptional lasting power. It has no special set of prerequisites to understand its message. Just be open, honest, reflective, humble, strong, the basic qualities of human nature as it was originally created by God and as it has spread throughout the world. All the world knows and accepts the wisdom of Proverbs:

> The one who makes a fortune by a lying tongue
>   is chasing a bubble over deadly snares.
> The one who shuts the ear to the cry of the poor
>   will also call and not be heard.

Whether we take the more "religious" route of Ezra (Cycle I) or the more "secular" way of Proverbs (Cycle II), we arrive at a healthy openness to the real world. We form family and ties with men and women everywhere. Perhaps, that was the intention of Jesus in his enigmatic reply sent by a messenger to his mother Mary and his brothers. Jesus' words may even have cut them to the heart and seemed a repudiation of his own immediate relatives. Jesus had this word brought to them:

> "My mother and my brothers are those who hear the word of God and act upon it."

Therefore, truly to know that word we must be in contact with everyone who is sincere, virtuous, obedient and responsive to life.

Prayer:

Lord, give us the faith and openness to unite our life in all its parts, secular and religious, with our worship of you. Always let us be turned towards your holy city and entering your courts for prayer. Through your help we will learn wisdom and walk in the paths of your command.

Wednesday, 25th Week

Ezra 9:5–9. At the time of the evening sacrifice, Ezra confesses the sins of the people. He acknowledges God's mercy for the remnant in the promised land and for the temple.

Prov 30:5–9. In praise of moderation and sufficiency.

Luke 9:1–6. Jesus sends forth the twelve to proclaim the reign of God and to heal the afflicted. They are to travel unencumbered, dependent upon alms.

Once again the diversity of the biblical message is impressed upon us. "All Scripture is inspired of God and is useful for teaching" (2 Tim 3:16). We need all of these options. The difference, therefore, is not a matter of right or wrong, nor of passages more inspired or less inspired. Scripture is most of all a pastoral document, and we have to decide, through prayer, guidance and community wisdom, which part of Scripture is best adapted to our current situation.

Ezra expects us to be satisfied with small achievements and Proverbs with healthy moderation. The gospel sends us forth like the twelve, poor, dependent and enthusiastic over the reign of God now in our midst. The gospel is certainly the most attractive situation, brimming over with contagious joy and simple trust. Yet there are moments in everyone's life when we have to grin and bear it and set our face to the wind. No one can smile so they stare sternly ahead. Other moments come when we steer the ship of life through quiet waters, our lives still aching from battling the waves! As parents, teachers and religious leaders, ours hopefully is the grace to bring the right text from the treasury of the Scripture.

Ezra, who first appears in today's reading (Cycle I) takes on the role of another Moses. He is the parent of Judaism as Moses was of the Israelite covenant. Although the Jews began their return to the Promised Land in 537 B.C., about all they accomplished was the rebuilding of a very modest temple. They were discouraged and covetous. They even sold one another into slavery for payment of a debt. The situation was still as Zechariah described it: "a day of small beginning" (Zech 4:10). With determination and even ruthless dedication to principle, Ezra straightened out the confusion and guided the people with clear direction. He reedited the Books of Moses and demanded compliance. He began a series of oral interpretations of the law that developed into the famous Talmud several centuries later.

First of all, Ezra confessed the sins of the people. He actually identified himself with the people in their guilt and wretchedness:

> My God, I am too ashamed and confounded to raise my face to you, O my God, for our wicked deeds are heaped up above our heads.

After this opening prayer he addressed the people. They almost remain in the category of slaves in that their social status in the Persian empire was exceedingly low, yet God's mercy has reached them.

- they are a remnant, a stake, firmly planted in the holy land;
- they have the good will of the Persian king
- the house of God has been rebuilt.

A sense of sober reality dominates this prayer and sermon of Ezra.

Sometimes all of us need to be told bluntly, first to admit our mistakes and to take responsibility for their sad effects, then to count our blessings. Things are not nearly as bad as we suppose. There is a future for ourselves and for our children and descendants.

The Book of Proverbs sobers us up in still another way! In this reading for Cycle II, we are no longer poor and disgraced as in the time of Ezra. We the new generation even have the opportunity to amass wealth and keep climbing upward. In this strong determination to get ahead, armed as we

are with prestige and learning, we are tempted to twist truth
and law to our own benefit and to the harm of others. We become greedy, and as we read elsewhere in Proverbs, greed,
like lust, starves the soul and it never has enough (Prov
13:19). We need to be warned:

> Every word of God is tested; . . .
> Add nothing to his words,
>   lest he reprove you, and you be exposed
>   as a deceiver.
> Put falsehood and lying far from me,
>   give me neither poverty nor riches,
> Lest, being full, I deny you,
>   saying, ''Who is the Lord?''
> Or, being in want, I steal,
>   and profane the name of my God.

These words were not minted for the low income days of
Ezra but for a later different period.

Finally, we come to the happy days of Jesus, sending
forth the twelve, overcoming demons, curing diseases, proclaiming the reign of God. Traveling missionaries are freely
cared for, so they need not carry bread or money, not even
staff and traveling bag. Whenever we meet such joy and
confidence, it is our privilege to rejoice and thank God. This
is not the proper time to call for moderation, nor to fast
and mourn like Ezra. Now and then God raises up a Francis
of Assisi, John XXIII and Mother Teresa. Occasionally
their shadow crosses our path in a member of our family or
parish, of our neighborhood or acquaintance. We should encourage their ideals, stand by them, support them, receive
them into our homes. Then the reign of God will be in our
midst.

Prayer:

Lord, you may scourge us, but you then have mercy. If you cast us down, you raise us up again. You scatter us but bring us together in our family. We rejoice in you, O Lord! Once beside you, your word becomes a lamp for my feet, withholding me from evil paths. Your law, Lord, I love.

Thursday, 25th Week

Hag 1:1–8. While providing for themselves, yet failing to be satisfied, the people neglect to build the Lord's temple.

Eccl 1:2–11. Nothing is new under the sun. Vanity of vanities. All things are vanity.

Luke 9:7–9. Herod was perplexed about Jesus and became very curious to see him.

People can be faced with economic confusion, as reflected in the prophecy of Haggai (Cycle I); or they are simply tired and unwilling to try anything new, as we find in Ecclesiastes (Cycle II); or again their religion consists of curiosity, born of perplexity and moral confusion, as was the case with Herod the tetrarch. No situation is hopeless, for then the Scriptures would not mention it. The Bible is definitely not the story of sin and hell but of sin and conversion.

''Economic confusion'' may not be the best way to pinpoint the scene before the prophet Haggai. His name means feastday, quite appropriate for the development within his five short sermons. Haggai began to prophesy around August/September 520 B.C., some nineteen years after the first caravan of Jews returned from exile. Those were nineteen long, discouraging years when the great vi-

sion of a new people of God collapsed and the people hardly
survived from month to month. Haggai describes the scene
this way:

> You have sown much, but have brought in little;
>   you have eaten, but have not been satisfied;
> You have drunk, but have not been exhilarated;
>   have clothed yourselves, but not been warmed;
> And the one who earned wages
>   earned them for a bag with holes in it.

Twice Haggai shouts at this tired, lethargic people: "Consider your ways!"

The prophet makes one simple demand: "Fetch lumber
and build the house" of the Lord. He says it in plain, una-
dorned Hebrew prose! All other prophets spoke in poetry
with eloquent symbols and parables. Haggai was not going
to pretend to read Shakespeare on a corner slum! He had no
aspirations to produce the golden poetry of an Isaiah or the
wrenching pathos of a Jeremiah. He is not concerned if
modern professors of Hebrew give a low "C" for rhetoric
and no better than a "C + " for public speaking. Alone of all
the prophets, Haggai lived to see his mission accomplished.
In 515 B.C. the temple was completed, as we read last Tuesday (Cycle I):

> The elders of the Jews continued to make progress
> in the building, supported by the message of the
> prophets, Haggai and Zechariah. . . . They fin-
> ished the building according to the command of
> the God of Israel and the decrees of Cyrus and
> Darius (Ezra 6:14).

Haggai reminds us, not only to put aside any pompous
airs and address the practical side of people's lives, but also

to realize the crucial importance of temple or church and of community and family prayer. Without a strong symbol that we are a people of God, with spiritual and moral aspirations, we will sink into materialism. Even in our poverty we will still cling to our trinkets and be jealous of others for theirs. Without community or family prayer, we will miss again the encouragement to be men and women of prayer. Without prayer we end up saying, what's the use? We repeat again those despondent lines heard within the prophecy of Jeremiah:

> Let us lie down in our shame,
>   let our disgrace cover us,
>   for we have sinned against the Lord,
>   our God (Jer 3:25).

Another type of ennui can set in when we have too much too easily. Etched into the memory of the world are those opening lines of Ecclesiastes or Qoheleth. The name is probably a title, given or accepted, which means in Latin or Hebrew: the assembly preacher. After reading the entire book, the assembly is not a liturgical one and the preacher is no ordained minister! This wise cynic, this troubling questioner, this tongue-in-check jokester, this affluent teacher, so prosperous as to have too much and to call it all a puff of wind, this sage keeps us guessing from the opening word:

> Vanity of vanities, says Qoheleth,
>   vanity of vanities! All things are vanity.

Qoheleth forces us to pray in a different way than Haggai; we are not called to liturgy and feastday but to take a second, hard, long look at life. The topic of ''prayer'' must not be distracted by sacred environment and religious

sounds! We are to contemplate life as it is and to admit that
it is all very boring—unless we *begin* to direct ourselves on
the way to true wisdom: "It is from the hand of God"
(2:24), from beginning to end, the work which God has
done" (3:11), "rather, fear God!" (5:6), "God made humankind straight, but people have had recourse to many cal-
culations" (7:29). He ends his twelfth and last chapter with
these words:

> The last word, when all is heard: fear God and
> keep his commandments, for this is all for man
> and woman, because God will bring to judgment
> every work, with all its hidden qualities, whether
> good or bad (12:13–14).

The end result may not seem like exalted spirituality, yet it
is no small accomplishment to shake loose the complacent
and *begin* the work of conversion.

Finally, we have the sad portrait of Herod the Tetrarch.
For him religion was a curiosity, a temporary pill to soothe
conscience, a clever way of winning allegiance. It is tragic
to think that his wish to see Jesus was fulfilled when Pilate
made friends with Herod by sending him the captive Jesus.
We are told that "Herod was extremely pleased to see Jesus" (Luke 23:8). Religion, like Jesus, can be used for politics and pleasure, the saddest way to relieve boredom.

Prayer:

Lord, teach us to number our days aright, that we may
gain wisdom. Break the spell of our melancholy and at daybreak fill us with your kindness. Grant that we may assemble as your faithful people. Let the high praises of
enthusiasm and joy sound from our throat, from our timbrels
and dance.

Friday, 25th Week

Hag 1:15—2:9. The Lord remembers his covenant. In a little while he will make the new temple more glorious than that of Solomon's.

Eccl 3:1–11. There is an appointed time for everything. God has put the timeless into the human heart without our ever discovering what God has done.

Luke 9:18–22. While people think that Jesus is one of the prophets, Peter confesses him to be "the Messiah of God." Jesus announces his suffering, death and resurrection.

The story of Everyman and Everywoman is told in today's readings. All of life's stages are represented here. Even though each of us individually will be identified with only one of these stages at *this* particular moment of our life, nonetheless, we must come to a peaceful acceptance of our past and we need to be prepared in advance for what lies ahead. Moreover as each of us lives in family, parish, religious community, neighborhood, work or residence, we mingle with others in all the stages of human existence.

Haggai (Cycle I) does not deny *memories* but puts them to their proper use. Without dodging the issue of discouragement, he asks the people:

> Who is left among you that saw this house in its former glory [the temple built by Solomon and demolished by the Babylonians]? And how do you see it now? Does it not seem like nothing in your eyes?

If the prophet can draw upon one memory, he is entitled to summon others. He refers next to the days of Moses and the covenant at Mount Sinai:

This is the pact that I made with you when you
came out of Egypt, and my spirit continues in your
midst. Do not fear.

We too have memories of God's goodness and graces, of
God's call and pledge to be with us always in pursuit of that
call. In order to summon these recollections, we have to be
at peace with ourselves and responsibly to possess each our
own "history." In order to evoke memories in others, we
need to understand them well, to have been a long, good listener, and to respect the good intentions of others through
their life.

By means of these good memories Haggai evoked a
recollection of Israel's *early days of dedication and accomplishment*, dedication through the covenant at Sinai and accomplishment during the glorious reigns of David and
Solomon. In our lives these are the days of adolescence and
young adult life. The Bible asks us to be enthusiastic about
this period of human existence, whether in ourselves or in
others. We should be excited about the achievement of
young people, never jealous nor critical. They will need
those golden days as happy memories at a later time.

Next comes the long stretch of *decision, acceptance*
and *patience*. For this we turn from Haggai to Ecclesiastes
(Cycle II). We quote a few of his lines:

There is an appointed time for everything,
    and a time for every affair under the heavens.
A time to be born, and a time to die,
    —to kill and to heal;
    —to be silent and to speak;
    —to love and to hate.

Ecclesiastes draws this long section to a conclusion by writing:

> God has made everything appropriate to its time,
> and has put the timeless into their hearts.

Ecclesiastes combines decisiveness (''an appointed time for everything'') with the ''timeless'' and monotonous. We never seem to complete the pursuit of our desires and objectives. We interpret this reaction as a healthy way of making decisions and an equally healthy way of knowing that ''here we have no lasting city; we are seeking one which is to come'' (Heb 13:14).

No life remains monotonous for long. Sooner or later *a severe trial* strikes. For Israel, the entire existence came down in fiery ruins. The temple of ''former glory'' lay a heap of ashes and rubble. Haggai, in Cycle I, repeats the phrase, ''Take courage!'' The exile purified the people, greatly reduced their material wealth and also greatly enhanced their *spiritual ideals* and *hopes*. God assures Israel:

> One moment yet, a little while,
> and I will shake the heavens and the earth . . .
> and the treasuries of all nations will come in . . .
> Greater will be the future glory of this house.

The New Testament will recognize this new ''moment'' in the coming of Jesus (Heb 12:26). Out of the scorching trials of the exile and the monotonous days afterwards God drew this statement of messianic hope. We too will be surprised by the spiritual insight achieved through suffering and perseverance.

In the midst of such trials, the questions will be put to us ever more insistently: "Who do you say that I am?" We will be called upon to renew our first dedication, to summon our memories, to overcome our monotony, to make our clearest decision. This is the most important of all "appointed times." Now we come face to face with the "timeless." "The heavens and the earth" are "shaken" and we confess, "the Messiah of God." We are now prepared to follow Jesus the last long stretch:

> The Son of Man must first endure many sufferings, be rejected . . . be put to death, and then be raised on the third day.

These final words of the gospel are most appropriate, not only for the continuation of the Eucharist—body broken and blood shed—but also for our meditations this Friday, the anniversary day of Jesus' death.

Prayer:
　　Lord, we hope in you always, even as we go about in mourning. We believe that you will send forth your light and your fidelity. As our rock and fortress, you will care for us, even when our life seems but a passing shadow.

Saturday, 25th Week

Zech 2:5–9,14–15. In a vision Jerusalem is seen as a home of peace where many nations come to dwell.

Eccl 11:9—12:8. Classic statement of old age (they who look through the window grow blind and one waits for the chirping of a bird) and of death (the silver cord is snapped and the golden bowl is broken). Vanity of vanities!

Luke 9:43–45. Jesus' prophecy of his death could not be grasped by the disciples, yet they were afraid to question him about the matter.

The Scriptures provide us with two, quite different signals about the future. Zechariah's prophecy is strong in symbolic expressions of hope, while Jesus speaks bluntly and sternly about his death. Ecclesiastes is not symbolic but rather very imaginative or rhetorical about old age and death. We see here another example about the demands which hope places upon us. Without the practical reminders given by Ecclesiastes and Luke, the hopes in Zechariah might deserve the charge of "pie in the sky," often enough thrown in the face of religion.

The selection from Zechariah (Cycle I) is taken from a series of visions in the early part of the prophecy. Visions are necessary for survival when times are bleak. Zechariah lived during the early postexilic period when the temple was still in ruins, the people ever more indifferent and their high priest, Joshua, was "clad in the filthy garments" of their sins (Zech 3:3). It was Zechariah who coined the phrase, "day of small beginnings" (4:10). Under the impact of the prophets Ezekiel, Jeremiah and Isaiah 40–55, Zechariah dreams about the future. As already mentioned, he had to dream visions in order to maintain his balance, psychologically and spiritually.

Because the vision turns out to be so wonderful and absorbing, Zechariah wanted two angels besides the "man with a measuring line," to accompany him and explain what is seen:

Jerusalem, so peaceful that no walls are necessary;

> Jerusalem, like an "open country" because
>   of the multitude of people and
>   domestic animals.
> Jerusalem, encircled by fire and possessing
>   the glory of the Lord in its midst.
>   The entire city becomes the temple
>   of prayer and worship.
> Jerusalem, home for "many nations [who] shall
>   join themselves to the Lord."

Zechariah is truly making the most of what lies in devastation before him. The temple and city walls had been demolished by foreign nations, but their absence becomes a prophecy of peace. The city is decimated, and the prophet dreams about multitudes. Foreigners had been hostile and vengeful; Zechariah sees them joining themselves to the Lord.

Zechariah is telling us that we never have a good reason for being gloomy and pessimistic. Each element of our sorrow can be transformed into a reason for hope. For this reason Zechariah was strong in tackling the problems of sin and deceit. He speaks out in the name of God:

> I am determined to favor Jerusalem and the house
> of Judah; do not fear. These are the things you
> should do: speak the truth to one another; let there
> be honesty and peace in the judgments at your
> gates, and let none of you plot evil against another
> in the heart, nor love a false oath. For all these
> things I hate, says the Lord (8:15–17).

The prophet effectively combined visions with earthy practicality. It may be more correct to state that his visions of hope would not permit him to accept dishonesty and bribes and so he appears as well as a stalwart moral reformer!

Zechariah strikes us as the type of young person to whom Ecclesiastes in Cycle II first addresses himself:

> Rejoice, O young man, while you are young
> and let your heart be glad
> in the days of your youth.
> Follow the ways of your heart,
> the vision of your eyes.

Very quickly, however, Ecclesiastes turns the brush of his pen away from the portrait of the young and begins to paint his extraordinary vignette of old age and death. The lines seem as bleak as the real Jerusalem before the eyes (not the vision) of Zechariah. We cannot help but think on our part of lonely old people, sitting all day long with their silent companions, staring into space:

> the sun is darkened
> the grinders are idle
> they who look through the window grow blind
> one waits for the chirp of the bird
> all the singing maidens are silenced.

We need Ecclesiastes' words lest we forget the aged and the dying. We too will one day take their ranks and we need to be told that such is the stuff of inspiration. Even to say ''vanity of vanities'' at these last years, repeats the words of the Bible. God must be present.

Certainly Jesus was there, with the lonely and the dying. He prepared himself and his disciples for the difficult time. His words were clear and intelligible: ''the Son of

Man must be delivered into the hands of men.'' If the disciples ''failed, however, to understand this warning [and] did not grasp it at all,'' they were unwilling to accept what their ears heard. For this reason they would not ''question him about the matter,'' lest Jesus reinforce what they thought he said!

Jesus did repeat the warning as he drew ever closer to Jerusalem. Hope for the resurrection grew out of the reality of death. Like Zechariah, Jesus could see visions to support the bleakness of life and arrive at life's finest moral ideals and eternal possibilities. Like Ecclesiastes Jesus faced up to the reality of death.

Prayer:

Lord, we acknowledge that you guard us like a shepherd guarding his flock. If we are scattered, you gather us together. You turn our mourning into joy. Help us to believe in you and to hope in you and so to realize that a thousand years in your sight are as yesterday.

Monday, 26th Week

Zech 8:1–9. Jerusalem shall again be filled with people, the aged and the young, with Israelites who have been scattered across the earth. ''I will be their God with faithfulness and justice.''

Job 1:6–22. In God's throne room Satan receives permission to try Job, first with loss of property and then with the death of his children. Yet, Job did not say anything disrespectful of God and did not sin.

Luke 9:46–50. With the example of a little child Jesus declares the least among you to be the greatest. Anyone who is not against you is on your side.

Children remain the constant topic and the key to reflection through all three readings. To provide an indication of the new Jerusalem, Zechariah pictures the city with "boys and girls playing in the streets" (Cycle I). In the prologue to the Book of Job the loss of sons and daughters brings forth lament: "Naked I came forth from my mother's womb, and naked shall I go back again" (Cycle II). Finally, in today's gospel Jesus turns to children to teach about the "greatest in the Kingdom of God."

Children take up where adults stop. Children manifest life and enthusiasm where many people in Zechariah's day were simply dragging themselves through life to the grave. The prophet's preaching about new life and bright future was badly received or at best accepted with a yawn. The people had followed his advice and that of Haggai and had rebuilt the temple. Yet it was on such a small scale that "many of the priests, levites and family heads, the old men who had seen the former house [of Solomon's construction] cried out in sorrow" (Ezra 3:12). "This [new vision of Jerusalem and the temple by Zechariah] seemed impossible in the eyes of the remnant of this people." Zechariah, however, quickly asks the question on the part of God, "Shall it . . . be impossible in my eyes also?"

Because of the children, the prophet returns in many ways to God's fidelity towards Israel:

- I am intensely jealous for Zion,
- I will return to Zion,
- Jerusalem shall be called the faithful city,
- I will rescue my people from east and west,
- They shall be my people and I will be their God, with faithfulness and justice.

Children are the pledge of the future, the source of happiness and hope, the teachers of true value and lasting treasures. Children set things straight for they put artificial pleasure and material possessions down to a low spot on the scale of values. If we are to believe in the hereafter, we must think of children. Children force us to think also in terms of family and that means the sharing of possessions with the wider family.

Children appear in our first selection from the Book of Job (Cycle II) and here our discussion moves in another direction. We are reading from the prose prologue, which with the epilog at the end, forms the context for the dramatic dialogue within the central part of the book. This prose section turns out to be the most ancient part and belonged to the patrimony of the Near East. We meet the somewhat naive situation in which Satan shows up in the heavenly throne room and argues with God about justice in the human family! God permits Satan to test Job, destroying first his property and then taking the lives of his sons and daughters.

Job is alone, totally alone. His wife appears later in the narrative but is hardly any consolation. Alone, yes; but also alone with God.

> Naked I came forth from my mother's womb,
>   and naked shall I go back again.
> The Lord gave, and the Lord has taken away;
>   blessed be the name of the Lord.

Children reach into the roots of life, into the womb where life develops. Children, therefore, make us ponder the mysterious source of life. As adults, we cannot control life as though we were God. At the same time we do not act solely on instinct, like animals. We must think and consider all of the responsibilities of life. Yet, there must also remain a secret part of life which belongs solely to God. Not only in the process of conception, pregnancy and birth, but also in many other important moments of our existence, we do our best when we follow intuitions or inspirations which take even ourselves by surprise.

Can we be like Job? When he was startled by the sudden news of his children's death and plunged into the dark mystery of life, he remained faithful to God.

Children, finally, encourage us adults to be faithful. They dispel our jealousies and disputes. Children quarrel, yes, but they quickly make up again. The gospel presents us with two scenes of envy and pettiness. The disciples were arguing, "which of them was the greatest." Or again they are upset because they see a man "not of our company," using the name of Jesus to expel demons and heal the sick. Jesus turns to children and says to welcome children is to welcome Jesus and even God the Father who sent Jesus. In this context Jesus says, "The least one among you is the greatest." This statement is all the more puzzling if it includes Jesus. Is he the least? He is the "child" of his Father, always in the attitude of receiving the Father's life and as a child he is receiving it totally.

Prayer:

Lord, you hear the prayer of the destitute and the groaning of prisoners. You show us your wonderful kindness. You will hear our prayer and make us again like children, trustful, full of life and hope, happy about the goodness of others. Test my heart and remove all malice from it so that I may be your servant, blessing you at all times.

Tuesday, 26th Week

Zech 8:20–23. Many peoples of every nationality shall take hold of every Jew by the edge of his garment and say,

"Let us go with you, for we have heard that God is with you."

Job 3 (*Selected verses*) Job curses the day of his birth and wishes that he had come forth from the womb stillborn.

Luke 9:51–56. The long journey narrative begins in Luke's gospel as Jesus proceeds towards Jerusalem. Rejected by the Samaritans, Jesus still does not want them cursed.

Today we are invited to participate in a journey to Jerusalem and the holy temple, there to worship God with many brothers and sisters. The spirit with which we travel forms the spirit with which we join in prayer at the temple (or church). This spirit, as we learn from the three readings, is not a generic kind of pious attitude which fits every moment and circumstance, but somehow or other this spirit is partially formed by the environment of our individual lives.

In *Zechariah* (Cycle I) we journey with the contagious excitement of a large group who want to "take hold of every Jew by the edge of his garment" as they say, "Let us go with you, for we have heard that God is with you." In *Job* (Cycle II) a sad, despondent person is among those who "wait for death and it comes not." Job longs for the final journey of death, where "the wicked cease from troubling and the weary are at rest." In the *Gospel of Luke* the long "journey narrative" is introduced; Jesus "firmly resolved to proceed toward Jerusalem and sent messengers on ahead of him." This journey becomes the context for understanding the preaching and ministry of Jesus. Everything which the Lord says or does is somehow a step towards Jerusalem, where "Jesus was to be taken from this world," a step towards Jesus' passion, death and resurrection.

If the larger setting, apparent in Zechariah and in the gospel, turns out to be a pilgrimage towards Jerusalem, "the place which the Lord your God, chooses . . . as his dwelling'' (Deut 12:5), then we have another motive, that of worship and adoration, of community prayer, of liturgically reliving the great moments of salvation in our own day and place. We of the twentieth and twenty-first centuries, are being asked to look upon all of our changes, transitions and ''journeys'' as a step towards union with Jesus and with all our brothers and sisters in worship. Each sorrow enables us to ''hang with Jesus upon the cross'' (Gal 5:24) and to be ''crucified with Christ'' (Gal 2:19). Every joy calls us to be with Christ, ''raised from the dead by the glory of the Father [so that] we too might live a new life'' (Rom 6:4). Whether in sorrow or joy we are joined with many brothers and sisters who assemble in worship for the Eucharist around ''the body [of the Lord] to be given for you'' and the ''blood to be shed for you'' (Luke 22:19–20), with Christ who has died, risen and is coming again in glory. These last words echo the proclamation of faith after the consecration of bread and wine into the body and blood of Christ.

Turning back to the Scriptures, we find that Zechariah catches the exuberant joy of ''Christ who will come again in glory.'' Zechariah, in this passage, represents one of the rare Old Testament moments which anticipates the conversion of the gentiles, honorably and enthusiastically with all the Israelites. Even though they are coming from ''every nationality, speaking different tongues,'' they all understand and speak the one language that proclaims: ''God is with you!'' For Zechariah to announce salvation in such a hopeful and generous way he had to be extremely courageous. We have only to recall the situation, again in his own language, ''a day of small beginnings'' (Zech 4:10), and yet he dreamed of the world and all its people. When it had been a monumental achievement for a few Israelites to return out of exile to the promised land, he sees all the nations converging upon the holy city. And he was correct. As we live within melancholy and discouragement, the Bible recalls happy moments that call us forward to a new Jerusalem.

At the same time the Bible gives us time for our sorrow and dejection; it provides us with the Book of Job! Among the stages of dying are those of anger and depression. These are real moments which cannot be denied or hurried. The selection from Job may seem so negative as to be blasphemous:

> Perish the day in which I was born . . . .
> Why did I not perish at birth? . . . .
> Or why was I not buried away like an untimely birth,
>   like babes that have never seen light?

At the very end of the selection, however, is a significant line. Job is one of those persons:

> whose path is hidden from them, and whom *God has hemmed in.*

Though we seem to go nowhere except to the grave, if we go thoroughly in God's presence, then mysteriously enough, the God who hears us like Job curse the day of our birth, is the God who is calling us to hang with Jesus on the cross, to cling to a body broken and to carry within oneself the blood that is being shed.

In the Gospel of Luke, we begin the long journey narrative. All the way to the end of chap. 19, Luke assembles anecdotes and sayings of Jesus which Matthew and Mark scatter elsewhere in Palestine. Luke thereby makes a theological (not a geographical) statement that every thing points mystically towards Jerusalem, that is towards our union with Jesus in his sufferings, death and glorious resurrection which happened at Jerusalem.

It is important to note that Luke opens this journey narrative with the incident at Samaria. These people in central Palestine had been rejected by the Jerusalem Jews and by this time they were fiercely hostile. Jesus will not permit his disciples to think of the destruction of the Samaritans. He gives them time, just as Job needed time to curse and to be angry! We learn in the Acts of the Apostles that many Samaritans were converted to Christianity, very quickly after Pentecost. After Stephen was martyred and while Saul was persecuting the church, we read:

> The members of the church had been dispersed. Philip, for example, went down to the town of Samaria and there proclaimed the Messiah [and] cured many people. The rejoicing in that town rose to fever pitch (Acts 8:4–8).

In his gospel Luke is preparing for this moment of glory!

The Bible, therefore, respects all different stages in life and enables us to see each of them as a following in the footsteps of Jesus.

Prayer:

Lord, we hear the song of the new Jerusalem where people from all over the world sing how ''one and all are born in her.'' Enable us to join in that song and to be at peace with men and women of all races and nations, with all our neighbors. Even if we are plunged into the dark abyss, grant us an awareness of your secret, holy presence. Then through our union with Jesus on the cross, we will rise to new glory.

Wednesday, 26th Week

Neh 2:1–8. Nehemiah receives permission from the Persian king to return to Jerusalem in order to rebuild its walls and to restore the ancestral graves.

Job 9:1–12,14–16. Job confesses God's omnipotent control of the universe and strong, mysterious guidance of human life.

Luke 9:57–62. Jesus responds to prospective followers by a series of stern statements.

We are offered an unique opportunity to reflect upon the ways of divine providence. Our response must blend heroic faith with practical decisions. As we integrate the three biblical readings or as we combine the gospel selection either with Nehemiah (Cycle I) or with Job (Cycle II), we reach a very wholesome attitude, thoroughly respectful of our human dignity and natural talents, and at the same time completely obedient, even humbly dependent towards God, creator and master of the universe.

In many ways Nehemiah had it made. He was a personal attendant or valet to the Persian king, Artaxerxes I (464–423 B.C.). An incidental detail found in today's reading indicates his rank or position at court. He first tasted the food or drink prepared for the king, as proof that nothing poisonous was being offered the monarch! He was daily in the royal retinue, and therefore he was always in a position to make requests or to interpret events and people! Yet, Nehemiah was "sick [and] sad at heart." The city of his ancestors lay in ruins.

The situation indeed was gloomy for any decent Jew. Even though the temple had been rebuilt between 520–515 B.C. at the urging of the prophets Haggai and Zechariah, the city was open to hostile or greedy invaders and no one could muster much energy to rebuild on a permanent scale. The great prophecies of Ezekiel and Second Isaiah, spoken during the Babylonian exile, must have seemed like whistling in the dark or else like reciting Shakespeare on the corner of a city slum!

Nehemiah as we already observed, was "sick [and] sad at heart," despite his personal security and even luxurious living at the Persian court. When the king asked: "What is it, then, that you wish, Nehemiah combined prayer with ingenuity. We read:

> I prayed to the God of heaven *and then* answered
> the king.

His request even got down to the practical nuts-and-bolts of letters of introduction to local governors along the route of his return and to "Asaph, the keeper of the royal park, that he may give me wood" for the city gates, temple-citadel and his own residence. Nehemiah's account ends with a reference that "the favoring hand of the Lord was upon me."

The Book of Job takes us back to the lonely stretch of nearly one hundred years after the exile as well as forward to personal crises in all of our lives. In today's reading Job is replying to Bildad, the second of his three friends who had "heard of all the misfortune that had come upon him [and had] journeyed together to give him sympathy and comfort" (Job 2:11). Chapter nine in many ways summarizes the entire Book of Job:

> no one can be justified before God,
> God is wise in heart and mighty in strength,
> He does marvelous things across the heavens
> and the sea,

Should he come near me, I see him not;
How much less can I give him any answer.

The magnificent poem to God's overpowering control of the universe, beyond human scrutiny and comprehension, which concludes the Book in chaps. 38–41, is already sketched for us in today's reading.

We, like Job, must live long within the dark cloud of mystery, in order to learn the way of faith and humility before God. Quick answers, like quick food and instant wealth, are generally not the best for physical health and psychological peace. Yet, once we have learned to recognize the interior groaning of the Spirit "as we await the redemption of our bodies" (Rom 8:23) and to be inwardly at peace with hopes as yet unfulfilled, then God calls us like Nehemiah to summon all of our human talents and to seize the opportunity to act with prudence and courage.

Human virtues plunge us again into mystery. As disciples of Jesus, we will be thrust into situations of courage and even martyrdom. These moments are not the daily fare of life. Very few people can live heroically on a continuous day-by-day basis, nor should life be planned that way. Yet, such excruciating moments come to each disciple, and then we need to turn and hear again the stern words of Jesus:

The Son of Man has nowhere to lay his head.
Let the dead bury their dead.
Whoever puts his hand to the plow but
   keeps looking back is unfit
   for the reign of God.

Jesus' statement even reaches heroically beyond the recommendations of the prophet Elijah who had replied affirmatively when asked by his own disciple to "kiss my father and mother goodbye, and [then] I will follow you'' (I Kgs 19:20).

Today's reading sets a pattern for one's entire life, a life that includes long delays, great opportunities for human talents, heroic decisions of faith. For this day's ''today'' we need to discern which of the readings are most appropriate, yet even today it is necessary to prepare for tomorrow and its new, unexpected demands.

Prayer:

Never let us forget Jerusalem, O Lord. It is the city of peace, justice and most of all your holy presence. At times our peace is shattered and justice is stolen from us; we sit and weep. Yet, we always wait upon you, O Lord. Do not hide your face from us.

Thursday, 26th Week

Neh 8:1–12. Ezra assembles the people to renew their loyalty to the covenant, to learn the meaning of the Torah, to worship God, and to share their good gifts with one another.

Job 19:21–27. Job again takes his case directly to God who will appear as his vindicator.

Luke 10:1–12. Jesus sends forth the seventy-two disciples who are to follow a stern discipline in announcing the reign of God.

We sense an urgency in the biblical readings. Ezra assembles *all* the people, even the ''children old enough to understand'' what was read from the Torah or ancient Books of Moses. Job wants his words to be ''cut in the rock forever'' ''with an iron chisel and with lead.'' Jesus sends forth the

seventy-two disciples with no provisions, lest they be bur-
dened in their stern and rapid announcement that "the reign
of God is at hand!" While all these scripture selections share
in this sense of crisis and the need to act at once in a decisive
way, they part company in the vision of the future. Ezra for-
sees a long stretch of time on earth and prepares the people
by renewing the covenant and by teaching them the Torah.
Job cuts through all human means of justification and
reaches directly for God's immediate presence. Jesus announces that Job's wish is fulfilled in the reign of God. Yet,
we also know that the reign of God, inaugurated by Jesus,
did not lead at once to a glorious paradise but rather to the
long period of church history. We still await the second
coming of Jesus!

Each of us stands in need of all three readings, not for
any single moment of our life, maybe not for today. One selection may seem to suffice at this time. Yet, we need to be
prepared for the many tomorrows ahead of us, lest we turn
aside and reject the Lord's messenger, and when it is too
late, we see only the dust of our mistake, shaken from the
messenger's feet. Jesus has said to these messengers:

> "If the people of any town you enter do not wel-
> come you, go into its streets and say, 'We shake
> the dust of this town from our feet as testimony
> against you. But know that the reign of God is
> near.' "

We cannot afford to be light-hearted and over-confident.
Time and the opportunities of special grace will pass us by!
At certain crossroads of life we are afforded the luxury of
much time, and like Ezra we can prepare punctiliously.
Other moments, just as serious in their outcome, come
quickly and leave us no time, only our good (or bad) in-

stincts for an immediate decision. Sometimes we have sufficient opportunity afterwards to correct mistakes, at other times like Job or like the cities who hesitate to receive the Lord's messengers, our decisions are "inscribed in a record" or even "cut in the rock forever." For the rest of our life, possibly for eternity, we must live with the consequences.

Ezra was right. Israel had to be instructed, disciplined and properly prepared for a long future. For over a hundred years since the return from the Babylonian exile, the people, repatriated in their homeland, were fiddling around half-heartedly. At the urging of the prophets Haggai and Zechariah they had rebuilt the temple yet its outline was so small that "the old people who had seen the former house [built by Solomon] cried out in sorrow" (Ezra 3:12). At Nehemiah's insistence the city walls rose again as a sign of permanency and strength, but now the people felt secure enough to exact heavy interest, force fellow Jews to sell sons and daughters into slavery and overlook the hungry. We still remember Nehemiah's words: "I was extremely angry . . . and rebuked them severely [who] remained silent, for they could find no answer" (Neh 5:6–7).

Ezra remains right even today. We need someone to stand up and to speak with authority.

> As the people remained in their places Ezra read plainly from the book of the law of God, interpreting it so that all could understand what was read.

In Ezra, however, the Torah did not bring sorrow. When he saw that "all the people were weeping," he corrected them again, this time in a different tone:

Today is holy to the Lord your God. Do not be
sad, and do not weep. . . . Go, eat rich foods and
drink sweet drinks, and allot portions for those
who had nothing prepared.

Ezra combined joy with discipline and so became the Founder of Judaism, the way of life which beats at the heart of the
Jewish people even today whether that heart weeps or
laughs.

While Ezra mustered human energy for the long haul
and parceled it out carefully for ordinary days and generously for festivals, Job is faced with the once-in-twenty
years challenge, maybe the once-in-a-lifetime ordeal. Human comforters, with their ancient wisdom and respected
advice, simply intensified Job's agony. Job does not want
theological explanations but—

Pity me, pity, O you my friends . . .
Why do you hound me as though you were divine?

Job must take his case directly to God. Each of us too at sin-
gular crises find "my inmost being . . . consumed with
longing." We are face to face with the awesome God in the
depth of our conscience.

Jesus too brings such an imperative into our lives:
"The reign of God is at hand!" Our reaction is as serious in
its results as that of "the fate of Sodom." Yet, once the decision is made, clearly and responsibly, we can settle into
our Christian life with the joy and at times the sorrow, with
the routine weekdays and special festivals for which Ezra
prepared. Once we have staked all of our responses and very
life—our "walking staff," "traveling bag," and
"purse"—and have taken the total risk for "the reign of
God," then the rest of our journey through life will benefit

from the gospel and especially from the presence of Jesus, "my Vindicator . . . whom I myself shall see."

Prayer:

Lord, I wait upon you with all my heart. I look towards you for pity and comfort. Your law, like your holy presence, will refresh my soul, enlighten my eyes and be sweeter than honey from the comb. Lord, you give joy to my heart.

Friday, 26th Week

Bar 1:15–22. From the time that the Lord led our ancestors out of the land of Egypt until the present day, we have been disobedient and only too ready to disregard the voice of the Lord, our God.

Job 38:1,12–21; 40:3–5. Only if Job is himself another god, walking the depths of the abyss and knowing the way to the dwelling place of light, can he challenge God.

Luke 10:13–16. If the miracles and wonders accomplished in your midst had been worked in Tyre and Sidon, these cities would have reformed long ago.

The scriptural readings transform today into a day of memories. Some of the recollections make us sad, others challenge us, still others shatter us like Job into "dust and ashes" (Job 42:6). Yet, each reading is "gospel" for us, that is, the good news of salvation, the wonderful presence of Jesus, the promise of a happy, transformed existence.

Today's selection from the Book of Baruch dates to the Babylonian exile (587–539 B.C.), and if we read the verse which precedes the liturgical text (Bar 1:14), we find ourselves in the midst of the autumnal feast of Tabernacles. A collection was being taken up, to be sent to Jerusalem for

sacrifices and for assisting the poor in the holy city. The
feast of Tabernacles was originally an octave of great rejoicing. We read in Leviticus:

> On the first day [of the octave] you shall gather fo-
> liage from majestic trees, branches of palms and
> boughs of myrtles and of valley poplars, and then
> for a week you shall make merry before the Lord,
> your God (Lev 23:40).

During the exile, however, as even later during the postexilic period, the joy that was appropriate for the feast even
precipitated sorrow. The contrast between the feast and the
reality of life was too great. During Ezra's day "all the people were weeping" and Ezra was compelled to order them:

> Go, eat rich foods and drink sweet drinks, and al-
> lot portions to those who had nothing prepared;
> for today is holy to the Lord. Do not be saddened
> this day, for rejoicing in the Lord must be your
> strength (Neh 8:9–10).

Under the circumstances of sin and disobedience to the
Lord, rejoicing would be completely out of the question. In
fact, it would provoke still more sorrow and punishment, if
God were like ourselves, holding grudges, punishing to the
last drop of blood, and repaying evil with evil. God is totally
different, as we hear God cry out with divine passion in the
prophecy of Hosea:

> My heart is overwhelmed,
>   my pity is stirred.
> I will not give vent to my blazing anger, . . .
> For I am God, no human being (Hos 11:8–9).

As we reread Baruch's confession, we realize that the fault is ours, not God's: we are flushed with shame; we have not heeded the voice of the Lord, our God (twice); we have been disobedient; we went off after the desires of our own heart. It is true, Baruch adds that ''the evils and the curse which the Lord enjoined upon Moses . . . cling to us even today.'' Yet, this curse did not keep Israel from entering and possessing ''the land flowing with milk and honey,'' God's lovely gift to his poor people. The same merciful God of the exodus is with us today. We are asked to repent, to reform our ways, to set our faces towards our good inspirations and fine hopes, yes, most of all to be men and women of hope.

Hopes do not make the future easy. Generally they challenge us to muster even that strength which we never thought that we possessed. Such is the case with Job. Today's selection (Cycle II) summarizes God's overwhelming address to Job ''out of the storm and whirlwind!'' Because Job had questioned God's providential care, God presumes that Job must be divine and so addresses Job as a fellow-god:

Have you walked about in the depths of the abyss?
Do you know the way to the dwelling place of
    light?
Do you command the morning light
    and show dawn its place?

We too will be ashamed to have questioned God's wisdom. We put our hand over our mouth. Yet we carry that wonderful memory of having taken part in the secret council of God, like Job and again like Jeremiah (*cf.*, Jer 23:18,22). If life's hopes and demands seem too divine and overtaxing on our human strength, we are being reminded how much we belong to God's family. Our memory convinces us of this.

Like Moses in the desert, we have experienced the goodness, even the miracles of God.

In the gospel, Jesus reminds us again of these miracles. Jesus holds out to us, melancholy and hopeless individuals, a new life, miraculously transformed.

Prayer:

Remember your ancient compassion and promise of forgiveness, O Lord. Help us, not because of our worthiness but because of the glory of your name, a name that promises salvation to the lowly. If only we will open our eyes, we will recognize salvation to the lowly. We will recognize your right hand, O Lord, holding us fast, even at the farthest limits of the sea.

Saturday, 26th Week

Bar 4:5–12,27–29. Jerusalem sorrows over her children in exile, because they "turned away from the law of God," "from God who had nourished you." Jerusalem pleads with them to "turn now ten times the more to seek him."

Job 42 (*Selected verses*). After Job repents of his doubts and complaints against God, he is blessed by the Lord more abundantly than ever before in his life.

Luke 10:17–24. When the seventy-two disciples return in jubilation over their miracles and success, Jesus rejoices as well in the secret graces reserved for the humble and merest children.

The secret, stirring beneath the surface in Baruch and Job, comes wondrously to the surface in Jesus' prayerful rejoicing in the Holy Spirit: "what you have hidden from the learned and the clever, you have revealed to the merest children.'' One aspect of mystery is always present when a city as stately and as endowed with promise as Jerusalem-Zion is seen in ''great mourning'' (Cycle I). Another side of mystery baffles us when a person as traditionally good and honorable as Job, is seen to ''repent in dust and ashes'' (Cycle II). Still another glimpse of mystery overawes us in the sight of Jesus in prayer!

Mystery, like a child, can never be handled properly with anger or pride, not with success and prosperity, not even with academic learning and syllogistic reasoning. Anger and pride deprive us of that delicacy and tenderness, so necessary to approach a child or any mystery in life. Learning and reasoning deal so much with what can be controlled that the intuitive and the wondrous are overlooked; success and prosperity so involve us in materiality and in worldliness, that our sense of the other-world or inner-world is blurred and denied. The three readings for this Saturday enable us to take the necessary time to stop and meditate, to let our spirit slip beneath surface concerns and quick answers, and to be at prayer with Jesus.

Baruch brings to mind the photos of Jerusalem's ancient walls that all of us have seen; some of us will remember our walks along those walls. So stately strong and silent, so old and wise, the walls of Jerusalem have seen it all, from the triumphant days of David to the battering rams of Babylonians and Romans, Crusaders and Moslems, and now the Israeli army. These walls seem so old as to be dead tomb stones, yet amazingly new life is always growing between the rocks, in the crannies, where green shoots are sprouting! Such is the spirit and tone of Jerusalem's prayer in Baruch. The prophet first addresses the people!

> You forsook the Eternal God who nourished you,
> and you grieved Jerusalem who fostered you.

Jerusalem first speaks not to Israelites but rather to the nations who fought against her:

> Hear, you neighbors of Zion!
> God has brought great mourning upon me.
> . . . my sons and daughter.
> With joy I fostered them;
> but with mourning and lament I let them go . . . .
> I am left desolate.

We begin to delve the mysterious darkness and new life within sorrow. If Jerusalem can speak in this kindly way to neighbors who harmed her and her children, Jerusalem is already a mother, begetting new life. Such tenderness cannot remain barren. With new hope Jerusalem then addresses her children, as yet hidden away in exile or in the dark womb:

> Fear not, my children; call out to God!
> He who brought this upon you will remember you.
> As your hearts have been disposed to stray from God,
> turn now ten times the more to seek him.

Very similar to sorrowful Jerusalem is the suffering image of Job (Cycle II). At this point Job is humbled by the mystery of God's overpowering providence. As we saw yesterday, Job had been presumptuous enough to question God, as though he, Job, were a divine colleague of Yahweh! Now he disowns his words and repents in dust and ashes. The mystery of someone as good as Job, "in dust and ashes"! How blessed we are to number such humble, great men and women in our own lives and among our own acquaintances. How we long to glimpse the mysterious depths of their heart and spirit! We know for certain what a great reward awaits them, even though they disclaim any credit for their beautiful lives. The conclusion to the Book of Job answers us. If we follow this example, we will be truly blessed.

Finally, the gospel allows us a rare glimpse into the deepest of all mysteries, the prayer of Jesus. The gospels, especially that of Luke, frequently enough speak of Jesus at prayer, but seldom do they do more than preserve a reverent silence around such moments.

The gospel reading begins with jubilation, miracles and exorcisms. The seventy-two disciples return after a marvelously successful missionary campaign. Jesus tells them to keep on rejoicing over all that they have done, but to rejoice most of all "that your names are inscribed in heaven." No happiness can compare to the bonds of personal love with God. The works and gifts of God are intended to lead us into the mystery of God's tender love, even of God's humble awareness for "merest children."

As Jesus is surrounded with all this bustle and excitement, wonder and triumph, he suddenly becomes silent, overcome by a hidden power. Rejoicing "in the Holy Spirit," he said:

> I offer you grateful praise, O Father, Lord of heaven and earth, because what you have hidden from the learned and the clever, you have revealed to merest children. Yes, Father, you have graciously willed it so.

We can only hope to remain so delicately sensitive and tender in the midst of triumph and achievement.

Prayer:

Lord, you listen to the poor and reveal the secret of your love to the weak. In all moments of our life, joyful or sorrowful, draw us to yourself that our hearts be merry in the mystery of your goodness and strong providence. Shine the light of your sacred wisdom into the paths of our lives.

Monday, 27th Week

Jonah 1:1–12; 2:11. Jonah, who worshipped the God of sea and dry land, attempts to flee from God on the open sea. When the pagan sailors finally threw Jonah overboard, the storm abated. A whale swallowed Jonah and brought him back to dry land.

Gal 1:6–12. Paul's gospel did not originate in human invention or schooling but in a special revelation from Jesus Christ, in whom God's gracious designs are made known. There is no other gospel.

Luke 10:25–37. The parable of the Good Samaritan explains who is my neighbor.

Today we are obliged by Scripture to deal with divine reversals in human life. It is not that God dramatically changes his mind but rather that God employs dramatic ways to keep us within his one and only gospel, his "gracious design in Christ," as we read in Galatians, or his unique revelation to Israel as the one "Lord, the God of heaven, who made the sea and the dry land."

Sometimes we attempt to trick God, like the lawyer who "stood up to pose to Jesus this problem [about] everlasting life," or we practically deny our correct theology by our wayward actions. We resemble Jonah who attempted to use the sea to flee away from "the God [of] the sea and the dry land." God has wonderful ways of bringing us back to our senses, extraordinary ways, in fact, to correct our orthodox theology by appealing to pagans and heretics! It really seems cruel, or at best whimsical on God's part, to advise us, who possess the truth, by means of our enemies who are wrong!

The dramatic reversals begin with the first reading (Cycle I) from the Book of Jonah. The paradoxes appear on the first line: all other prophets speak in poetry, while Jonah is written in prose; all others preach to Israelites, Jonah to foreigners; other prophets usually fail in converting Israel, Jonah succeeds in converting foreigners. While the original Jonah announced a *material* extension of the Kingdom of Israel over gentile territory "from Labo-of-Hamath to the sea of the Arabah" (2 Kgs 14:25), the prophecy of Jonah speaks of a *spiritual* extension of God's kingdom while preserving the political independence of Assyria. Last but not least, elsewhere in the Bible, Assyria is the most hated and feared of all foreign nations, second only to Babylon. In the Book of Jonah the Assyrians are more open to God's grace than the Israelite prophet!

God is determined to teach Israel a stern, profound lesson by the foreigners. While on board the boat, Jonah sleeps and must be wakened by the pagan foreigner:

> "What are you doing asleep? Rise up, call upon your God! Perhaps God will be mindful of us that we may not perish."

Even after the lots fall on Jonah and it is evident to the pagans that Jonah is guilty in "fleeing from the Lord," they still hesitate in "shedding this man's life" and throwing him into the sea, lest they themselves be guilty in "shedding innocent blood."

Dramatic reversals take a different twist in Paul's letter to the Galatians (Cycle II). Paul insists upon the authentic orthodoxy of his gospel, namely that in Christ Jesus,

> there does not exist among you Jew or Greek,
> slave or free person, male or female. All are one
> in Christ Jesus (Gal 3:28).

This statement, which we will read again on Saturday of this week (Cycle II) represents the key to Paul's gospel and entire ministry. This insight came directly to him. Paul did not learn it from Peter or any of the other apostles, nor would it have come from the earlier preaching of Jesus. Jesus had said so clearly to the twelve apostles when he "sent these men on mission":

> Do not visit pagan territory and do not enter a Samaritan town. Go instead after the lost sheep of the house of Israel (Matt 10:5).

God's covenant with Israel, however, was to be completed and perfected by reaching out and embracing first the Samaritans, among the first outsiders to be converted in the Acts of the Apostles (Acts 8:1), and then the Greeks and even the despised Romans, who occupied the Jewish homeland and were destined to destroy the Holy City, Jerusalem. Paul turns to these foreigners, not only for subjects to convert, but also for leadership and styles of worship. Israel could not learn simply or exclusively from her own major traditions what God intended as the full and final meaning of her covenant.

Paul received his gospel directly from God, as he protests vigorously in Galatians against all opponents, yet God was continually offering hints or flashing signals of this universal, missionary outreach. One of these signals was shot across the bow of the Old Testament ship of state by the author of the Book of Jonah. Another comes from Jesus in today's gospel. A lawyer, well trained in theology, posed a problem to Jesus about everlasting life, one of the deepest and most serious of all theological questions, and then tried to justify himself because he had already known that the answer consisted in the first and second greatest commandments. He asked: "Who is my neighbor?" Jesus turned to the Samaritan for an answer, to those people, despised and rejected by Israel as heretics and spoilers of the Torah!

Today Jesus turns to *our* "Samaritan" or "Assyrian" neighbor, the people whom we hate or look down upon, who are ignorant and willfully wrong, who have harmed us and taken advantage of us. Listen, Jesus tells us. Listen to them as they teach you how to pray and to follow God's holy will. Listen as they silently turn aside and care for their wounded enemy along the road. Listen, Jesus tells us, because we who are correct can be so biased and self-righteous, so proud and pious that we miss those signals of wonder and goodness flashed through the darkness to keep us on the course of God's "gracious design in Christ."

Prayer:

At times, Lord, in the raging and foaming sea, where I think there can be only breakers and billows of death, you send a whale to swallow me, to take me in the opposite direction and to save me. In strange ways the opposite direction is the right one. Give me the patience and humility to perceive this mystery. Then I will realize that the assembly of the just include people whom I hated, feared and despised. Thus you complete your covenant in our midst.

Tuesday, 27th Week

Jonah 3:1–10. At the preaching of Jonah, the people and king of Nineveh repent and so the Lord does not destroy their city.

Gal 1:13–24. Paul's zeal in persecuting the disciples of Je-
    sus, his conversion, and three years later his journey to
    Jerusalem "to get to know Cephas."
Luke 10:38–42. At the home of Martha and Mary, Jesus de-
    fends Mary "who seated herself at the Lord's feet and lis-
    tened to his words" while Martha busied herself with all
    the details of hospitality.

    While good intentions can drive a person to overactiv-
ity and even to misguided zeal, inflicting injury upon others,
the Scriptures still defend human activity and good works as
essential to salvation. For interpreting today's scripture
readings we must not only keep this healthy balance in mind
between contemplation and action, but it is also very helpful
to remember that each of us, simultaneously, are Martha
and Mary, Paul *and* Peter, Jonah *and* the the Ninevites!
Each of these persons becomes a symbol for us. This outlook does not deny the reality of the people; it simply points
out that "*everything* written before our time in the Scriptures was written for our instruction, that we might derive
hope from the lessons of patience and the words of encouragement" (Rom 15:4).
    Jonah was a man of action, not always good action, but
certainly decisive and effective. As we saw yesterday, when
he was ordered to Nineveh to preach repentance, he
promptly acted, but in the wrong direction! He could have
avoided all trouble by ignoring the Lord's command and
sleeping longer than usual in his Jerusalem home! In Galatians Paul too was a man of action. He was one of those people always at the eye of the hurricane! And in today's
gospel, Martha was no different than other people in Luke's
rendition of the Good News, who threw parties and state
dinners for Jesus or for a good cause—beginning with Si-
mon Peter's mother-in-law (4:39) to the father of the prodi-

gal son (15:22–24), to Zacchaeus the tax collector (19:5–6)
and Jesus' own preparations for the Last Supper (22:7–13).
Silent contemplation is the exception, not the rule, in the
Old and New Testament.

We need to reflect still more carefully upon the readings. In the Book of Jonah (Cycle I) repentance did not consist simply in the ritual acts of sackcloth and ashes. All persons were required to ''turn from their evil ways,'' a phrase
repeated twice in this short book, therefore an idea essential
for this account of conversion. Both ritual and moral action
were expected. In Galatians (Cycle II) Paul was not converted to pray but rather ''that I might spread among the
gentiles the good news concerning Jesus.'' And as already
mentioned, Martha fit the pattern of many good, active people in the Gospel of Luke.

As we read once again from the Scriptures, the role of
Mary begins to emerge in all these cases. First of all, we
need to take note of Moses, the founder of biblical religion,
who ''passed into the midst of the cloud as he went up on the
mountain [of Sinai] and there he stayed for forty days and
forty nights'' (Exod 24:18). Later we are told that during all
this time spent by Moses in writing the law, he refrained
from ''eating any food or drinking any water'' (Exod
34:28). The king of Nineveh also called for fasting, penance
and prayer on the part of everyone. He stipulated:

> Neither human being nor beast, neither cattle nor
> sheep, shall taste anything; they shall not eat, nor
> shall they drink water. Human being and beast
> shall be covered with sackcloth and call loudly to
> God.

In the case of Paul, we are told that immediately after
his conversion, ''I went off to Arabia.'' Here in silence and

prayer, he lived with the Lord Jesus. This may have been the time and place when he "was snatched up to Paradise to hear words which cannot be uttered, words which no one can speak" (2 Cor 12:4). He read and re-read the Scriptures, so that when he composed the Epistle to the Galatians, the words about himself form a filigree of earlier prophetical passages, especially from Jeremiah and the Songs of the Suffering Servant:

> Before I formed you in the womb, I knew you,
>> before you were born I dedicated you,
>> a prophet to the nations I appointed you (Jer 1:5).
> The Lord called me from birth,
>> from my mother's womb he gave me my name (Isa 49:1).

Turning now to the gospel, we are not surprised at Jesus' words to Martha:

> "Martha, Martha, you are anxious and upset about many things; one thing only is required. Mary has chosen the better portion."

In a very true sense, Jesus was speaking to the "Mary" that should exist in Martha and belongs to each person. First of all, it is not good to be so active as to be "anxious and upset." Then, we are always in need to be reminded of the secret, inner vision of our lives. An hour's contemplation each day gives heart and soul to the other twenty-three hours. We must not forget the first impulse, the initial conversion, and the early fervor. Like Paul we must always remember our years "in Arabia"; and like Israel the memory of Moses' forty days and forty nights of fasting and prayer before the Lord on Sinai should never fade away. The prophecy of

Jonah calls us to reform our lives and call out prayerfully to the Lord.

The ''better portion,'' also called ''the one thing necessary,'' in no ways makes the other portion unimportant or unnecessary; it makes our activity full of spirit and soul, direction and wisdom, love and tenderness. We each need to be both Martha and Mary.

Prayer:

Lord, as we cry from our depths of sorrow and guilt, we also sense within us the depths of your kindness and plenteous redemption. As we look further in ourselves, we find how fearfully, wonderfully made we truly are. Wonderful, Lord God, are your works, Fill our works with your spirit of prayer, concern and peace.

Wednesday, 27th Week

Jonah 4:1–11. Jonah complained and three times wanted to die, because the Lord, a compassionate God, spared Nineveh. Jonah is more concerned about the life of a gourd plant then about the people of Nineveh which included 120,000 infants.

Gal 2:1–2,7–14. Paul staunchly defends his ministry to the gentiles and even corrects Peter to his face when the principles are compromised by vacillation and fear. Paul also wanted the understanding and cooperation of the parent church at Jerusalem.

Luke 11:1–4. The Lucan version of the Our Father stresses daily needs and daily temptation.

If the Kingdom of God is to extend throughout the universe, then the interior quality of faith, patience, and trust in

God must be stressed. Externals are absolutely necessary to manifest interior life. Where there is no breath nor pulse, a person is assumed to be dead. When exercise and work are neglected a person easily becomes sickly, open to disease, and in danger of premature death. While we emphasize religious principles and interior well-being, we cannot neglect their daily application and visible manifestation. Scripture today asks us to meditate upon this healthy balance between principles and their application. In many ways we continue yesterday's reflections that were prompted by the example of contemplative Mary and activist Martha!

We have already noted the paradoxical ways of the Book of Jonah. The prophet who claimed to "worship the Lord, the God of heaven, who made the sea and the dry land" (Monday of this week), pretends to "flee . . . away from the Lord" by taking a long sea voyage! Today's paradox shows up still more poignantly. Jonah knew his Mosaic Torah very well and easily quoted by heart from a key passage:

> The Lord, the Lord, a merciful and gracious God,
> slow to anger and rich in kindness and fidelity,
> continuing his kindness for a thousand generations
> (Exod 34:6–7).

Therefore, Jonah feared to preach in the name of such a God, who would be true to this revelation of divine being and have compassion on Jonah's enemies, the people of Nineveh. The dialogue and action in the book now centers upon the object of God's compassion. Jonah is willing to bypass the Ninevites, but he becomes quite angry when God fails to save the gourd plant. "Certainly," thinks the selfish prophet, God must show his abundant compassion upon this little shade tree, especially when it is shading Jonah from the fierce noon sun and burning east wind!

God's reply blends good theology with almost whimsical tenderness:

> You are concerned over the plant. . . . Should I
> not be concerned over Nineveh, the great city
> [with] more than a hundred and twenty thousand
> infants, not to mention the many cattle?

God's "principles" reach to the smallest and most defenseless people, even to the cattle, grazing quietly in the field!

In the Epistle to the Galatians (Cycle II) Paul demonstrates the origin and validity of his "gospel" that gentiles are "coheirs" with Jesus in the promises of Abraham. Paul did not instigate a secret revolt but, "prompted by a revelation" he laid out for the scrutiny of the original band of apostles and disciples "the gospel as I presented it to the gentiles." It is summarized in a famous statement, to be read on Saturday of this week:

> Jew or Greek, slave or free, male or female, all
> are one in Christ Jesus (Gal 3:28).

While the Torah led the Jewish people to the fulness of time and retained its constant value, like "everything [else] written before our time," to endow us with patience and encouragement (Rom 15:4), nonetheless gentiles were redeemed immediately by faith in Jesus. Circumcision and dietary laws were no longer obligatory. Paul was so convinced of this new freedom in Christ Jesus, that "when Cephas [or Peter] came to Antioch [and would not sit and eat with gentiles], I directly withstood him, because he was clearly in the wrong.''

When principles were at stake or were compromised by a person's actions, Paul was adamant. He not only corrected Peter but he stood up against the top leaders in the church, against the disciples of James, leader of the Jerusalem church, even against Barnabas who ''was swept away by their pretense,'' Barnabas who had brought Paul out of his seclusion at Tarsus and had started him on his apostolic career at Antioch (Acts 11:25–26).

In order to harmonize the principles of God's Kingdom with daily life, freedom in Christ Jesus with the demands of the apostolate, we need patience and forbearance with people's difficulties and long-existing habits. We require assistance, day by day, even minute by minute. Life is not concentrated on the single moment of death or of Christ's second coming, but is to be embraced each day. Luke, therefore, adapted the *Our Father*, so that the Greek verbs no longer refer to a single, crucial moment as in Matt 6:9–13 but to the extended and continuous practice of the faith. Like Peter in today's reading from Galatians, we too succumb to temptation and sin. Our good intentions are marred by fear and false motives. We need the strength of daily prayer and even of daily Eucharist. Luke's *Our Father* quickly became the prayer before holy communion in the early church. The blend of principles with daily needs was to leave no single moment of life unaffected.

Prayer:

Lord, we should never be afraid to follow your will unreservedly. You are always true to yourself, tender and full of love. Our only fear lies in our unwillingness to love as universally and as compassionately as you do! Strengthen us each day with your daily bread, so that we can go out to the whole world and tell the Good News of our salvation in Christ Jesus.

Thursday, 27th Week

Mal 3:13–20. The just are tempted by the prosperity of the unjust, as though religion brings little or no benefit. Yet on the day of the Lord the sun of justice will arise with its healing rays.

Gal 3:1–5. Paul reasons with the Galatians: did you receive the Spirit through the observance of the law or through faith in what you heard?

Luke 11:5–13. Jesus teaches the need to persevere in prayer, confident of the heavenly Father's gift of the Holy Spirit to them who ask.

Perseverance is more than the way to the great Day of the Lord; it also assures us that we already possess what we seek. No one can keep on asking all through the night if they were not already being sustained by God's Holy Spirit. We already treasure this Holy Spirit within our bodies, the temple of God (1 Cor 3:16). If we believe, we are functioning under the impulse of God's mysterious presence. Faith accepts and acts upon that which remains unseen. St. Paul wrote to the Romans that "all who are led by the Spirit of God are children of God" and this "Spirit witnesses within our spirit that we are truly God's children" (Rom 8:14,16). Paul brings this discussion around to our theme of perseverance: "hoping for what we cannot see means awaiting it with patient endurance" (Rom 8:25).

We have been using the more religious, moral word, "perseverance." In today's gospel, Luke brings our discussion much closer to earth by citing a more secular word, "persistence"! While "perseverance" connotes the way to heaven and the faithful fulfillment of one's moral obligations, "persistence" almost has an unappropriate taste of stubbornness about it. Such indeed is the tone and attitude of Jesus' short parable.

The iron law of this country and culture demands an open door even to "someone who comes . . . in the middle of the night." Nonetheless, according to the customs of every land throughout the world, we do not bang on the door of a neighbor in the middle of the night in order to obtain some bread. Jesus is not arguing what is right or wrong. The point of a parable is always reserved for the last line or final statement. The neighbor obliges, not because of friendship but because of the other person's persistence, and gives that one as much as he needs.

Perseverance and persistence, then, carry a note of annoyance and trouble, but most of all there is an enduring faith that hopes will not be frustrated. A bond of the spirit between the neighbors is being deepened beyond the laws of friendship. A new grateful love and loving admiration must ensue, once the shock of midnight banging and family disturbance levels off!

Jesus takes the parable a few steps further. He appeals to parents' care and attention towards their children. Does a mother give a snake when a child asks for fish, or a father a scorpion when the child wants an egg? Jesus acknowledges the basic goodness and fidelity of every human being, yet he also wants our relationship to deepen and to be still more reliable:

> If you, with all your sins, know how to give your children good things, how much more will the heavenly Father give the Holy Spirit to those who ask him.

Where Matthew's gospel reads, "will your heavenly Father give good things," Luke adapts the account to focus on the Holy Spirit. God gives part of himself, his own Holy Spirit. Perseverance enables us to wait long enough, so that our own good actions manifest a divine goodness and reach beyond our dreams and expectations.

Paul also, in Cycle II, does not want his converts to slip back into their earlier habits. Not that these ways were all that wicked, only that they were not good enough. We should not regulate our external actions simply by external norms. The spirit of love should reach beyond custom and habit, and like the neighbor who persists knocking through a long stretch of darkness, we too should extend our hopes to new and even to heroic expressions of love. How can it not be otherwise, "you before whose eyes Jesus Christ was displayed to view upon the cross." With such love before our eyes, how can we draw any limits to what we can expect of ourselves and of our neighbor. "God lavishes the Spirit upon you and *works wonders* in your midst."

As mentioned already, the way to such "wonders" is ensured by persistence, and persistence always implies a certain amount of stubbornness and annoyance. It also brings a dose of scandal and discouragement. As the prophet Malachi points out (Cycle I), law-abiding people begin to ask:

What do we profit by keeping God's command?
Must we call the proud blessed?
Can evildoers tempt God with impunity?

Putting it this way, Malachi makes it clear that "good people" need to be purified and corrected. Religion, like friendship and love, is not a commodity to be "used" nor should its effectiveness be gauged by external results.

Another series of phrases from Malachi point out the true results of religion and enable us to appreciate the presence of God's Holy Spirit:

- they shall be mine,
- my own special possession,
- I will have compassion,
- the sun of justice with its healing rays.

Only by waiting, persistently and perseveringly, can these beautiful virtues, within us from birth, be nurtured and grow to maturity, in all of us as a family of faith in one another and in God.

Prayer:

Happy are those who hope in you, Lord. We are like trees, planted beside hidden streams of water. As we persevere through dry and difficult periods, we will continue to yield the good fruit of peace and patience. Through all this time you will remember your promises, rid us of fear, and enable us to serve you devoutly through all our days.

Friday, 27th Week

Joel 1:13–15; 2;1–2. A solemn fast is proclaimed at the time of a devastating locust plague. This catastrophe evokes the tradition of the fearful ''day of the Lord.''

Gal 3:7–14. Justification by faith according to the promises made to Abraham. The law puts one under a curse. Christ himself became a curse for us, to relieve us of the curse leveled against every infraction of the law.

Luke 11:15–16. Jesus casts out devils by the finger of God,

not by Beelzebul, as his detractors claim. Other sayings follow about evil spirits.

Today's biblical readings combine many different statements, sometimes related only externally by a word for devils or evil spirits or by means of a plague which induces the people to consider the traditional concept of "day of the Lord." Sometimes we meet only a single sentence, like "the one who is not with me is against me," and in other instances we are given a mini-essay on the topic, as in Joel or Galatians. As we read all of these biblical passages we are confused!

At once we can remind ourselves that the Bible is complicated like the rest of life. There is no single, easy, obvious answer. One of the most frequent methods of answering a question, among the rabbis and with Jesus, is to ask another question. While we, on our part, seek answers, the Bible endeavors to induce a meditative attitude in God's presence. This God is beyond our comprehension and rational control, as we are told so eloquently in the Book of Sirach (or Ecclesiasticus):

> More than this we need not add;
>   let the last word be, God is all in all!
> Let us praise him the more, since we cannot
>   fathom him,
>   for greater is he than all his works (Sir 43:28–29).

The wonder of God's providence comes to us in many different ways in the Scriptures: in external events or in our reactions to them. There develops in us a sense of faith and an appreciation of God's mysterious yet controlling presence within human life, even within a serious locust plague, as we read in the prophecy of Joel. For the biologist this book is a goldmine of information about locusts if only some of the rare, technical Hebrew words can be deciphered, as in the verse:

> What the cutter left,
>   the locust swarm has eaten;
> What the locust swarm left
>   the grasshopper has eaten;
> What the grasshopper left,
>   the devourer has eaten (1:4).

Such words as cutter, locust swarm, grasshopper and devourer are only ''approximate'' hypotheses for the Hebrew. It is also possible that Joel is referring to the different stages of a locust's life, from larvae to flying insect.

What interests the Bible and ourselves is not so much the biological question but rather the way by which Scripture advances from a national disaster to a solemn religious service for all the people, and from this liturgical ceremony to a long-standing tradition that God will transform the universe on an awesome ''Day of the Lord.'' Quoting from the prophecy of Zephaniah where this idea may have originated, Joel proclaims:

> Yes, it is near, a day of darkness and of gloom,
>   a day of clouds and soberness!
> For great is the day of the Lord,
>   and exceedingly terrible;
>   who can bear it? (Joel 2:2,11).

No one can bear it, left alone to one's own resources and willpower. Therefore, we are forced to turn to God, and in

God we do not find a destructive force but a transforming love. Joel quotes from the ancient covenant with Moses on Mount Sinai:

> The Lord, your God, gracious and merciful, slow
> to anger and rich in kindness, relenting in punish-
> ment (Joel 2:13; Exod 34:6–7).

Somehow or other, when we are pushed to the limits of our energy and patience, only then can we realize that God's hopes for us are supernatural and reach beyond the horizons of this earth. Paul picks up this idea (Cycle II) and moves with it in an entirely different direction than the prophet Joel.

Paul's doctrine about justification by faith does not deny the efficacy and necessity of good works, but like the prophets whom Paul quotes very frequently, we cannot remain satisfied with human works, no matter how good they are. If we do, we place ourselves under a curse. Works are visible and so can always be judged. They will seldom achieve the perfection and goals of the laws that govern them. Therefore, Paul quotes from the Book of Deuteronomy, a book normally very moderate and compassionate towards human frailty and needs:

> "Cursed be that one who fails any of the provi-
> sions of this law!" And all the people shall an-
> swer, "Amen!" (Deut 27:26)

After Deuteronomy thus concluded the twelve curses, it proceeded to enumerate the many blessings upon the faithful Israelite who observed the law. Those blessings reach beyond Israel's talents and accomplishments. Like Paul, therefore, they warn us that we must be reaching beyond ourselves, and by faith we experience a superhuman force at work within us.

Jesus too went the full way of a perfect human action, yet he ultimately died, to manifest the ''curse'' that lies upon redemption confined to human resources. If Jesus thus became a ''curse'' for us, it was to point out that salvation lies beyond death in the resurrection and gift of the Spirit. Like Abraham, we must believe that God can transform our ''dead'' or ''barren'' bodies into sources of new life that lasts forever.

Human life then deals with life beyond death and with life beyond the vision of our human eyes. It confronts supernatural forces of goodness and evil, devils and angels! Jesus wrestles with these mighty powers and must silence his adversaries who speak out of jealousy and fear:

- by Beelzebul, he casts out devils
- even a strong person can be overpowered
- unclean spirits return to proud people and the last stage is worse than the first.

We cannot rely simply on our fear of others, nor upon our own unaided strength, not even upon our goodness and virtues. God is always calling us from the human situation to a fearful ''Day of the Lord.'' This call can come any day, but it will certainly be heard at death and at some other, crucial transition in our existence.

Prayer:

Lord, we declare your wondrous deeds. Left to ourselves even to our best self, we are caught in the snares of pride, jealousy and false confidence. You, Lord, are always mindful of your covenant, when you pledged yourself to be a God of compassion. You strengthen your faithful people to reach by faith beyond their finest works and to realize your justice and glory in their midst.

Saturday, 27th Week

Joel 4:12–21. The prophet announces a time of terrifying judgment in the Valley of Jehoshaphat and after that a time of everlasting peace, prosperity and joy on God's holy mountain of Zion.

Gal 3:33–39. After Christ all the baptized are equally children of God, Jew or gentile, slave or free, male or female.

Luke 11:27–28. More blessed than the womb that bore Jesus is the one who hears God's word and keeps it.

God seems to wield a sword of sorrow in all three readings. Joel announces a severe judgment against the nations in the Valley of Jehoshaphat. (The Hebrew word itself means "Yahweh judges.") In Galatians Paul brings to an end the privileged role of Israel, a people who had suffered much over eighteen hundred years to remain God's elect. From now on, writes Paul, "all are one in Christ Jesus." Luke, for his part, almost seems to have in mind the prophecy of Simeon to Mary that "you yourself shall be pierced with a sword" (Luke 2:35). How else than by a shock of bewilderment and seeming rejection could Mary have interpreted Jesus' response to a woman who shouted such spontaneous praise for the mother who bore Jesus, whose breasts nursed him. Jesus replied: "Rather blest are they [all of these people before me, all those other people across the world] who hear the word of God and keep it."

Perhaps it is crucial to our understanding of Scripture to take note that each time the sword reaches into the sources

of life it opens up a mysterious aspect of human existence.
In the prophecy of Joel the sword of God's word, announcing the terrifying "day of the Lord," lays bare the initial
force of first creation. Joel seems to go back to God's creation of the universe. He also reverses the process:

> For near is the day of the Lord, . . .
> Sun and moon are darkened,
>   and the stars withhold their brightness.

Elsewhere in the same prophecy of Joel the image is expanded still more forcefully as God declares:

> And I will work wonders in the heavens
>   and on the earth,
>   blood, fire, and columns of smoke;
> The sun will be turned to darkness,
>   and the moon to blood,
> At the coming of the day of the Lord (Joel 3:3–4).

Particularly the image of "moon to blood" assures us that
God is speaking through symbols. Even if symbols are not
to be taken literally, they are to be taken seriously. "Blood"
is invested as "the seat of life" (Lev 17:11). Joel warns us
that the life of all the created universe must be re-conse-
crated to God in the valley of decision. We are forced to re-
think our entire existence, including our relation to the sun
and moon, symbolic of our actions in daylight and at night.
We evaluate our loyalty to family, country, race and church,
perhaps, the meaning of the phrase, "the Lord is a refuge
. . . stronghold . . . on Zion, my holy mountain." We re-
consider our relationship with foreigners or with business,
employment and government, possibly what God has in
mind for us in the references to Egypt, Edom and Judah. In

all of these rich symbolic expressions, Joel compels us to re-think the heart and source of all our relationships, obligations and hopes. We are to see them anew in God and be enriched in remarkable ways, so that

> on that day,
> the mountains shall drip new wine,
> and the hills shall flow with milk.

The sword of God's word in Joel reaches into the creation of the universe, certainly in favor of Judah. It cuts more deeply into the sensitive heart of life in Paul's Letter to the Galatians (Cycle II). It strikes down any false or artificial boundaries between "Jew or Greek, slave or free, male or female." Again Paul writes:

> All of you who have been baptized into Christ have clothed yourselves with him . . . If you belong to Christ, you are [all] the descendants of Abraham.

Abraham, who had once been told to "go forth from the land of your kinsfolk and from your father's house" (Gen 12:1), is now called "home" and is reunited with kinsfolk everywhere. His offspring in Israel form one family with all their first ancestors and with all of Abraham's other descendants through Ishmael and Esau.

The pain and humility by which divisions and grievances are healed are usually more severe and more difficult than the sorrow and pride which initially provoked the differences. Paul summons us to this excruciating "valley of decision," to heal old wounds and family disputes, to become "one in Christ Jesus."

No one escapes the sharp sword of God's words, not

even the blessed mother of Jesus. She cannot stop with her role of physical motherhood, nor with her gentle, life-giving care of the infant Jesus at her breasts. She too was expected to listen continually to God's word and to act upon its new inspirations. In fact, Mary is presented just that way in Luke's gospel. She appears in Luke's infancy narrative, treasuring God's word, spoken through her wide reach of neighbors, and reflecting on them in her heart (Luke 2:19).

We too will find our deepest sources of strength and security, even our well tried goodness and virtue, somehow or other insufficient. We must listen again this day to God's word and act upon it with new faith and confidence. "Blest are they who hear the word of God and keep it." This new moment may seem and may actually be as dramatic as Joel's fearful "day of the Lord." We will reach out, as Paul advises us, with new bonds of love and find a family across the world, as close to us as brothers and sisters.

Prayer:

Lord, each moment, but especially those decisive moments of important decisions, enable us to acclaim you as king and ruler of our lives. We see the whole world rejoicing, almost running away with excitement, as this new light dawns in our hearts. We proclaim your wondrous deeds and are determined, with new faith, to serve you constantly.

Monday, 28th Week

Rom 1:1–7. Paul has been set apart to proclaim to gentiles the good news, which is none other than Jesus, according to the flesh a descendent from David but according to the Spirit seen as Son of God by the resurrection.

Gal 4:22—5:1 (*Selected verses*). Through faith we are born free, the fruit of the promise. It was for liberty that Christ freed us.

Luke 11:29–32. The people of Nineveh and the queen of the south will rise at the judgment and condemn this generation because a greater than Jonah and Solomon is here.

The theme of today's mass may be summarized in this prophetic way: some people with little or no understanding of Jesus manifest a gentleness and prayerful spirit, an honesty and reliability, a generosity and concern for us which puts to shame many Christian believers, including ourselves. The gospel gives us excellent symbols for the non-Christian nations. Jesus of course was comparing the gentiles with his Jewish compatriots, but the gospels were written for Christian communities.

The queen of the south represents the continent of Africa, long known to the Israelites through their references to Kush or Ethiopia. This distant land was impenetrable and forbidding to Israelites who feared the open sea and only rarely constructed a fleet of ships possibly under Solomon (1 Kgs 9:26–29) and another futile attempt under Jehoshaphat (1 Kgs 22:49). Ethiopia comes to Solomon in the person of the queen of the south (1 Kgs 10:1–13). As discussed already, the people of Nineveh were the hated Assyrians, who destroyed the ten northern tribes (2 Kgs 17) and even scorched Judah with widespread destruction (2 Kgs 19). These people, among the cruelest in biblical history, could be converted by the obstinate and stubborn Jonah! Yet, a greater than Solomon and Jonah was here. At the judgment the queen of the south and the citizens of Nineveh will rise along with ourselves, and they will condemn us. With so little they accomplished so much. We who see and hear what kings and prophets desired to see and hear and yet never saw nor heard (Matt 13:17), we with so much accomplish so little.

Some explanation for this unnatural situation can be found by reflecting on St. Paul's letter to the Galatians (Cycle II) and to the Romans (Cycle I). In many ways the Galatians epistle was a trial run for the ideas developed more extensively in the Roman epistle. ''Romans'' is probably Paul's most careful synthesis of his gospel; it will be read for the coming four weeks, the 28th to the 31st in ordinary time (Cycle I).

''Galatians'' introduced an antithesis which ''Romans'' will make famous, the opposition between flesh and spirit, the way of nature and the way of promise. This image has its origin in a series of Old Testament passages which speak of several heirs to the promise born of very elderly or sterile couples: Isaac, son of Abraham and Sarah in their old age (Gen 18:11); Samson, whose mother had been ''barren and had borne no children'' (Judg 13:2); Samuel, whose mother, ''Hannah was childless'' up to that time (1 Sam 1:2). The prophet applies this tradition to Jerusalem, deprived of all her children by the Babylonian exile and unable to receive a happy family in the homeland:

> Rejoice, you barren one who bear no children;
> > break into song, you stranger to the
> > pains of childbirth!
> For many are the children of the wife deserted,
> > far more than of her who has a husband (Isa 54:1).

Paul's style of reasoning in Galatians is very strange for us. In fact, he turns history on its head, he who knew Israelite history extremely well. He is arguing as a Rabbi who can make surprising turns and leaps and counterleaps. Paul traces the Jewish people and Sinai to Abraham's son Ishmael by the fertile Egyptian woman, Hagar; gentiles and Jerusalem are related to Abraham's son Isaac, conceived by the barren Sarah.

Each of us contains then two births within ourselves. We are born of the flesh in the natural order of human conception; we are born of the spirit in the supernatural order of faith. The first follows a law that is irreversible—conception, birth, life in the flesh; in this sense we are enslaved by the law of nature. Paul compares this order to Judaism with its multiple laws for each moment of human existence. Our second birth through the Spirit far surpasses our human ability and potency. It contains many wonderful surprises and it leads to eternal life. Flesh is doomed to die; spirit is promised eternal life. The spirit co-exists with our human, fleshly self and liberates us from its slavery to death.

This same double birth is found in Jesus according to Paul's opening words to the Romans. Jesus "descended from David *according to the flesh* but was made Son of God in power, *according to the spirit of holiness*, by his resurrection from the dead." Salvation comes through the Spirit, not only in Jesus' case but actually throughout the Old Testament when children of promise are conceived miraculously, like Isaac or Samuel. Jerusalem was revived after the exile when everything seemed lost, by the "enduring love [of] the Lord, your redeemer" (Isa 54:8), the same Lord who also says in this passage of Isaiah:

> My love shall never [again] leave you
> nor my covenant of peace be shaken,
> says the Lord who has mercy on you (Isa 54:10).

Jesus was raised from the dead by the Holy Spirit. The flesh of Jesus was transformed into an instrument of eternal joy for Jesus and through Jesus for each of us.

This spirit exists with all men and women throughout the world. We also have the benefit of the Scriptures, the sacred liturgy and a long tradition of saints. All of us can remember wonderful moments in our own individual lives when the Holy Spirit brought us the fruits of love, joy, peace and many others, and as we will read on Wednesday of this week (Cycle II) "against such there is no law" (Gal 8:23). With so much we are able to anticipate eternal life and its joy here on earth. The Spirit of Jesus, far greater than Solomon or Jonah, dwells within the fleshly temple of our bodies.

Prayer:

Lord, through the Spirit you make heaven our salvation in acts of kindness and faithfulness. As each stirring of the Spirit we can sing a new song to you. From the rising to the setting of the sun, blessed be your name. You look down from heaven and raise our lowly self from the dust that we may live eternally.

Tuesday, 28th Week

Rom 1:16–25. God's eternal power and divinity are visibly manifest by the world he created. Failure to glorify God leads to many immoral excesses. The justice of God by which we are saved begins and ends with faith.

Gal 5:1–6. In Christ Jesus neither circumcision nor the lack of it counts for anything; only faith which expresses itself through love.

Luke 11:37–41. Interior cleanliness is far more important than exterior cleanliness. If you give what you have as alms, all will be wiped clean for you.

In the central part of today's reading from Romans (Cycle I), we begin with the *visible* manifestation of "God's eternal power and divinity'' within the created world and then we are gradually led to the ''invisible realities,'' the marvels of God himself. The gospel, on the contrary, seems to say that the condition on the *inside* of the cup is more important than the outside, the spirit of generosity more effective than the washing of hands. Romans moves from the outside inwardly, the gospel from the inside outwardly. Galatians (Cycle II) seems to hit the happy medium: ''only faith which expresses itself through love.'' There ought to be a harmonious blending of faith and love, flesh and spirit, interior and external cleanliness. If such an integral and peaceful wholeness exists in us, then Paul's ideal of perfect liberty will be ours.

The Epistle to the Romans cannot be easily and simply interpreted. For many of us Paul's ideas seem to slip as he glides from one aspect of salvation to another. We can bring the ideas back into focus if we recall the key phrase, prominently in Galatians (3:11) and now repeated as a dominant theme for the entire Epistle to the Romans: ''The just one lives by faith.''

Paul is quoting from the prophet Habakkuk, a ''minor prophet'' who was responsible for a signal change in Israelite prophecy. Up till his time (605 B.C.) the ''word of God'' addressed by the prophets to the people, was always in the form of a divine message or oracle. Habakkuk and Jeremiah, contemporaries, revised the process, flung their human questions back to God, and these became the ''word of God''! After Habakkuk's second question, however, God responded properly as God, closed the conversation with a statement that was to be inscribed with letters so large (as on a billboard) that one can read it ''on the run'' (Hab 2:3). The messages ''will not disappoint,'' says the Lord. Therefore, ''if it delays, wait for it.'' It was simply: ''the just one lives by faith.''

"Faith" here implies fidelity and trust over the long run. It recognizes that the mysteries spread across the universe are also deeply imbedded in each person's soul. "Faith" is related to a Hebrew word, frequently translated the "justice" or "fidelity" of God. In this case "justice" does not denote our obedience to laws, rewards for obedience and punishment for disobedience. Rather, justice signifies that God, humanity, and the entire created universe live up to what they are. Actions flow from nature. Human nature denotes the intricate set of relationships, powers, and promises making up our being. God, therefore, is just when he lives up to his covenantal promises, given to Moses on Mount Sinai and quoted very frequently not only in these meditations but also throughout the Old Testament:

> The Lord, the Lord, a merciful and gracious God,
> slow to anger and rich in kindness and fidelity,
> continuing his kindness to a thousand generations
> (Exod 34:6–7).

When St. Paul writes: "in the gospel is revealed the justice of God which begins and ends with faith," he means to say that God fulfills these covenantal promises in a way beyond all expectation, yet true to his own compassionate self in the gift of Jesus. The gospel goodness *is* Jesus, who was born and died according to the flesh, that our flesh might rise with him through the Holy Spirit to new life.

This Holy Spirit is interiorly present throughout the universe, slowly but surely revealing God's invisible realities. Even gentiles and all people who are without the benefit of the Scriptures, are living within this marvelous cycle of life. Because of an inward supernatural life, the outward natural life is already able to reveal the compassion of God and so to lead men and women to the proper use of their body and all physical realities. Even though we begin with the outward manifestations, we are quickly involved in the inward life of the spirit. Thus the stakes of life are high. It is not a matter of ''natural goodness'' but of fidelity to a supernatural spirit within each person. The law of the flesh must give way to the law of the spirit. We are set free from laws about circumcision and legal cleanliness, clean and unclean foods, so that we can follow the more demanding law of the spirit, which is love and everlasting fidelity.

This law, Paul writes to the Galatians, ''expresses itself through love.'' Jesus makes the demand more explicit: ''give what you have as alms.'' Love, therefore, is to be concerned about the needy and generous in attending to them. Then, Jesus concluded, ''all will be wiped clean for you.'' This is a curious reply. The poor and the needy generally have a much more difficult time with cleanliness than the wealthy and the leisure class. The poor work longer hours, are involved with dirt, grease and dust, and do not have at hand all the conveniences of running water, hot and cold, privacy and energy. Could this be the reason in part why Jesus did not properly wash his hands before sitting down to eat at the Pharisee's house? We have no way of knowing.

God's *justice* surrounds us in sun and wind, family and community, scripture and tradition. This justice begins and ends with *faith*, our recognition of God's ''invisible realities'' all around us. We can then blend and harmonize our entire existence, within ourselves and with our neighbor, peacefully, freely, generously and honorably.

Prayer:

The heavens declare your glory, O God. The mystery of your fidelity gushes like spring water from the rocks; it breathes like the evening wind around about us. Let me keep your law continually, and then I will walk in liberty, delighting in what is best.

Wednesday, 28th Week

Rom 2:11. "By your judgment against another you convict yourself." God's kindness is an invitation to repent. Anguish on everyone who does evil, honor and peace for everyone who has done good, the Jew first, and then the Greek.

Gal 5:18–25. Paul contrasts what proceeds from the flesh with the fruits of the spirit. "Those who belong to Christ have crucified their flesh with its passions and desires."

Luke 11:42–46. Woe to Pharisees and lawyers who insist upon the impossible burdens of trifling legal details yet neglect to help others to lift this burden by seeking the justice and love of God.

The Scriptures insist upon freedom and the primacy of love. Yet they prudently warn us against the excess of libertinism and individualism. In today's selection from Galatians (Cycle II) Paul minces no words in stating what "obvious[ly] proceeds from the [undisciplined] flesh: lewd conduct, impurity . . . jealousy, factions, envy, drunkenness, orgies and the rest."

Jesus' words in the gospel are carefully nuanced. While contrasting the way that the Pharisees paid tithes, all the "while neglecting justice and the love of God," Jesus concludes that the latter are to be insisted upon as more important, but he immediately adds, "without omitting the other." Jesus did not mount any campaign against the Jewish or Mosaic law. In fact, he observed it carefully and always had a sensible reason for departing from it. When he permits a freer way of acting, he is generally defending his disciples, e.g., plucking and rubbing grain on the Sabbath (Matt 12:1).

As we return to the readings and meditate more deeply, we first note the trap which we set for others and for ourselves in stressing external details and in judging accordingly. The more that we multiply rules and regulations, the more *we* take control of other people's lives. With control over other people's lives there comes a propensity to judge. At the same time we ourselves are in ever greater danger of imagining ourselves to be holy persons because we are exact in externals. Our insistence upon externals, moreover, makes judgment easy. There is always a law with which to measure actions.

As already mentioned, Jesus did not deny the validity of rules and regulations, in this case, the requirement to "pay tithes on mint and rue and all the garden plants." In fact, we should not be in the habit of "omitting" these things. Yet Jesus did see an initial and more important need for justice and the love of God. "Justice," as was mentioned yesterday, has a special theological meaning: for God, fidelity to himself as a gracious and kind Lord; for ourselves, fidelity to our calling as servants of God, compassionate within a family of love.

It is good for us to question our motives in obeying rules and in seeking to be proper and correct in external details. Some consider the appearance of a home more essential than the happy life within the home. We ourselves may look good because that is expected of us. Another way of assessing our motives is to see how frequently we judge others. If we are in the habit of passing judgment on family, community and people at large, we have probably lost touch with our own humanity, the instrument of salvation. The worth or value of human beings ultimately derives from the motives and values within their heart.

As we read further within today's selection from Romans, we meet several important sentences which throw new light upon the question of judging others. Paul writes:

> Yes, affliction and anguish will come upon everyone who has done evil, the Jew first, then the Greek. But there will be glory, honor and peace for everyone who has done good, likewise the Jew first, then the Greek. With God there is no favoritism.

''With God there is no favoritism.'' This phrase reminds us of the different scale of values and the important cultural diversity between Jew and Greek. It is so easy, at least at first, for a person from one culture or one background, to judge severely a person from a different culture or background. There are absolute truths, of course, but on the scale of values these truths will take different places within different cultures. For some education and property are prime values. For others vocational or service jobs and family ties come first. ''With God there is no favoritism.'' Therefore, no culture, lifestyle or scale of values is better than another.

Furthermore, each person has the capability of living a good life, whether Jew or Greek. We are asked to look for this goodness in others before we drag them before our hastily convoked court of law. Jesus, moreover, adds another bit of important advice. Before we begin to judge others harshly, we are asked first to ''lift a finger to lighten'' their burden. Perhaps, if we tried for an hour, not to mention a lifetime, to carry their burden of problems and trials, we would be in such admiration of their goodness and patience, that negative attitudes would be choked off.

Prayer:

Lord, only in you is my soul at rest. You are my rock and my salvation. I will not be disturbed, when others judge me rashly or quickly. Lord, keep me from judging others, so that I may always be assured of your mercy. If I follow you in kindness and in fidelity, in integrity of heart and wholesome living, then I will be like a tree planted near running water, always relying upon your justice and love.

Thursday, 28th Week

Rom 3:21–29. The justice of God has been manifest apart from the law and our works. All have sinned, Jews and Gentiles alike, and are now undeservedly justified by faith in Jesus Christ. Through his blood God made him the means of expiation for all who believe.

Eph 1:3–10. God chose us in Christ before the world began, to be holy and blameless in his sight, full of love, and through his blood to bring all things in the heavens and on earth into one under Christ's headship.

Luke 11:47–54. In opposing Jesus and plotting his death, Pharisees are guilty of the blood of all the prophets since the foundation of the world. Lawyers have taken away the key of knowledge and so have stopped others from entering God's rule.

Romans (Cycle I) and Ephesians (Cycle II) are important theological documents. In Romans Paul explores the basis of his gospel and entire ministry: namely, that all, whether Jew or Greek, are justified by faith in Jesus. Ephesians may be a composite document drawn both from Paul's writings and preaching. Here it begins with an early church hymn; a mini-confession of faith is woven into these lines of wonder and adoration. By contrast, while Ephesians opens with a hymn, the gospel is similar to the ''woe'' or ''curse'' passages of the Old Testament.

Many rich theological phrases bring depth and strong Old Testament resonance into Paul's writings, each with its own specific background and nuance of meaning. Such words include: justice of God (see Tuesday of this week), the glory of God, redemption, blood, law or Torah blessing, choice or election by God, predestination, divine favor, mystery, fullness of time, Christ's headship. For our meditation we choose one of these, namely *blood*, which occurs in all three readings for today:

- through Christ's blood God made him the means of expiation for all who believe (Romans);
- In Christ and through his blood we have been redeemed (Ephesians);
- the blood of all the prophets shed since the foundation of the world (Luke).

Romans and Ephesians clearly assign a positive meaning ''life'' to the blood of Christ, and we will find the same interpretation in Luke's gospel.

As mentioned already in these meditations, the key text on blood in the Old Testament is provided for us in the liturgical book of Leviticus. At once we realize that we are dealing with symbolism. Blood evokes a whole series of meanings and emotions.

> Since the life of a living body is in its blood, I
> have made you put it on the altar, so that at-one-
> ment may thereby be made for your own lives, be-
> cause it is *blood, as the seat of life, that makes at-
> one-ment* (Lev 17:11).

Blood, therefore, as life, and not as the symbol of death,
unites us with God and with one another. Blood consequently was sprinkled on the altar and on the people when
the covenant was sealed between Yahweh and the Israelites
(Exod 24:6–8). The meaning of this symbol can be appreciated by considering the human body. Each of us is a single, living person when warm blood flows from heart to
head and hands and feet uniting all the members.

We will be helped in remembering that the basic Hebrew word for *redemption* is *blood-bond*. ''Redeemer''
originally signified the members of a single family, clan or
tribe and their consequent obligations by reason of their
bond of blood (Lev 25).

When Paul writes to the Romans, ''through his blood
God made Christ the means of expiation for all who believe,'' he is saying that Christ's death and resurrection have
established a bond of life in all who are one in Christ Jesus.
The *focus* of attention is not on Christ's death (even though
this agonizing event is not to be overlooked), but on the new
life which the risen Christ suffuses into our midst. Because
this ''life'' or ''blood'' of Christ is so pure, vigorous and divine, we are cleansed of all impurities within our system and
are granted a supernatural energy and perception.

If life comes from this mysterious source, ''what reason is there then for boasting?'' If this life or blood is trans-
fused immediately by faith in Jesus, and is not dependent
upon previous good works nor upon the direction of the Mo-

saic law, then everyone who professes Jesus as redeemer is at once acting as child of God and member of God's elect family. Membership in this family unites equally ''Jew and gentile, slave and free, male and female'' (Gal 3:28).

The Letter to the Ephesians not only stresses the same bond of unity which blood establishes, but it also extends this unity to a time ''before the world began.'' ''God chose us in Christ before the world began.'' There is no other answer. If this gift of life in Christ Jesus is wholly *undeserved*, a phrase used today by Paul in Romans, then it can be explained only in the mystery that God *freely* decided to love us and to gift us with life, before we even existed, even ''before the world began.'' This sweep of the eternal ages, which brings all of time and all human beings together in Jesus, is a frequent referent in Ephesians. If only our love for others could be swept along so freely and so effectively.

Jesus also returns to the theme of blood in his ever more bitter controversy with a group of Pharisees and lawyers. When he condemns them for erecting monumental tombs over the graves of the prophets, it is not that Jesus is opposed to honoring the prophets. Typical of the blood-symbolism, Jesus wants to honor the dead, not so much by concentrating upon their dead bones nor even upon their dead memory, but rather by continuing their life and imitating their selfless concern for others, especially for the poor and for others in desperate need. By our life we are meant to reveal the dedication and strength of their martyrdom. By our total union with our neighbor, even with foreigners and enemies, we manifest their radical disposition to die for the justice of other people's dignity and goodness.

Prayer:

Out of the depths we cry out to you, O Lord. The depths of love and life, the depths of dedication and surrender to your life, the depths of suffering that all may live in peace and dignity. In this mystery of life we wait for you, O Lord, more than sentinels wait for the dawn. In this mystery of life, Lord, let all the ends of the earth see your salvation and sing joyfully to Jesus, our Redeemer in blood.

Friday, 28th Week

Rom 4:1–8. ''When a person does nothing, yet believes in that one who justifies the sinful, faith is credited as justice.'' Such is the way Abraham was justified.

Eph 1:11–14. We are sealed with the Holy Spirit, the pledge of our inheritance, the first payment against the full redemption of a people that God has made his own to praise his glory.

Luke 12:1–7. Do not be fearful! What you hear or say in secret, proclaim from the rooftops. Do not be afraid of those who kill the body but cannot touch your soul.

We center upon an interior dignity, strength and holiness that far surpass our worth or good works, that seem to swallow up our weakness and sinfulness, that leave us fearless before all human judgment, at ease before our divine Judge, living on earth yet already enjoying heavenly peace.

There is a word in today's reading from Ephesians (Cycle II), that implies something like our English phrases, ''down payment,'' ''first installment,'' ''possession by credit.'' Changing the image, we might best express the idea by thinking of a pregnant woman. She already possesses, but not yet! She has an assurance or guarantee, but must wait! She can discern the future by already feeling the child's life now, but is still guessing what the future will really be like. In Ephesians we are said to be "sealed with the Holy Spirit," who is:

- the pledge of our inheritance,
- the first payment against the full redemption.

The gift of the Holy Spirit is exactly that, a gift! Paul can offer no credible explanation, except that "we were chosen," "in the decree of God," "according to *his* will and counsel," "predestined." All of these phrases point out that we were loved before we loved in return, that we were carefully, with will and counsel, chosen to be God's very own people. Our entire life then with its intrinsic goodness and good actions is a praise to God's glory, in no way to our own glory. If our entire life and its growth and fulfillment are due entirely to God, then how free and uninhibited we can be. All that we do and say and think are for "the praise [of] his glory."

The uplift or exuberant language of Ephesians flattens out a bit as we turn to the Epistle to the Romans (Cycle I). Romans is like cooked-over food, still very delicious, but still a bit old, even stale, and lacking the initial zest. Perhaps, this example is not the best. Ephesians *too* as an epistle is the result of serious reflection upon important themes of St. Paul, except that we are still in the initial hymnic section of chapter one. Another reason why Romans tends to be sober and cautious comes from the atmosphere of controversy. Paul is still battling against the "Judaizers" of the early Church who demanded the full observance of the Mosaic law from every disciple of Jesus.

In Romans Paul turns to the example of Abraham, an excellent type of justification by faith rather than by works. Not only does the Torah state clearly: "Abraham *believed* God, and it was credited to him as *justice*," but it is also an indisputable fact that Abraham preceded Moses, perhaps by as many as six hundred years, and therefore did not observe the Mosaic law and its later elaborations. This part of Paul's argument is so obvious that he may seem guilty of overkill. Yet, even before the time of Jesus, one tradition held that Abraham knew by advance revelation the entire Mosaic law, obeyed it and so was blessed. Such seems to be the position of the sage Sirach (or Ecclesiasticus).

> Abraham, father of many peoples, . . .
> He observed the precepts of the Most High, . . .
> In his own flesh he incised the ordinance [by
>   circumcision], and when tested, he was found
>   loyal.
> *For this reason*, God promised him with an oath
>   that in his descendants the nations
>   would be blessed (Sir 44:19–21).

Paul, however, disregards this later tradition and takes his case back immediately to Genesis. First came God's choice and call (Gen 12), then Abraham's faith (Gen 15) and only later did he demand circumcision (Gen 17) and prove himself faithful in the test (Gen 22).

If God's gift to Abraham, and like Abraham now to the gentiles, was so freely bestowed and so very generously, then Paul and ourselves will no longer think of past sins. Nor will we be concerned about offenses against a law that is no longer binding on us. Paul's language is worth noting: "David *congratulates* the one to whom God credits justice without requiring deeds." If our guilt is not worth thinking about, neither by us nor by God, than our guilt does not exist. In Christ we have been chosen, predestined, and transformed by the interior gift of the Spirit, the heavenly pledge already with us on earth.

The exuberance and liberty of spirit returns again in the gospel. Whatever is said in the dark or whispered behind closed doors we are to proclaim from rooftops. Do not fear anyone who kills your body but never touches you! If God, merciful and kindly, is concerned about sparrows, then "fear nothing. You are more precious than a whole flock of sparrows!"

Justification by faith then liberates us more than from the law. It makes us totally free, happy and already in heaven.

Prayer:

Whenever I turn to you, O Lord, even in time of trouble, you fill me with joy! You have taken away my guilt. I can be glad and rejoice. This joy is mine, Lord, because you have chosen me to be your very own. Of such kindness the earth is full.

Saturday, 28th Week

Rom 4:13,16–18. Abraham, hoping against hope, became the father of many nation. He believed in God who restores the dead to life and calls into being those things which had not been.

Eph 1:18–23. May God enlighten your innermost vision that you may know the great hope to which you are called: our Lord Jesus Christ, head of the church which is his body, the fullness of him who fills the universe in all its parts.

Luke 12:8–12. Whoever speaks against the Son of Man will be forgiven, but not that one who speaks against the Holy Spirit. Do not worry how to defend yourselves. The Holy Spirit will teach you at that moment all that should be said.

When we think of Abraham, hoping against hope (Cycle I), his vision seems almost ridiculous, stretching across the universe. Who would ever think that this elderly couple, Abraham and Sarah would not only be the parents of ''a great nation'' and possess a land into which they had just wandered like many other migrant Asiatics, but also that ''all the communities of the earth shall find blessing in you'' (Gen 12:2–3). A person without Abraham's faith would strike out the word ''almost'' and call this man's hope simply ''ridiculous.''

Whenever a situation turns out to be humanly hopeless, the Bible draws our attention to Abraham and Sarah. Such situations of dramatic transition or of utter destitution do not come often in individual lives, and within church history even less rarely. Yet, there is a certainty about the cycle and the return of ''zero'' hour for traumatic decision-making. Death is one such moment for everyone. Radical conversion is another. A decision for marriage, priesthood, religious life or particular secular career is still another.

When Israel seemed lost before the Philistine onslaught, God raised up David, the youngest son of Jesse, from a tribe up till now inconspicuous and unimportant in Israel. Many of the traditions in the Book of Genesis about the creation of the world, the formation of the human race, the call and journey of Abraham from the land of the gentiles were gathered together and developed into a continuous narrative at the royal court of David and Solomon. These accounts are called the Yahwist (J) tradition.

Abraham appears again, four or five centuries later during the Babylonian exile. The fate of Judah seemed hopeless. Very few nations that had been deported like Israel survived historically. A great prophet appeared at this time, unknown by name and therefore called Second or Deutero-Isaiah because his poetry was appended as chaps.

40–55 to the Isaiah scroll. The passage is long but also too important not to quote for our meditation. God is speaking:

> Listen to me, you who pursue justice,
>   who seek the Lord,
> Look to the rock from which you were hewn,
>   to the pit from which you were quarried;
> Look to Abraham, your father,
>   and to Sarah who gave you birth.
> When he was but one, I called him,
>   I blessed him and made him many.
> Yes, the Lord shall comfort Zion
>   and have pity on her ruins;
> Her deserts he shall make like Eden,
>   her wasteland like the garden of the Lord;
> Joy and gladness shall be found in her,
>   thanksgiving and the sound of song.

The first word, God's justice, is paralleled by the last words, joy, gladness and thanksgiving, which express God's full or just response to his promises. The words, rock and pit, are similar to ruins, deserts and wasteland. The center lines concentrate upon Abraham and Sarah whose lonely marriage was transformed into a tent teeming with many offspring by God's special blessing. Second Isaiah's words may also have sounded ridiculous, yet because the prophet "hoped against hope" and placed unwavering faith in the Lord, death gave place to life and "the wasteland [was transformed] like the garden of the Lord."

St. Paul calls us to "look to Abraham . . . and to Sarah," so that the Lord may have pity on all our ruins and turn our desert existence into a paradise like Eden.

Paul assures us:

God restores the dead to life and calls into being those things which had not been.

He then concludes:

Hoping against hope, Abraham became the father of many nations, just as it was once told him.

Abraham himself never witnessed this marvelous fertility. He saw only his son Isaac. In a unique way, Abraham's faith had to reach beyond death to the resurrection of the dead. For this reason Jesus appeals to the example of Abraham for belief in the resurrection.

The Epistle to the Ephesians extends and clarifies Abraham's hope. Paul prays that we be enlightened to ''know the great hope'' in Christ:

- the wealth of his glorious heritage,
- the immeasurable scope of his power in us,
- Christ, raised from the dead and seated at God's right hand,
- Christ, head of the church which is his body, the fullness of him who fills the universe in all its parts.

Not only does Abraham's faith reach still more wondrously across the universe and is the source of wealth and power, but most of all it vibrates with the personal presence of Jesus. ''Hoping against hope,'' Abraham did not look forward to material things or stupendous deeds, but he saw a vision of Jesus. For the sake of Jesus we risk everything and receive everything in return.

With such ''innermost vision'' and with such intimate union with Jesus, then we realize how disastrous is a word

spoken against the Holy Spirit and how easily we will be inspired with courageous and insightful vision at any moment
of crisis. ''The Holy Spirit will teach you at that moment all
that should be said.''

Prayer:

You remember your covenant forever, Lord. Despite
our faults and ingratitude you are true to yourself and to your
ancient promises, that your bond of love extends through the
universe. Your name is glorious over all the earth. With our
brothers and sisters we sing your praise.

Monday, 29th Week

Rom 4:20–25. Like Abraham our faith will be credited to us
   if we believe in Jesus' resurrection, this Jesus who was
   handed over to death for our sins and raised up for our justification.
Eph 2:1–10. God brought us to life with Christ and in Christ
   when we were dead in sin. This is not our doing, it is
   God's gift. We are God's handiwork, created in Christ Jesus.
Luke 12:13–21. Avoid greed in all its forms. A person may
   be wealthy, but possessions do not guarantee life.

If the Scriptures insist frequently on justification by
faith, they are not condemning works, as though our only alternative is to believe and do nothing but pray! We have
only to consider the gospel example of Jesus; he went about
doing good, preaching, healing, listening, defending, encouraging, giving alms to the poor. If faith means the absence of works, then many of the prophets went astray,

especially those like Isaiah who preached a strong message of faith.

Paul's favorite author was the prophet Isaiah, responsible for that stirring, if almost untranslatable couplet:

> Unless your faith is firm,
> You shall not be affirmed (Isa 7:9).

This same prophet also insisted upon good works. When Isaiah condemned Israel's liturgy as presumptuous and useless, he still gave a chance for conversion. Its conditions, of course, were not better rubrics for the liturgy, nor for that matter more faith! Twice in the same chapter he wrote this solution:

> Make justice your aim: redress the wrongs,
> hear the orphan's plea, defend the widow (Isa
>   1:16,23).

During the readings on faith, a theme so frequent in Paul's epistles, we ought to attend to false motivations and excessive expectations in our works. These problems arise when we do very well in our works and accomplish much. If our deeds are performed in a slovenly way, carefree and irresponsible, then we have no temptation to substitute works for faith. When, however, we are very successful, then we begin to think—perhaps subconsciously—that our good works are accomplishing so much that God is dependent on us—maybe God becomes unnecessary! Yet we want to keep a veneer of religion about us, so we multiply our religious works. To such as these Paul writes:

> I repeat, it is owing to God's favor that salvation
> is yours through faith. This is not your own doing,

it is God's gift; neither is it a reward for anything
you have accomplished.

This citation comes from Ephesians (Cycle II) where
the "problem" of *good* works is pursued still further. Good
works not only induce pride, but they bring with them, like
the touch of dominoes, a series of sins and collapses. Many
of our sins result from the excess of our virtues. The good
administrator over-administrates and handles *all* problems
by administration, whether administration is the best rem-
edy or not. A good teacher teaches us to boredom by teaching so incessantly. The ones who are loving and tender,
compassionate and warm-hearted, will tend to be too soft,
discipline goes out the window and they themselves may be
swept off their feet in sensuous temptations.

It takes talent and ability to commit sin; men don't do
evil in their sleep or if they are mentally handicapped. It
takes much talent to commit a bigger sin! Even the best of us
use our special talents too continuously and too narrowly
and fail to appreciate the need of cooperation and wisdom
from others. To all of us then Paul writes in Ephesians:

God is rich in mercy; because of his great love for
us he brought us to life in Christ when we were
dead in sin.

Our sins, moreover, may be more than our good intentions gone awry. "We lived at the level of the flesh, following every whim and fancy, and so by nature deserved God's
wrath like the rest."

Returning to our "good works," many talents and
grand accomplishments, we ought to find at the very moment of success a vision or an expectation of doing more or

doing it still better. This moment is very difficult, trying for a person's patience, even provoking frustration. How do we tell good persons that they are not good enough! Yet through Christ God has planted within us a dream and a hope beyond our unaided human ability. Paul expressed it this way again in today's reading from Ephesians:

> We are truly *God's* handiwork, *created in Christ Jesus* to lead the life of good deeds *which God prepared for us in advance*.

By surrendering to this goal of our hopes, we rise from the dead in Christ Jesus and achieve beyond all expectation.

The example of Abraham urges us to think beyond the humanly possible and to seek this goal of faith. Paul writes about it this way in Romans (cycle I):

> Abraham never questioned nor doubted God's promises; rather he was strengthened in faith and gave glory to God, fully persuaded that God would do whatever he had promised . . . .

This expectation of the heroic and the best beyond our human ability is not our daily fare. Men can't survive if their most normal, daily actions entail a continuous need to steel oneself for the impossible. Yet, underneath all of our thoughts and actions is this abiding resource, to remain faithful in ordinary things till death (perhaps the most heroic feat of it all) and *at times* to clench the fist, tighten the jaws and plunge into heroic battles for goodness and justice.

The gospel reminds us of still other faults of "good" people. They can be greedy and miserable about preserving what they have amassed diligently and properly. They can find total security in wealth and respectability. To this streak in most of us, Jesus gives this warning:

> Avoid greed in all its forms . . . .Possessions do not guarantee life . . . [Do not] grow rich for oneself instead of growing rich in the sight of the Lord.

Prayer:

Lord, you grant us the promises you once gave to Abraham. Strengthen our faith to be like our ancestor Abraham, so that we may in our present earthly life live under the Spirit of Jesus and may reach even beyond death. Lord, throughout our life let us remember that we are your handiwork; make our lives a blessing to your holy name. Lord, increase our faith.

Tuesday, 29th Week

Rom 5:12–21 (*selected verses*). Through Adam, sin and death exist in everyone; through Jesus Christ, grace and justice exist in everyone who believes. Grace has far surpassed sin.

Eph 2:12–22. In the flesh of Christ, nailed to the cross, God has broken down the barrier of hostility between Jew and gentile. Together we form a holy temple, a dwelling place for God in the Spirit.

Luke 12:35–38. It will go well for those servants whom the master finds wide-awake at his return. He will set them at table and wait on them.

By the time that Luke wrote his gospel, the early church was no longer obsessed with the proximate return of

Jesus in glory. The urgency of waiting vigilantly for the Lord Jesus is no longer directed to this once-for-all manifestation of the glorious Jesus which would end the present condition of the world and would usher in the final, everlasting kingdom. As in the case of the Our Father (see Wednesday, 27th Week), Luke here thinks of the daily return of the Lord Jesus in our neighbor and in contemporary events.

We must be waiting, *always* ready to open the door of our heart, of our time and of our other possessions, should Jesus come even at midnight or before sunrise. Whatever happens anytime, anywhere, must be received as though Jesus were coming in person.

Jesus then overturns oriental custom and sets us back to the drawing board of our own theology and organization of life. Normally, when the master returned, the servants waited on him. Jesus recognized this custom at another time in addressing the disciples (Luke 17:7–10). Now the reverse is true:

> The master will put on an apron, seat the servants
> at table, and proceed to wait on them!

In our service of receiving others in our heart or home, we will benefit the most! When we think to be doing heroic service to others, they will heap good gifts upon us.

Perhaps the greatest gift will come through our realization that our family extends to many brothers and sisters. Paul addresses this idea very clearly in Ephesians (cycle II):

> You are strangers and aliens no longer. No, you
> are fellow citizens of the saints and members of
> God's household.

Very intense suffering goes into this enterprise. No one forms family and community with others, even with one's own flesh and blood, without carrying the cross with Jesus and being nailed to it. Our sufferings become one with Jesus, in so far as his goodness inspires us to follow his example, his Holy Spirit sustains us, and our faith accepts these extraordinary hopes and abundant love. What was said of Christ breaking down the barrier between Jew and gentile can now be repeated of ourselves as we open our lives hospitably to all who knock at our door:

> He is our peace, who made the two of us one by breaking down the barrier of hostility . . . in his own flesh . . . through the cross which put enmity to death.

Our suffering to restore and maintain the bonds of brotherhood and sisterhood is one with Jesus. Our flesh hangs with him on the cross. Paul has already written to the Galatians:

> I have been crucified with Christ, and the life I live now is not my own, Christ is living in me. I still live my human life, but it is a life of faith in the Son of God who loved me and gave himself for me (Gal 2:19–20).

Our sufferings, like Christ's become a sacred sacrifice. Our bodies are built into a "temple, . . . a dwelling place for God in the Spirit." Charity and hospitality have formed us into a world family, dying and rising to new life in Jesus, consecrated as a sacred temple for adoration and holiness in the Spirit.

Finally, if we are *all* one, humanly in the flesh with one

another, divinely in the Spirit through faith in Jesus, then we can understand better Paul's words to the Romans (cycle I). We are *all* one through Adam and again through Jesus. Through Adam we share in the sins, prejudices and weaknesses, inherent in our family, race, nationality and church. Through Jesus there is "overflowing grace" that makes us just. Paul writes, "Despite the increase of sin, grace has far surpassed it, . . . leading to eternal life, through Jesus Christ our Lord." As we overcome our sins through grace, we suffer with Jesus on the cross; as we are even more fully united with *all* our brothers and sisters, we suffer still more, till the last barriers to peace and charity be broken down. Even the initial attempts at forgiveness and understanding are the working of God's Holy Spirit and the grace flowing from Jesus, risen from the dead and exalted at God's right hand. Each attempt then is a sacred action within God's holy temple. Each moment of our life takes place in "a dwelling place for God in the Spirit."

Prayer:

Here I am, Lord. I come to do your will. I hear your knocking at my door, as each person or event comes across my life. Together we form a vast assembly of worship. In this holy temple kindness and truth shall meet; justice and peace shall embrace. At the heart of this sacred service we see the cross of Jesus which has broken down all barriers.

Wednesday, 29th Week

Rom 6:12–18. Submit yourself as obedient slaves of justice. Offer yourself to God as a person who has come from death to life.

Eph 3:2–12. Paul is commissioned to preach to the gentiles
the unfathomable riches of Christ, the mystery unknown
in former ages but now revealed by the Spirit to the holy
apostles and prophets.

Luke 12:39–48. Be on guard. The Son of Man will come
when you least expect it.

From the point of view of Romans (cycle I) we are
"men and women who have come back from the dead to
life," and the risen Christ dwells within us. Luke seems to
say in the gospel that Jesus has gone on a long journey and
has disappeared across the horizon. The Epistle to Ephesians (cycle II) brings these two divergent ideas together. Simultaneously, we already possess the mystery of Christ in
us, and we are still seeking the fullness of this mystery. As
we already read from Ephesians, Friday 28th week, we are
"sealed with the Holy Spirit, [our] *promise*, . . . the *pledge*
of our inheritance, the *first* payment against the full redemption."

As we read again the gospel selection, the divergence
does not seem so severe as at first. We are advised to live
daily, even moment by moment, as though the Son of Man
were at the door, already knocking and ready to come in!

Another key to the readings occurs in the word "servant" or "slave," at least for Romans and Luke's gospel.
Paul advises us to be "obedient slaves of justice." The biblical word, "justice," embraces much more than integrity
and concern in the distribution of this world's goods. "Justice" goes back to God's promises to the patriarchs and to
Moses and to God's fidelity in being true to them and to
himself. To Moses on Mount Sinai Yahweh proclaimed
himself as "a merciful and gracious God . . . rich in kindness and *fidelity*" (Exod 34:6). Therefore, as "obedient
slaves to justice," we must live with an awareness of God's

marvelous plan of salvation. This grace reaches far beyond our understanding: it sweeps us "off our feet." We are dead people come back to life. The risen Christ lives within us. If we are "slaves of justice," we are true to our most inward self, to our authentic personality, to our image of God before creation, to the most wonderful possibilities of our life in God's dreams for us.

The key word, *slave*, also occurs repeatedly in the gospel. Here Jesus tells the parable of the unworthy steward who began "to abuse the housemen and servant girls, to eat and to get drunk." This steward is a slave himself, only of a higher class position. To be true to his office, this "slave" is not expected to be swept "off his feet" in ecstatic flights of faith, but rather to attend to most elementary norms of justice and concern for others. The steward-slave was to look after the property and "to dispense the ration of grain in season." In this way he will be a just and faithful steward.

The biblical sense of justice then includes the wide sweep of God's plans for the universe and the immediate needs of righteousness, honesty and human rights. We should not be absorbed in immediate details nor lost in distant theological horizons. We need to look at the ground at our feet and towards our neighbor, but it is also necessary to see each against the background of the mountains and the sky.

In writing to the Ephesians (cycle II), Paul concentrates on the mountains and the sky. He is lost in a wonderful insight, an extraordinary revelation. We should note the repetition of such phrases as:

- God's secret plan,
- the mystery of Christ, unknown in former ages but now revealed by the Spirit,
- the unfathomable riches of Christ,

- the mysterious design which for ages was hidden in God, the Creator of all,
- God's manifold wisdom [and] age-old purpose.

As we interrelate all of these references to mystery and secret plan, we realize that it has existed before creation and controlled God's making of the universe. It exists now throughout the world, whether people realize it or not, accept it or not.

Linked up with the gospel, then, the selection from Ephesians takes on still another nuance or interpretation. The master comes unexpectedly from all corners of the universe. Jesus is knocking at our door, literally everywhere. He is rising to new life in people and places where we would never suspect it to happen. Such is "God's secret plan." We, the chief steward of the house, must not mistreat nor abuse anyone. We need to care tenderly for each person. We need to be very solicitous about the use of God's good earth. Any moment, any time Jesus will come and knock.

Prayer:

Lord, you do not leave us as prey to sorrow and evil. You rise in us to new strength and goodness. You are our help, you who made heaven and earth and placed a mystery of salvation across the world. With faith we open the door and find you there. With joy we will receive refreshing water from you, the fountain of salvation. Then your glorious achievements will be known throughout all the earth.

Thursday, 29th Week

Rom 6:19–23. Freed from sin and slaves of God, you tend towards eternal life. This is the gift of God in Christ Jesus our Lord.

Eph 3:14–21. May you grasp fully with all the saints the breadth and length and height and depth of Christ's love and experience this love which surpasses all knowledge and so attain to the fullness of God himself.

Luke 12:49–53. I have come to light a fire on the earth. I have a baptism to receive. What anguish I feel till it is over. I have not come for peace but for division.

The imagery or symbolism of today's readings sets up a series of paradoxes or even contradictions. For instance, in Romans (cycle I) Paul speaks of being slaves of God; in this case the Lord is a slave master. The divine title modulates full circle to that of father or parent in Ephesians (cycle II). Normally, a parent who drives and orders children as though they were slaves has forfeited love and controls by fear and authority. Again, Ephesians enjoins us to grasp or know that "which surpasses all knowledge"! We seem to be set up for a major act in frustration. Jesus' words that "I have not come to establish peace but division" openly clash with his other assurance " 'Peace' is my farewell to you, my peace is my gift to you" (John 14:27). We also recall the statement in Ephesians (Tuesday of this week), "Christ is our peace who has made the two of us one by breaking down the barrier of hostility that kept us apart." We must meditate longer, allow the Scriptures to sink more deeply within us and so experience their reconciliation "through the workings of his Spirit" in a new and profound way.

The reading from Ephesians centers on God's love for us in Christ Jesus. Love always reaches beneath logical considerations, carefully articulated reasons and rational control. If we are obliged to explain fully to another's satisfaction or even to our own, why we love someone, such love is shallow and suspect. In Ephesians, therefore, love is surrounded with mystery (see Eph 3:4). Yesterday we read in cycle II:

> . . . to preach to the gentiles the *unfathomable* riches of Christ and to enlighten everyone on the *mysterious* design which for ages was *hidden* in God, the Creator of all.

This same sense of *mystery* breaks through the darkness like a galaxy of midnight stars, signaling to us the wondrous love of God for us in Christ Jesus:

- the Father from whom every family in heaven and on earth takes its name,
- the riches of his glory,
- Christ dwell in your hearts through faith,
- experience this love which surpasses knowledge,
- God can do immeasurably more than we ask or imagine.

To sum it up: we experience a love which we cannot understand, explain or control.

Love such as this truly makes "slaves" of us, but not a slavery wherein people grovel in fear but a slavery which sets us joyfully on the way to eternal life. We are freed from shame and the earlier forms of degradation. Our bodies acquire a new dignity as they become "servants of justice for this sanctification." If we are swept beyond our control and risk everything for the sake of life in Christ for all eternity, we experience a love beyond comprehension. All this is "the gift of God," undeserved yet bountifully given, never merited yet received in such a way that we experience a new integrity and sense of responsibility that surrounds us, body and soul.

In the gospel Jesus too appears enslaved to love and to the Father's holy will. The language is strong in its echo of interior emotions:

- How I wish the blaze were ignited!
- What anguish I feel till it is over [or, fully accomplished]!

Jesus was being swept beyond his human understanding, almost beyond his human tolerance and patience. The references are clearly to his passion and death, particularly as Luke develops the theme of Jesus' ministry. Since 9:51 (see Tuesday, 26th week) Luke portrays Jesus as "firmly resolved to proceed towards Jerusalem" where he "was to be taken from this world." Yet, when the time came for the fulfillment of this plan and thus the quieting of this anguish, Jesus was plunged into a deeper agony. He prayed in the garden of Gethsemane:

"Father, if it is your will, take this cup from me."
. . . In his anguish he prayed with all the greater intensity, and thus his sweat became like drops of blood falling to the ground (Luke 22:42,44).

We can return to Jesus' other words in today's gospel with a deeper appreciation of their force and implication:

Do you think that I have come to establish peace on the earth? I assure you, the contrary is true; I have come for division.

In Gethsemane Jesus' own soul was torn apart, so that "his sweat became like drops of blood." It is not surprising that serious division will split families into quarreling factions, each misunderstanding the other. The motivation is love, and love so great that it "surpasses all knowledge." How can anyone properly and satisfactorily explain that which is beyond the clear thoughts even of the believer?

Yet, such division is only temporary. In the flesh of Jesus, where the separation was felt most severely, we find a unifying power that breaks down all barriers and makes one chosen people of Jew and gentile, male and female, slave and free. All are one in Christ Jesus. Only in this way can the justice of God, the fulfillment of God's promises and of God's personal love and fidelity, be accomplished.

Prayer:

Happy are we, O Lord, as we meditate on your law and walk with hope. Even in time of drought and division, the roots of our tree of life are planted deeply in the stream of your promises, O God. And as we look about, from the tree of the cross and its sufferings, we see anew how the earth is of your goodness. You are faithful in all your works, even though they may cause suffering and division. Your eyes are always upon us who hope in your kindness.

Friday, 29th Week

Rom 7:18–25. What happens is that I do not the good I will to do, but the evil I do not intend. Who can free me from this body under the power of death?—God, through Jesus Christ.

Eph 4:1–6. One body and one spirit, one hope given to all of you by your call, one Lord, one faith, one baptism, one God and Father of all, who is over all and works through all, and in all.

Luke 12:54–59. If you can judge rain or hot weather in the offing, why can you not interpret the present time?

"One hope given to all of us by reason of your call"—these words in Ephesians (cycle II) set the context for meditating upon Romans (cycle I) and upon the gospel. As mentioned often enough in these reflections, hope is the most difficult of virtues to appreciate and safeguard. Faith and love in many ways are more obvious. Faith can be clarified by studying Scripture and Church documents. Love can be rather obvious through bonds or relationships and through the manifest needs of our neighbor. Hope is the most intangible. Paul writes about it in a selection from Romans to be read on Tuesday of next week: "Hope is not hope if its object is seen . . . And hoping for what we cannot see means awaiting it with patient endurance" (Rom 8:24–25).

Hopes cannot be quickly identified by prophecy. It is interesting to note that the very next section of Ephesians, read tomorrow in the liturgy, quotes an Old Testament passage by reversing it. While the Hebrew original states that God "ascended on high [and] received men as gifts," Paul quotes from a later Aramaic version that God "ascended on high . . . and gave gifts to men." Hopes are like the distant horizon which is ever the same sky and yet is continually changing in color and shifting in cloud formation and in the position of stars and moon. Sunrises and sunsets, clouds and stars all indicate the intricate and exquisite beauty of the heavens but no single moment catches the full splendor and majesty. Speaking theologically, we are always hoping beyond that which we see.

There are other problems about hopes, beyond their shifting and modulating form. Hopes vary with a person's age, health and family. They also vary from person to person. Even identical twins can reach towards their future differently. Hopes induce ambition and action, hopes stir up desires and plans, hopes make people selfish or fearful. Hopes induce important personality changes. Hopes easily degenerate into greed and selfish passion.

Little wonder then that when Paul writes about the "one hope given to all of you by your call" he also admonishes us:

> Live a life worthy of the calling you have received, with perfect humility, meekness, and patience, bearing with one another lovingly. Make every effort to preserve the unity of the spirit.

How desperately we need these virtues, especially patience and forebearance, as we live with gifted people, who effervesce with energy, plans and super-action.

In writing to the Romans (cycle I) Paul takes another view of hopes and hopeful, gifted people. He views the situation, not from a distance but from the inside, namely, within himself, one of God's most gifted and creative apostles, but a thorn in the flesh for many early Christians, especially Peter and others of Jewish extraction. Sometimes he feels that "no good dwells in me" and he becomes frustrated and despondent. Other times he reacts so impulsively that "I do what is against my will." Paul agonizes at length over this situation:

> My inner self agrees with the law of God, but I see in my body's members another law at war with the law of my mind; this makes me the prisoner of the law of sin in my members. What a wretched person I am! Who can free me from this body under the power of death?

Yet, Paul does not end up in futile desperation. He adds: "All praise to God, through Jesus Christ our Lord!" The body, for Paul, is not evil. It is "a holy temple in the Lord" as we read from Ephesians on Tuesday of this week. Paul witnesses to those moments of confusion, precipitated by the hopes for what is unseen, by the energy to do always the best and by the ever present danger of stubbornness, impulsiveness, pride and selfishness.

The impulsiveness that can be dangerous can be turned into a necessary virtue, as we see in today's gospel selection from Luke. Some important moments do not come a second time. Failure to act is the same as to lose the opportunity. Some graces belong to the "day" and the "hour," the "proper time"! These are all favorite biblical phrases: day of the Lord, my hour and the "time," in the same sense of the Greek work *kairos*. *Kairos* is not just any moment (for that, the Greeks used the word *chronos*) but a very special moment with tremendous implications.

If we link today's gospel with other statements of Jesus about being alert and vigilant: "The Son of Man will come when you least expect him" [Wednesday of this week], then we realize that we must carefully discern the situation and act promptly, for the sake of charity, of forgiveness, of conversion, of confidence, of trust, of fidelity. The stakes are high, and we cannot dodge the decision. Again, not to act is to act negatively and poorly. As the saying has it, "Not to decide is to decide."

God does not expect the impossible, only that we exert the same care and decisiveness as when we "interpret the portents of earth and sky." We are to act for God with the same decisiveness as we dispatch other practical decisions in our life. The natural virtue is put to the service of the religious activity, the body is at the service of the soul!

Prayer:

Lord, let me never neglect your precepts but take delight always in your holy will. You are good and bountiful. I need never fear any evil from serving you. Even my mistakes will be treated compassionately. Your kindness is always present to comfort me. Lord, in all our actions we seek you, and in finding you we realize the fulfillment of all our hopes.

Saturday, 29th week

Rom 8:1–11. God sent his son in the likeness of sinful flesh as a sin offering, thereby condemning sin in the flesh . . . so that we can live according to the spirit. The Spirit who raised Jesus from the dead will bring to life our mortal body.

Eph 4:7–16. Christ, risen from the dead, sends his gifts into our midst, giving us apostles, prophets, evangelists, etc. Let us profess the truth in love and grow to the full maturity of Christ the head, the members joined firmly together.

Luke 13:1–9. Those who suffer are not necessarily those who sin. All must bring forth good fruit. Otherwise, the tree will be cut down.

Today's scriptural selections can be appreciated better if read within the background of the close union of people among themselves and with God. The Bible seldom thinks of an individual as isolated, but always as a member of a race or nation, family or clan; in the New Testament this relationship with one another in God reaches to all members. The Epistle to the Romans (cycle I) builds upon a major position expressed already in chapter 5 (Tuesday of this week): ''Through one person, Adam, sin entered the world . . . so death came to everyone inasmuch as all sinned; much more did the grace of God and the precious gift of the one person, Jesus Christ, abound for all.'' We all share the same flesh and we are all gifted by the same Holy Spirit. ''Flesh'' for St. Paul, like the Hebrew word *basar*, indicates weakness and instability; without back bone, muscles and sinews, flesh collapses like a balloon or a wet cloth. ''Spirit'', again like the Hebrew word, *ruah*, indicates life, strength, permanence, purity and sacredness. Spirit—the bone, blood and breath of human life—gives character, tonal quality, dignity and integrity.

The bonds uniting us in flesh and spirit show up all the more prominently in chapter 4 of Ephesians (cycle II). Yesterday we read the litany of ''one's'': one body, one spirit, one hope, one Lord, one faith, one baptism, one God and Father of all. Today the results of this unity are manifest. Together we form the one ''body of Christ,'' still growing to full stature and forming ''that perfect human being who is Christ.'' ''Through him the whole body grows . . . members joined firmly together.''

The gospel passage for today is not as clear, yet somehow or other we realize that the Galileans, slaughtered under Pontius Pilate, or those other persons, ''killed by a falling tower at Siloam,'' suffered because of a mysterious yet real bond with other men and women. Therefore the innocent suffer with the guilty. While it is true that sinful people always suffer, the reverse is not true, that suffering people are always sinners. Yet, people in pain and discouragement are suffering the effects of someone's sinfulness. The bonds of flesh, nationality, race and family are that close.

As we re-read today's selection in Ephesians, another

clue is given us. While all of us together form the one body
of Christ, we have each received specific gifts. Paul enumerates a few of these:

> apostles, prophets, evangelists, pastors and teach-
> ers in roles of service for the faithful to build up
> the body of Christ.

This diversity is to the honor of Christ's body, just as
the variety of parts in the human body provides for rich and
varied functions. Paul developed this analogy while writing
to the Corinthians:

> Now the body is not one member, it is many. . . .
> As it is, God has set each member of the body in
> the place he wanted it to be. If all the members
> were alike, where would the body be . . . The eye
> cannot say to the hand, ''I do not need you'' (1
> Cor 12:14–21).

When the analogy is applied to the Christian community, a
double reaction takes place. Sometimes each member rejoices in the others and is assisted by them. At other times
the variety of gifts and roles provokes jealousy, fear, antagonism, and domination. The administrator over-administrates, the teacher solves all problems speculatively, the
practical-minded person rejects study and reflection, the
spiritual-minded person leaves everything to prayer. Each
gift must function ''in roles of service for the faithful to
build up the body of Christ,'' and therefore must cooperate
and depend on others, even while serving them.

If we share a common bond of flesh and spirit, as we
read in Romans, then we are simultaneously dragged down
and built up by one another. Usually at one and the same

time another person's talents help us, complement us, annoy us and threaten us! If Jesus united himself with all the diversity within our flesh and our spirit, then his devotion and obedience manifested at once the glory and the tragedy of our common bond of flesh and spirit. We already read Paul's statements in Galatians (Friday, 27th week):

> Christ has delivered us back from the power of the law's curse *by becoming himself a curse* for us (Gal 3:13).

Paul even went so far as to write:

> For our sakes God made Jesus who did not know sin, *to be sin*, so that in him we might become the very holiness of God (2 Cor 5:21).

As we live closely as brothers and sisters, all of us in one family and in one spiritual blood-bond, with one another and with Jesus, we suffer together, we lift one another up and with Jesus we are all instruments in sharing the glory, strength and fruitfulness of the resurrection. Together we sorrow for one another's sins, together we hoe and fertilize the soil around the tree of our life, the one tree with many branches, so that together we bear fruit. If we do not suffer and transmit life together, we are like the persons whom Jesus warned: "You will all come to the same [dreadful] end unless you reform." Or again, "If the tree does not bear good fruit, it shall be cut down."

Prayer:

Lord, we are the people that longs to see your face. Keep us from desiring what is vain. Enable us to be your ministers to one another, making our hands sinless and our hearts clean. Then your glory will be revealed across the earth. With joy we will go up to your house; worshipping you in your earthly temples and celebrating eternally in your heavenly home.

Monday, 30th Week

Rom 8:12–17. Led by the Spirit of God, we are all God's children, and with Christ we cry out, "Abba!" [that is, "Father"]. We are heirs with Christ, provided we suffer with him so as to be glorified with him.

Eph 4:32–5:8. Be kind to one another and mutually forgiving. Be imitators of God. Follow the way of love, even as Christ loved you. Let no lewd conduct or lust of any sort be even mentioned among you.

Luke 13:10–17. Jesus cures a woman, badly stooped, on the sabbath. The chief of the synagogues becomes indignant, but everyone else rejoices at the marvels Jesus was accomplishing.

In a very practical, even earthly way the Spirit of God moves into our hearts and through our lives. Chapter 8 of Romans (cycle I) is sometimes called the "Gospel of the Holy Spirit" and like any of the four gospels, it shows us the power of God *within our lives*. Ephesians (cycle II) calls for human virtues, by which we mean actions and attitudes closely associated with our earthly existence. The gospel, finally, argues from common sense against religious authorities for a better interpretation of the Ten Commandments. Today then the devout lay person, without theological education, gifted with wholesome integrity and good natural virtues, has his or her day in court. God listens to them attentively and makes their statement the inspired word of the

Bible. The secular automatically becomes sacred, the earth is appreciated as God's creation, the temple where "all say, 'Glory!' " (Ps 29:9).

The woman, "badly stooped" and "drained [of] her strength," is a too common sight to anyone who has traveled or lived in under-developed countries. The grandmother or grandfather must lean step by step upon a cane, lest they collapse to the ground from their bent back. They have spent themselves, drained their strength and twisted their body out of shape, by back-breaking labor in rice fields, hour by hour transplanting individual young stalks, or at harvest picking up the stray shoots of rice. They have looked so long at the earth that they cannot physically look up to the heavens.

What wisdom, strength and compassion these grandmothers and grandfathers have absorbed from mother earth. Even the passing traveler pities them, the long time resident admires them so much that a certain kind of healthy jealousy displaces the pity. Bent over, these grandparents are spiritually strong. Their words carry an enormous common sense, their decisions cut through idle discussion and questioning. Their calloused hands handle the infant grandchild with delicate care, their weakened eyes still carry a sparkle of pride and peace.

Jesus saw one such woman while teaching on a sabbath day in one of the synagogues. Jesus knew what was proper to do on the sabbath. After all, as the eternal Word of God, Jesus had presided over creation and even now he could not rest till every man and woman was re-created to the divine image. In the Ten Commandments, according to the Book of Exodus, the reason for resting on the sabbath lies in the fact that God had completed the divine work and so "rested on the sabbath day" (Exod 20:11). On this particular sabbath, therefore, Jesus could not enjoy his "sabbath shalom" until the work of creation was completed and this woman was remade to the divine image.

> When Jesus saw her, he called out [a creative word, as once at the dawn of first creation] and said to her, "Woman, you are free of your infirmity." He laid his hand on her, and immediately she stood up straight and began thanking God.

Jesus' action was prompted by divine wisdom and eternal memories of what the sabbath was supposed to be. When "the chief of the synagogue [became] indignant that Jesus should have healed on the sabbath," Jesus' defense of himself comes from the impulse of a merciful heart and the common sense imbedded in his flesh:

> O you hypocrites! Which of you does not let his ox or ass out of the stall on the sabbath to water it? Should not this daughter of Abraham here . . . have been released from her shackles on the sabbath?

In a more explicit theological reflection Paul recognizes this interior presence of God's spirit in humankind: "The Spirit gives witness with our spirit that we are children of God" (cycle I). In tomorrow's reading from Romans, the text is even more pointed: "The whole created world eagerly awaits the revelation of the children of God . . . All creation groans and is in agony even until now." Jesus' words to the stooped woman echo this instinctive groaning; his direct calling out to her responds to the way that the created world eagerly awaits the revelation.

The Epistle to the Ephesians also deals with the same groaning of the spirit (cycle II). It advises us to practice the typically good virtues of human nature: kindness, compassion and forgiveness. Yet it also elevates and transfigures those natural virtues with supernatural light: ''Follow the way of love, even as Christ loved you.'' It sternly warns against sins that common sense and wholesome human stock will immediately condemn, such as: lewd conduct, promiscuousness or lust.

To sum up our meditation: supernatural goodness heightens our awareness of natural goodness and actually builds upon it. Our crippled or handicapped neighbors often hold the key to our understanding of God's revelation in Jesus.

Prayer:

Lord God, you are the parent who loves orphans and defends widows. You bear the burden of our weakness and re-create us anew to your image and likeness. Let me always delight in your law and meditate on your desire to bring wholeness and joy to all your children. Allow me to aspire to that wonderful hope of imitating you and your son Jesus in love and forgiveness.

Tuesday, 30th Week

Rom 8: 18–26. We hope for what we cannot see, yet the object of our hopes already exists within us, as we groan and eagerly await the full effects of our adoption as God's children in Christ Jesus.

Eph 5: 21–33. Love between spouses foreshadows the mystery of Christ's love for the church and his sanctification of it through union with human nature and suffering in his flesh.

Luke 13:18–21. The reign of God is likened to a mustard seed, planted in the garden, and the yeast kneaded into dough.

Similar to yesterday, the scripture calls us to recognize our dignity and our great hope as God's creatures. Deep within our human nature God has planted a seed that will grow in surprising ways. God has also kneaded supernatural "yeast" that will transform us in a way similar to dough that becomes fresh bread, the staff of life! Therefore, "the whole created world eagerly awaits the revelation" of what is already stirring within it, like an unborn child in the pregnant mother, we ourselves as children of God (Romans, cycle I). Marriage, one of the most basic, elementary institutions of humankind, contains within itself the mystery of Christ's love for the church (Ephesians, cycle II).

These texts explode with magnificent, exciting possibilities in almost all directions. They state very clearly that every human being across the planet earth carries within himself or herself the seed of eternal life, the source of transformation into Jesus Christ, hopes beyond their understanding. Every man and woman, united in marriage, lives within a sacred mystery, sacred not only because God is the author of sexuality so that male and female complement one another, but sacred as well because every marriage foreshadows the union between Christ and the church. In these passages of the Bible we are reminded that all persons, for instance, all those millions of non-Christians throughout the world, already carry within themselves the seed or image or hope of eternal life in Christ Jesus. The extraordinary goodness which we find among the "pagan" world of Buddhists or Hindus, or the strong monotheistic religion of Islam, represents inward groaning and eager expectation of the Spirit of Jesus.

We must apply this passage of St. Paul to our neighbors and friends, even to those people who annoy, bother or scandalize us. *Wherever* any goodness is to be found, mixed, perhaps with ignorance, prejudice and human weakness, *there* in that place is the Holy Spirit. Because of the faulty or defective surroundings, we may not perceive this Spirit clearly and directly. Yet, each small act of kindness, sympathy and help is enough to testify to a strong hope that here the Holy Spirit is present. If we cannot always see clearly, then we are helped by Paul's other words in today's selection:

> Hope is not hope if its object is seen; how is it possible for one to hope for what one sees? And hoping for what we cannot see means awaiting it with patient endurance.

We need to pray so that we can place great hopes in others, especially in those people whom we tend to discount or even to dislike. Therefore, we need to pray as well for the "patient endurance" with which Paul concludes the first reading (cycle I).

We do not discover this hope by looking heavenward but by attending to the earthly, physical form of human life. St. Paul also wrote to the Romans: "We await the redemption of our bodies." Today's reading from Ephesians (cycle II) adds that the use of our bodies to form marriage, family and homelife, by marital love, tender concern, care for a home, physical labor and employment—all of these bodily actions are spirited by the example and the immediate presence of Jesus. *Wherever*, then, there is faithful, fruitful marriage, *there* is the holiness of Jesus and the foreshadowing of Jesus' love for the church. Both aspects of love, within marriage and within the church, result in holiness. It is helpful to apply to marriage, as is intended in this passage from Ephesians, what is said of Christ's love for the church:

He gave himself up for her to make her holy, purifying her in the bath of water by the power of this word, to present to himself a glorious church, holy and immaculate, without stain or wrinkle or anything of that sort.

Other statements about wives' ''submissive[ness] to their husbands'' should be interpreted according to the culture and customs of that ancient age. This same larger section of Ephesians also speaks of slaves and their obligation to ''obey your human master'' (Eph 6:5). No one would quote this section of the Bible to support slavery, also a part of the custom and culture of that time.

If we seek the reign of God, then we must reverence the hidden mustard seed that will develop into a tree of holiness in other peoples' lives. We must be like the woman who so kneads the yeast into the dough that other people's lives rise with freshness, life and dignity.

Prayer:

Lord, you do marvels for us. Your goodness produces such wonderful results among us that sometimes we are like people in a dream. If we sow the tiny seed of hope in tears, we believe that we will reap rejoicing. Wherever there is hope and love, happy marriages and children like olive plants around the table, there we see the blessed presence of the Lord.

Wednesday, 30th Week

Rom 8:26–30. The Spirit helps us in our weakness to pray as we ought, with groanings that cannot be expressed in

speech. All things work together for the good of those
who have been called.

Eph 6:1–9. Advice to parents and children, masters and
slaves. Each one must respond to the other with reverence, sincerity and patience.

Luke 13:22–30. Come in by the narrow door. People will
come from distant places and will take their place in the
kingdom of God, while others who considered themselves very close will be excluded.

Two opposite reactions are induced in us as we meditate on today's biblical readings. From one point of view,
the way of salvation does not seem too difficult, especially
when we read in Romans (cycle I) that "the Spirit helps us
in our weakness" and that "all things work together for the
good of those who have been called," or again when we
read in Ephesians (cycle II) that our normal human relationships can continue, provided we act within them with appropriate patience, reverence and honesty. Yet, when we turn
to the gospel the opposite impression is left with us, and it
almost seems foolish to try to attain eternal life. Luke sums
up the section by that fearful and puzzling one-liner: "Some
who are last will be first and some who are first will be
last."

This statement from Luke may give us the cue for har-
monizing all three readings and for delving deeply into their
meaning for ourselves. It is better not to interpret the various
difficult statements in an external simple way. These statements are like proverbs which have been repeated over a
long period of time, have been wittled down to the fewest
number of words, and are meant to provoke our thinking
rather than to give quick answers. They are like icebergs
more important for what they conceal than for what they reveal! We listen again to these familiar, mystifying words:

Lord, are there few in number who are to be saved?
Try to come in through the narrow door. Many, I
   tell you, will try to enter and be unable.
Some who are last will be first and some who are
   first will be last.

Is the Lord saying that in each of us there exists some
hidden, tiny hopes or inspirations which will be our salvation? Right now we may overlook them or even try to silence the ideas or expectations. We crowd them out with
many activities and distractions, with many excuses and arguments. Perhaps, ''the narrow door'' which leads us to a
new, transformed existence is that inspiration:

- to forgive a person who has hurt or even injured us,
- to help a neighbor or relative in their old age or sickness,
- to follow a call to dedicate some part of our time to
  religious or charitable service, perhaps to follow
  some vocation of service within the church or within
  a humanitarian organization,
- to spend more time each day in prayer and in Bible
  reflection.

Each of us can add to this list. A decision that seems small,
may also turn my life around. I will find myself surrounded
with new friends ''from the east and the west, from the north
and the south.'' What I had put in last place in my scale of
values, now appears first; my former first values now seem
unimportant in last place! The largest part of myself will be
saved by the least part, the tiny inspiration.

From this background we now re-read the passages
from Romans and Ephesians. ''The Spirit helps in our
weakness.'' The tiny inspiration enables us ''to pray as we

ought'' and to express ''with groanings that cannot be expressed in speech.'' Only the one ''who searches hearts knows what the Spirit means'' in inspiring us to forgive, to be helpful, to pray or to follow a way of service for others. This small inspiration or narrow door that leads to life witnesses to a *special call from God* within us. Paul's words take on a wonderful, consoling meaning:

> We know that God makes all things work together
> for the good of those *who have been called* according to his decree.

In this way God has ''predestined us to share the image of his Son.''

The reading from Ephesians (cycle II) may seem further away from this interpretation of Jesus' proverbial remarks. Paul seems to be saying the obvious and certainly wants to be understood clearly:

- Children, obey your parents in the Lord.
- Parents, do not anger your children.
- Slaves, obey your human masters.
- Masters, stop threatening your slaves.

Yet, Paul allows important, qualifying remarks to slip into these apodictic commands. Parents are to train and instruct their children in a way *befitting* the *Lord*. ''Slaves, obey your human master with . . . the sincerity *you owe to Christ*.'' So render your service as to ''*do God's will* with your whole heart as *slaves of Christ*.'' ''Each one, whether slave or free, will be *repaid by the Lord*.'' ''Masters . . . remember that you and your slaves have a *Master in heaven* who plays no favorites.'' These qualifying italicized remarks, ''befitting the Lord,'' transform the substance of each statement and lay the groundwork for removing institutions like slavery.

Again, therefore, what seems accidental, gives new direction, and what hardly drew our attention, turns out to be the "narrow door" that leads to salvation.

Prayer:

Lord, you are faithful in all your works. You achieve them in us by inspiring and calling us in hidden ways. You lift us up in this way and change our lives. Even though I seem overcome, I turn to you and feel new hope in your loving kindness.

Thursday, 30th Week

Rom 8:31–39. Is it possible that God who did not spare his own Son but handed him over for the sake of us all will not grant us all things besides? Who will separate us from the love of God that comes to us in Christ Jesus?

Eph 6:10–20. Put on the armor of God, for our battle ultimately is not against human forces but against the evil spirits in regions above. Pray in the Spirit, using petitions of every sort.

Luke 13:31–35. Certain Pharisees warn Jesus against Herod's plans to seize him. Jesus laments over Jerusalem, its rejection of prophets and its coming destruction, but ends with its future recognition of the Messiah.

The Scriptures mince no words in warning us about the serious battle against evil in which we are all engaged. Whether we speak graphically in terms of "trial or distress, or persecution, or hunger, or nakedness, or danger, or the sword'' (cycle I) or in more religious symbolic language, ''principalities and powers, the rulers of this world of darkness, the evil spirits in regions above'' (cycle II) we cannot miss the obvious. The battle for goodness and integrity is fought seriously against overwhelming odds.

As we read through the same biblical passages a second time however, we discover a motif of confidence. We are almost made to feel that the battle is over and won. Paul writes:

> If God is for us, who can be against us?
>> Who will separate us from the love of
>> Christ? (cycle I)
> Draw you strength from the Lord and his
>> mighty power. Put on the armor of
> God so that you may be able to stand
> firm against the tactics of the devil
> (cycle II).

The battle has turned into an exciting adventure. We all delight in trysts of love. We cannot help but remember the melodic, haunting lines of the Song of Songs. One of the most memorable comes to mind:

> Set me as a seal on your heart,
>> as a seal on your arm;
> For stern as death is love,
>> relentless as the nether world is devotion;
>> its flames are a blazing fire.
> Deep waters cannot quench love,
>> nor floods sweep it away.
> Were one to offer all one owns to purchase love,
>> that one would be roundly mocked (Song 8:6–7).

These lines, at once serious and playful, confident and cautious, are yet another way, this time highly poetic and musical, to express the themes of today's reading.

On our part we must take seriously the double position: 1) "our battle ultimately is not against human forces but "against principalities and powers"; and 2) nothing "will be able to separate us from the love of God that comes to us in Christ Jesus, our Lord."

We dare not trifle with temptation, evil and sin. It is disastrous to discard the possibility of hell. These "eternal truths" are not toys, to be played with and then tossed aside and ignored. Nor are they fairy tales to amuse, scare and control children. We are reading from the Word of God, written for adults to ponder and to use as the launching pad of important decisions.

Neither does the excelling love of God make the struggle automatically easy. We are required to face, each in our own way: "trial or distress, or persecution, or hunger, or nakedness, or danger, or the sword." These problems and sorrows will still rend our heart and bring tears to our eyes. Yet they are not excuses for giving in to depression, panic, frustration, moodiness and the host of other frequent reactions to crises.

When Paul quotes from Ps 44, in the midst of the passage from Romans, he draws upon a psalm of severe personal and national crisis. Some of its lines even seem close to despair:

> You have cast us off and put us in disgrace,
> You make us the mockery and the scorn
>   of those around us,
> All the day my disgrace is before me,
>   and shame covers my face.
> Awake! Why are you asleep, O Lord?

Paul, however, rebounds with new strength and reverses the idea, making use at the same time of similar military language as in the psalm: "Yet in all this we are more than conquerors because of him who loved us."

Love then is the second ingredient in our double attitude. We must keep ever before our eyes the image of Jesus on the cross and the love which prompted such obedience to the will of God the Father:

> Is it possible that he who did not spare his own Son but handed him over [to death on the cross] for the sake of us all will not grant us all things besides?

In Ephesians (cycle II) still more helps are provided for us in our grueling struggle against "the rulers of this world of darkness." Here we single out the prayer of petition and intercessions:

> Pray constantly and attentively for all in the holy company. Pray for me. . . . Pray that I may have courage.

The gospel beings us squarely down to earth again. It refers to the intrigues of "that fox," Herod. It recognizes the certainty of Jesus' struggle with death:

> On the third day my purpose is accomplished. . . . no prophet can be allowed to die anywhere except in Jerusalem.

The word Jerusalem, however, does not bring hatred and bitterness, only sorrowing love and eventual hope:

How often have I wanted to gather your children
together as a mother bird collects her young under
her wings! . . . You shall not see me until the time
comes.

Eventually, love wins out!

Prayer:

I believe, Lord, that you will save me in your kindness.
I am wretched and poor, harassed and weary, but you will
always take your place beside me and deal kindly with me.
Blessed are you, O Lord, my refuge and deliverer, my
shield in whom I trust. I will sing a new song to you.

Friday, 30th Week

Rom 9:1–5. There is great grief and constant pain in my
    heart for the sake of my kinspeople, the Israelites. To
    them belong the adoption, the glory and the promises.
    From them came the Messiah.
Phil 1:1–11. God who has begun the good work in you will
    carry it through to completion. How much I long for each
    of you with the affections of Christ Jesus.
Luke 14:1–6. While at dinner on the sabbath Jesus was
    watched closely over his observance or non-observance
    of tradition. He took the initiative and cured a man who
    suffered from dropsy. The others even refused to discuss
    the case with him!

Many different reactions of love are offered for our reflection: *the love of sorrow and regret* over the failure of the
people to recognize Jesus as messiah (cycle I); *the warm affection* of Paul for his favorite church, Philippi (cycle II);

the stern and strong love of Jesus towards the man with dropsy, despite the hateful and spying tactics of certain pharisees (gospel).

For Paul Judaism remained a ''mystery,'' the word with which he will summarize the lengthy discussion in tomorrow's reading from Romans (11:25). Particularly in chapters 9–11 he tackles the thorny issue head on and writes very deliberately. We are obliged, on our part, to recognize and maintain Paul's language. He formulates the relation of Israel as a continuing, irrevocable bond. Often in the Bible God's promises to his chosen people are expressed in absolute style; God's word is not conditioned, nor can it be annulled by Israel's sins:

> The Lord, the Lord, a merciful and gracious
>   God . . . rich in kindness and fidelity
>   . . . forgiving wickedness and crime and
>   sin (Exod 34:6–7).
> How could I give you up, O Israel?
>   I will not give vent to my blazing anger,
>   For I am God, no human being (Hos 11:8–9).

Ps 103 explicitly considers Israel's sins. It draws upon the Mosaic covenant to restate the Lord's forgiveness:

> He has made known his ways to Moses,
> Merciful and gracious is the Lord,
> He will not always chide
> Not according to our sins does he deal with us
> As a parent has compassion on children,
>   so the Lord has compassion on those
>   who fear him.

Paul continues this tradition and affirms the absolute nature of God's choice of Israel. Here we quote directly from the Greek text of Romans where the present tense of the verb is unmistakably present for the promises to Israel; the verb changes to past tense only in reference to the appearance of Jesus within Judaism:

> To them [the Israelites] *belong* the adoption, the glory, the covenant, the law-giving, the worship and the promises; to them *belong* the patriarchs, and from them *came* the Messiah [I speak of his human origins].

Indeed, Paul too loves his people even to the point of wishing ''to be separated from Christ for the sake of my brothers and sisters, my kinspeople, the Israelites.'' Yet, if the Messiah or ''Christ came from them,'' Paul cannot be separated from Christ under any condition.

After his conversion Paul suffered greatly from his kinspeople. Yet he could never stop loving them, admiring them and extolling their dignity before God.

Paul writes just as intimately and lovingly to the Christians at Philippi, certainly his favorite church. The words tumble out without restraint, an unusual style for epistolary or public correspondence:

> I think of you . . . constantly rejoicing.
> I hold all of you dear.
> I long for each of you with the affection
>   of Christ Jesus.
> My prayer is that your love may more and
>   more abound.

We are grateful for this insight into Paul's character. He was no stoic, no distant ascetic, no hard-nosed theologian, no stern administrator. He was much more, even if those traits do appear at times. Because Paul was so affectionate and sensitive, he could not write calmly nor react phlegmatically. The excitable side of Paul's character is manifest in his correspondence with the Corinthians and the Galatians. Paul paid a heavy price for his apostolate, not only in physical pain (labors and imprisonments, beatings, shipwreck, hunger and thirst, etc.—2 Cor 11:23–27), but also in his interior life ("that daily tension, pressing on me, my anxiety for all the churches"—2 Cor 11:28).

Even in writing to the Philippians, Paul combines his affectionate concern with the spread of the gospel. One sentence expresses this relationship very well:

> I give thanks to my God every time I think of you —which is constantly, in every prayer I utter—rejoicing as I plead on your behalf, at the way you have all continually helped promote the gospel from the very first day.

Paul, therefore, experienced all the heights and depths, the vicissitudes of strong faithful love within marriage, family and community.

While the gospel account is written in the literary style of a "conflict story," we should not overlook the silent interchange of love and confidence between two people seated opposite each other at table: between Jesus and the man with dropsy, seated "directly in front of him." What turmoil of hope, gratitude and affection must have raced through the sick man. He sat silently, no words are recorded between him and Jesus, as Jesus asked the lawyers and Pharisees, "Is it lawful to cure on the Sabbath or not?" When Luke adds, "At this they kept silent," the silence must have exploded with a thousand and one reactions. On the part of Jesus and the sick man the silence spoke more eloquently and certainly more appropriately than words, how strong is love and how determined is compassion. Jesus was risking his entire ministry and the most powerful people in Judaism, for the sake of an unnamed ''man who suffered from dropsy,'' a man who is quickly lost to sight after he is cured: ''Jesus took the man, healed him, and sent him on his way.''

Each action bespeaks totally unselfish love: ''he took him; he healed him; he sent him on his way.'' Jesus did not attempt to possess and profit from his love or from his miracle. We must always love, whether overcome with regret, or swept along by affection, or surrounded by confrontation.

Prayer:

Lord, you will never betray your promises to us; you assure us of your continued fidelity. You give peace within the borders of our heart and fill us with the best. You bless us within our holy city and home. You give food to those who fear you. You are forever mindful of your covenant. We thank you, Lord, with all our heart.

Saturday, 30th Week

Rom 11:1–29 (selected verses). In regard to the ''mystery'' of Israel, their transgression has meant riches for the gentiles. Yet, God's gifts and his call toward Israel are irrevocable.

Phil 1:18–26. I long to be freed from this life and to be with Christ, for that is the far better thing; yet it is more urgent that I remain alive for your sake. That Christ is being proclaimed is what brings me joy.

Luke 14:1,7–11. Take the lowest place at a wedding party. The one who humbles himself shall be exalted.

Scripture urges us to listen anew to a quiet call at the center of our being. Here we are "with Christ" and here we long for that fuller union with Christ after our death. "All that matters is that in any and every way . . . Christ is being proclaimed." As we will see in today's Scripture, it is so easy to be distracted from Jesus. The Scriptures do not refer so much to serious, wilful sins but to those lesser sins that plague "good people". Often enough it seems easier to convert a great sinner from grave offenses than to convince a "good person" to repent of small transgressions.

The church at Philippi must have asked Paul about people who preach Christ, yet are not of their ranks. We are reminded of a similar episode in the gospel (Luke 9:49–50) and in each case jealousy is the fault which God will not tolerate among his disciples. Paul replies that the proclamation of Christ, "whether from specious motives or genuine ones," "is what brings me joy."

Paul is reducing the entire gospel to that single word, "Christ", who lives as our risen saviour. In Matthew the gospel was summarized by the phrase the "kingdom of God" but in Paul simply as "Christ":

> . . . the splendor of the gospel, showing forth the
> glory of Christ, the image of God. It is not our-
> selves we preach but Jesus Christ as Lord (2 Cor
> 4:4–5).

Unlike the evangelists (Matthew, Mark, Luke and John) Paul's gospel does not record the words and deeds of Jesus. Rather Paul finds the gospel, that is, the risen Jesus, alive now within the community. Every action and word among the believers becomes an action or statement of the "body of Christ." Jesus, therefore, was that fully alive and that continuously present in the Christian that Paul writes to the Philippians:

> I have full confidence that now as always Christ
> will be exalted through me, whether I live or die.
> For, to me, "life" means Christ.

Paul's other statement to the Galatians comes to mind:

> The life I live now is not my own; Christ is living
> in me. I still live my human life, but it is a life of
> faith in the Son of God, who loved me and gave
> himself for me (Gal 2:20).

What joy filled the heart of Paul and what holiness was transmitted to others, by simply mentioning the name "Christ." With this name Paul swept aside jealousy and envy among the faithful.

Christ is now the treasure and the vocation of the gentiles. This unusual turn of events brings Paul to think of his own people, the Israelites, who as a group refused to recognize Jesus as Lord and Messiah. Many of them, as we read in the early chapters of the Acts of the Apostles, did become disciples. Yet, as a nation, they were overcome by blindness. That is Paul's word. It not only contains an enormous amount of kindly judgment, but it also indicates that "God has not rejected his people whom he foreknew, for his gifts are irrevocable."

Rather than discuss the baffling "mystery" of Judaism, our meditation here can focus upon Paul's word, "blindness." How much anger and impatience would be spared, how much kindness and gentleness manifested, and it should be added, how much truth would be comprehended, if we would stop judging people's motives. Even if we are absolutely correct, our approach to others would be so much more in accord with the Scripture, if we would only attribute good intentions and divine grace to those who differ with us. "God has not rejected his people whom he foreknew." Secondly, the divergent viewpoint in our neighbor may enable us to see our own position of faith all the more clearly. "Blindness has come upon part of Israel until the full number of Gentiles enter in."

Paul adds: "Then Israel will be saved," but only when we ourselves are fully dedicated to the gospel which is the person of Christ. What hinders conversion then is not our ignorance of truth but our lack of joy and enthusiasm "in Christ."

The disciples of Christ erect barriers to the gospel by jealousy (Philippians), by gloom and judgmental attitudes (Romans), and by their greed for honor and prestige. Too many good people want to be known and recognized for their goodness, too many of us pull rank and "sit in the place of honor." In today's parable Jesus is kind enough to adapt himself to this common weakness of saintly people. "Sit in the lowest place . . . so that the host will say, 'My friend, come up higher,' [then] you will win esteem." It seems that Jesus is saying: if you must win esteem, at least go about it in a proper, civilized way!

The gospel ends with the most difficult commandment of all, humility. The commandment to be humble is the stumbling block of believers and even they have to see an exaltation offered as a reward!

Everyone who exalts himself shall be humbled,
and the one who humbles himself shall be exalted.

Prayer:

Lord, you never abandon your people. Despite our calling and our giftedness, we become jealous, judgmental and proud. Let us listen again to your instruction and seek you and you alone in all that we do. As we turn inward and attend to your holy presence, we find our souls thirsting for you, my living God.

Monday, 31st Week

Rom 11:29–36. Paul concludes the discussion about Israel and the gentiles by recalling God's mercy and the unsearchable ways of divine providence.

Phil 2:1–4. That his joy be complete, Paul begs for unanimity, humility and love that rule out rivalry or conceit. Each of us should look towards the interests of others.

Luke 14:12–14. In preparing a banquet invite beggars, the crippled, the lame and the blind. You will be repaid in the resurrection of the just.

Because God will reward us far beyond what our actions deserve, we should not be overly concerned about the exact measure of our merits. We remember the discontent of the laborers in the vineyard, at least those who had worked all day and received the "just" wage, while those who had worked but an hour received as much. The gist of this parable is found in the final statement: "Are you envious because I am generous?" (Matt 20:15—see Wednesday, 20th week). If God is generous it behooves us not to argue our rights. What if he gave us only what we deserve? This parable was repeated in the early church to answer the question: "Why do the gentiles now receive the same blessing of discipleship in Christ as the Israelites who had toiled in the vineyard of the covenant for almost two millennia?'' In the reading from Romans (cycle I) Paul concludes the entire discussion about Israelites and gentiles by stressing the disobedience of all which was the occasion of God's mercy for all, a powerful example of God's inscrutable judgments and unsearchable ways.

The disobedience of all. Israel's earliest period of wandering in the Sinai desert was pockmarked with grumbling and disobedience. Only three days after being saved from Egypt and led through the Red Sea, Israel complained about the bitter water in the desert and so in Exod 15:23 the place came to be called Marah (= ''Bitter''). Several verses later we read again:

> Here in the desert the whole Israelite community grumbled against Moses and Aaron [and] said to them, ''Would that we had died at the Lord's hands in the land of Egypt, as we sat by our fleshpots and ate our fill of bread! But you had to lead us into this desert to make the whole community die of famine'' [Exod 16:2–3].

God's response to such grumbling and disobedience was mercy. Chap. 16 of Exodus then describes the appearance of the manna.

The gentiles have a similar history. ''You [the gentiles] were once disobedient to God and now you have received mercy.'' Earlier in Romans, Paul had described how ''formerly you enslaved your bodies to . . . degradation . . . things of which you are now ashamed'' (Thursday—29th week). We have only one adequate explanation for God's direction of our lives—*the mystery of divine mercy*.

Mercy is always visible and palpable. We see and feel it. We need to reflect further on Paul's sense of *mystery* in

God's mercy. What is it, we ask, that God is communicating to us *in faith* when we experience mercy? The mystery is there, beyond all doubt. Paul draws upon a number of favorite Old Testament texts to announce the mystery: Isa 40:13; Ps 139:6, 17–18; Wis 9:13. He writes:

> How deep are the riches and the wisdom and the knowledge of God! How inscrutable his judgments, how unsearchable his ways! For ''who has known the mind of the Lord? . . . Who has given him anything so as to deserve return?''

From the background of Isaiah, chap. 40, we find the mystery in God's near broken heart over the extreme suffering of Israel and in Israel's need to wait upon the Lord. In fact chap. 40 begins with, ''Comfort, give comfort to my people, says your God,'' and ends with, ''They that hope in the Lord will renew their strength.'' From Ps 139 we learn that the mystery extends from conception. ''You knit me together in my mother's womb,'' to every moment of one's lifetime. ''Your eyes have seen my actions; in your book they are written.'' And from the entire discussion in Romans about Jews and gentiles, we admit that the mystery of God's mercy reaches to *all of our relationships* with others:

> Blest are they who show mercy;
> mercy shall be theirs (Matt 5:7).

In writing to Philippians (cycle II) Paul translates the general call to ''show mercy'' into specifics: unanimity, one love, united in spirit and ideals, no rivalry or conceit, think humbly of others as superior, look after the interests of others rather than your own. By following these norms we do not deprive those who receive our mercy of their human dignity; they remain our brothers and sisters, members of our one large family. Paul also explains the attitude and the bond of spirit that should characterize the family setting for mercy:

> In the name of the encouragement which you owe me in Christ, in the name of the solace that love can give, of fellowship in spirit, compassion and pity, I beg you make my joy complete.

We notice how exquisitely Paul combines the obligation and the dependency of family life. In one and the same breath he refers to that ''which you owe me'' and that which ''I beg you'' to do!

The gospel now gives a concrete example of what the precept of showing mercy means:

> When you have a reception, invite beggars and the crippled, the lame and the blind.

If we allow ourselves to be overtaken by our memory, we will recall moments when God invited us in our crippled, beggarly state to a banquet of joy—the joy of an undeserved family, the joy of forgiveness, the joy of new life. We recall, too, times of depression when we were blind to hope, paralyzed without energy to go forward. Yet God called us, gently laid his hand on our feeble eyes and legs; and we found our hopes revived, our strength restored.

If Jesus assures us that ''you will be repaid in the resurrection of the just,'' we can affirm that promise from our own experiences. We have already felt the power of the resurrection within ourselves.

Therefore, as stated at the beginning of this meditation, we are very wise, not to act or do for others so that they can repay us, but rather to act and help others freely. God's recompense to us may be locked in mystery, but it will overtake us with the wonders of the resurrection even now on earth.

Prayer:

Lord, we, your lowly people, look to you in your great love. You hear the poor and never spurn your own. So absorb me in your mercy, Lord God, that mercy will always direct my thoughts and actions towards my neighbor. As I hope in you, I feel as secure and peaceful as a child on its mother's lap.

Tuesday, 31st Week

Rom 12:5–16. We though many are one body in Christ. We have gifts that differ according to God's favor. Love one another with the affection of brothers and sisters.

Phil 2:5–11. Your attitude must be Christ's. Though he was in the form of God, he emptied himself and took the form of a slave, obediently accepting death on a cross. Therefore, God highly exalted him.

Luke 14:15–24. God invites poor people from the streets and the alleys, from the highways and the hedgerows. Those invited first, who turned down the invitation, shall not taste a morsel.

Hopes are freely suffused in us by God and they offer undeserved possibilities. We cannot ignore them, nor reject them, without being seriously harmed in the process. In fact, it can be disastrous to toy around with important hopes. The moment may pass us by, and we can never recover the lost opportunity. Furthermore, hopes are not bestowed on us by God simply for our private, individual enjoyment. Unless they are shared, they are lost! Though the matter is serious, Paul still exhorts us: "Rejoice in hope!"

The reading from Romans (cycle I) begins with the need to share our hopes and gifts, so obviously true because "we, though many, are one body in Christ and individually members one of another." Each gift, compared to a member of the human body, must serve the entire body and be exercised in such a way that the hand is never thinking of the hand but of the mouth to which it offers food, and the mouth is never so absorbed with chewing food as to overlook whether the stomach and intestines can digest the food and nourish the other parts of the body, including the arm and mouth.

Paul enumerates seven of the gifts bestowed on individual members of the church, the body of the Lord:

- *prophecy*, in accordance with faith, so that the bond of unity in Christ be strengthened;

- *ministry*, to represent the church in serving others in their material or physical needs;

- *teaching*, that the mystery of Jesus be ever more profoundly appreciated;

- *exhortation*, like parents joyfully encouraging their children in their talents;

- *almsgiving* from one's private resources, generously and graciously;

- *administration* which should recognize its subordinate place on the list of gifts and act "with love";

- *works of mercy* cheerfully.

Not only does the entire church depend upon the right functioning of each member within the body, but each member will shrivel, become sick and harm the entire organism unless properly exercised.

In Philippians (cycle II) Paul draws upon an early church hymn to "Jesus Christ as Lord" and as we meditate upon it today, we realize better how totally we like Christ must submerge ourselves within the loving bond of community and there exercise a heroic obedience to God's holy will for us. If we are members of "one body in Christ," as we just read in Romans, then how necessarily our "attitude must be Christ's."

- As eternal Word in the Holy Trinity, Jesus "did not deem equality with God something to be grasped at," and neither should we as individual members of the church be arguing our equality, rights and privileges.

- Jesus emptied himself of divinity and was born in human likeness. We are advised to be so thoroughly a living member of the church that we are emptied of self-serving and we live and think in the interest of Christ's body.

- Jesus obediently accepted death, even death on the cross. Jesus' words come to mind: we gain our [total, eternal] life by [freely] losing it [our individual, isolated, earthly life].

- At Jesus' name every knee must bend. Our adoration will be absorbed into our entire heavenly life, and even here on earth we proclaim JESUS CHRIST IS LORD!

The Gospel reinforces each of these reflections. We should not argue our own individual roles against Christ's invitation in the church and in our community. We should remember how helpless and impoverished we would be, left to being just an arm or leg or ear or mouth! Finally, if we do not act upon grace and divine initiative, the opportunity may never return.

Prayer:

Lord, we find our peace in you. Protect us from our tendency to be proud and haughty; keep us from reaching beyond ourselves and our service to community with things too lofty and too selfish. We praise you, Lord, in the unity of our faith, in our bonds as one body, in our consciousness of being your lowly ones, eating their fill at your heavenly banquet.

Wednesday, 31st Week

Rom 13:8–10. Owe no debt to anyone except the debt that binds us to love one another. Love never does any wrong; it is the fulfillment of the law.

Phil 2:12–18. Prove yourselves children of God, innocent and straightforward. God begets in you every measure of desire or achievement. You give me cause to boast.

Luke 14:25–33. No one can be my disciple unless that one renounce all possessions, even father and mother, spouse and children, indeed one's very self.

Fortunately we do not read the gospel selection alone but can balance it with other passages from Scripture. True, there are moments, very infrequent and most difficult, when the gospel must be heard in stark, heroic loneliness, but initially and normally we should approach today's gospel from the bonds of union of family, community and church. Together with family and friends we form the one body of the Lord, and as Paul wrote elsewhere to the Corinthians: "the eye cannot say to the hand, 'I do not need you,' any more than the head can say to the feet, 'I do not need you' '' (I Cor 12:21).

In the concluding chapters of Romans (chaps. 12–16) Paul follows a general practice at the end of his epistles of becoming very practical and of urging fidelity to Christian virtues. In today's selection (cycle I) he quotes from the Ten Commandments, and then adds:

> [all] other commandments are summed up in this [one commandment]: "You shall love your neighbor as yourself."

Love is the one and only debt which Paul will tolerate in the community. This one obligation so "binds us to love one another," that no one is superior to any other. All persons have gifts, unique to themselves, and by exercising and sharing these gifts, all make their proper contribution. Each is dependent upon the other and each enriches the other. There is written into our human nature a law of mutual help and mutual subordination. Love then is the fulfillment of such a law, for love preserves and cherishes the unity essential for a healthy body.

Earlier, in reading from Ephesians (Saturday, 29th week) this idea of unity was stressed:

> Through Christ the whole body grows, and with the proper functioning of the members joined firmly together by each supporting ligament, builds itself up in love (Eph 4:16).

With less symbolic language, Paul points out in Philippians (cycle II) how the body functions smoothly and healthily. He advises us:

> In everything you do, act without grumbling or arguing; prove yourselves innocent and straightforward, children of God beyond reproach [even] in the midst of a twisted and depraved generation.

In this setting of love and trust, Paul introduces us to several ideas disposing us to understand the gospel that *seems* to cut through love and disregard trust.

Paul refers to "the day of Christ," *i.e.*, that of his death. At that time he will even be able "to boast that I did not run the race in vain or work to no purpose." He also adds these important words:

> Even if my life is to be poured out as a libation over the sacrificial service of your faith, I am glad of it and rejoice with all of you. May you be glad on the same score, and rejoice with me.

Jesus' statement, therefore, about "turning one's back on father and mother, spouse and children, brothers and sisters, indeed one's very self," can never be interpreted against the continual, biblical insistence upon the first two commandments of love for God and for one's neighbor. Who is a closer neighbor than one's family?

Every stern action that affects one's family and community must be directed by love for family and community. The action is really for their welfare because a manifestation of one's own loyalty to Jesus. Pain and death are for "the sacrificial service of faith" within the bonds of love set up by God within the total body of Christ, the Church.

There are times, hopefully rare, when we deliberately act in such a way that suffering is inflicted on others. Parents discipline children, good friends correct one another. Jesus calls each of us to take up our cross and follow him. Like Jesus, we too should suffer with those whom we cause to suffer; and like Jesus our mutual bearing of the cross is life-giving and transforming. This heroic form of love is the ultimate fulfillment of the law.

Prayer:

Lord, make me generous in sharing my gifts. Let me delight in your commandment to love and be your instrument in shining the light of your goodness through the darkness of this life. Then in all my needs I will find you to be my refuge. I will see your goodness in the land of the living.

Thursday, 31st Week

Rom 14:7–12. Both in life and in death we are the Lord's. That is why Christ died and came back to life again. We are not to judge brother or sister; every knee must bend before the Lord.

Phil 3:3–8. Though uncircumcised, the gentile church has inherited the promises of circumcision. Paul, for his part, can boast of being of the stock of Israel. However, he rates all as loss in the light of the surpassing knowledge of my Lord Jesus Christ.

Luke 15:1–10. More joy in heaven over finding the one lost sheep or the one lost silver piece than over the ninety-nine others who had no need to repent.

Typical of Luke's Gospel, Jesus never passes up an opportunity for a party or a dinner! Many of Jesus' great discourses in the third gospel were delivered at the dinner table of a wealthy or influential person! Jesus concludes the two parables in today's gospel when the happy retriever of lost goods "arrives home, invites friends and neighbors in and says to them, 'Rejoice with me!' " Jesus then proceeds to compare this happy occasion with "joy in heaven."

The gospel describes the joy in finding the lost sheep and lost silver pieces. It even concludes each short parable by saying that:

> There will be more joy in heaven over one repen-
> tant sinner than over the ninety-nine righteous
> who have no need to repent.

Rather than discuss the seeming inequity of this heavenly re-action, we reflect on another aspect of the parables and then are in a better position to think favorably of the entire story.

Each of us at once is a bundle of ninety-nine sheep always accountable and under control, and the one lost sheep always wandering off and seldom if ever under control. We all contain ideas and talents which we have come to under-stand and carefully direct. We can always foretell their line of action and the outcome. They are always with us and we are proud of them. Because of them we receive compliments and awards. These constitute ninety-nine righteous percent of ourselves that has "no need to repent."

Fortunately God has also suffused an unpredictable, unruly and oftentimes lost talent or quality in our being. Stretching the parable a bit, we might say that this *easily* lost part about ourselves can be a special moment of time or a unique opportunity or even a stranger crossing our path. If it is a moment of time, then it is so fleeting that it is over with before we know it!

All of us possess some wonderful talents and beautiful

inspirations, for ourselves or the church, for our family, neighborhood or country, that seem too good even to talk about. They might be spoiled or injured by ridicule or simply by cool indifference. Or they might turn out to be so demanding on ourselves that we try to suppress them. Often those talents or inspirations can become the crucial turning point in our lives. They may be an inspiration to forgive another and be reconciled, to volunteer assistance, to form a program of prayer, to make a clear decision for marriage or priesthood or religious life or single career.

If we act upon these moments of grace, then our entire life, attitude, scale of values, ways of thinking, everything about us will be transformed. Forgiveness and reconciliation bring that peace which had eluded us for a long time! If we offer a helping hand, we may meet a friend whose love and goodness will turn our life around one hundred and eighty percent.

Jesus assures us that the lost sheep and lost coin in each of us can be found. We must leave aside the ninety-nine other more perfect or more jealous parts of ourselves and seek this one, precious but lost sheep or coin.

There is another aspect of the parable that is disturbing and fearful. Are we willing not only to revolutionize our entire life for God but are we also able to leave much of the customary, controllable parts of our existence and plunge into a wilderness for the lost sheep? Are we ready to "light a lamp and sweep the house [of our existence] diligently" till we discover the lost coin?

The gospel gives us a healthy viewpoint for re-reading the selection from Romans (cycle I). Every part of ourselves and of our existence "in life and in death" belongs to the Lord. "That is why," Paul goes on to say, "Christ died and came to life again." If we suffer greatly as we detach ourselves from the ninety-nine percent of ourselves, "Christ too died''; if we rise with new enlightened outlook upon finding and claiming our lost sheep, Christ also ''came to life again.''

With this background we can also understand Paul's injunction against judging one's brother or sister, or as he wrote elsewhere, against judging himself (1 Cor 4:3). We judge from the evidence. What we see is the ninety-nine; the one other is lost! Our judgment seldom takes into consideration the rediscovering of the lost sheep or coin. This latter cannot be seen. It is lost!

In awe and surprise we find ourselves, bending the knee and praising God, when we set out in search and eventually find what had been lost.

The other ninety-nine will be reabsorbed and transfigured in Jesus. They will live in new, exciting ways. They will be found for Jesus and be lost in the wonder of his holy name! Paul writes for us:

> Those things I used to consider gain I have now reappraised as loss in the light of Christ. I have come to rate *all* as loss in the light of the surpassing knowledge of my Lord Jesus Christ.

When the lost is found and ninety-nine are inspired with new meaning, then Paul is correct that ''we [gentiles] are the circumcision.'' We were once lost and are now found; we even become ''the circumcision,'' that means, the inheritors of Jewish faith and hope.

Prayer:

Lord, you are my refuge. You search for me when I am lost. Why then should I fear! I shall see your good things in the land of the living. Whether alive or dead, lost or found, at home or abroad, we look to the Lord in strength. We want to serve you constantly! We rejoice and recall your wondrous deeds.

Friday, 31st Week

Rom 15:14–21. Paul preaches only what God has done through him among the gentiles; his is the priestly duty of offering the gentiles as a pleasing sacrifice, consecrated by the Holy Spirit.

Phil 3:17–4:1. We eagerly await the coming of the Savior. He will give a new form to this lowly body of ours and re-make us according to the pattern of his glorified body.

Luke 16:1–8. The worldly take more initiative than the other-worldly. The owner gave his devious employee credit for being enterprising.

We are asked to reflect upon the attitude with which we act. All too frequently we become workaholics, distracting ourselves from any serious consideration about our motives or about the source of our strength, even about the purpose and result of our excessive activity. A hurricane is sweeping through our lives and is driving other people as well. The Scriptures declare that ''by waiting and by calm you shall be saved'' (Isa 30:15), for this frenetic motion to be correct. At the same time the Scriptures do not canonize inactivity. We have the example of Paul, apostle of the gentiles, central figure and ''world traveler'' in the second part of the Acts of the Apostles (Acts 13–28), prolific writer of letters, many of which are preserved in the New Testament. In today's selection (cycle I) he even wrote that ''I can take glory in Christ Jesus for the work I have done for God.''

Because Paul's action, like his letters, was undertaken ''rather boldly,'' we can confidently study his writings for

the correct attitude or spirit with which to direct and modulate our own activity. Several magnificent lines or phrases
come to our attention at once in the reading from Romans:

- God has given me the grace to be a minister of Christ
  Jesus among the gentiles.
- I will not dare to speak of anything except what
  Christ has done through me . . . by the power of
  God's Spirit.
- Gentiles are to be a pleasing sacrifice, consecrated by
  the Holy Spirit.

The spirit then which motivated Paul was quite con-
sciously the Holy Spirit, ''the Spirit of adoption'' through
which we become ''heirs with Christ'' (Rom 8:15, 17). Paul
was a ''minister of Christ Jesus,'' and achieved only ''what
Christ has done through me.''

In many ways Paul surrendered to the Spirit and so
acted as Christ's minister. Courage drew Paul to undertake
the more difficult tasks, to preach where Christ's name was
not yet known, and through this courage Paul would be
compelled to turn repeatedly to the Holy Spirit for assistance
and guidance. Courage brings us to the further boundary
where fear catches up with us again and Paul like ourselves
must choose between panic or faith in God. Facing difficult
and draining demands Paul did not succumb to feverish motion nor to a blind drive to get it done, but rather they at-
tracted Paul into the quiet corner of his heart, for long
stretches of contemplation, ''eagerly awaiting the coming of
our savior,'' as well as for short God-filled moments in between the words and movement.

Paul, moreover, controlled and directed his activity
along a path of humbly recognizing and seconding what God
was already doing in others. He looked upon the gentiles as

"consecrated by the Holy Spirit." Paul was to inspire, aid and minister to the new life within the heart of the believer. "We were as gentle as any nursing mother fondling her little ones" (I Thess 2:7). This final goal of apostolic activity moved Paul always to be delicately aware of what *God* was accomplishing in others. As Paul furthered this action of God in others, he appreciated the special talents, charism and function of each person. In this way "preaching" became a "priestly duty," for it enabled the movement towards God in the heart of the believer to become "a pleasing sacrifice." Therefore, Paul writes that "I can take glory in Christ Jesus." The work which Paul does is lost within the work which Jesus is doing in the heart of others.

To follow Paul then was the same as to follow Christ; Paul was at once the instrument of the Spirit and "the minister of Christ Jesus." For this reason Paul wrote to the Philippians: "Be imitators of me, my brothers and sisters" (cycle II). Yet, when Paul imitated Jesus, he seldom referred to Jesus' earthly life. Paul's gospel was quite different in tone and content from the gospels of Matthew, Mark, Luke and John. Paul's Jesus dwelt within him. Paul's Jesus also was to come again; Paul was preoccupied with this second coming at the end of time. Later Paul perceived the risen Jesus within the wondrous possibilities of the apostolate. This latter is the case in writing to the Philippians:

> Our citizenship [is] in heaven; it is from there that
> we eagerly await the coming of our savior, the
> Lord Jesus Christ.

The apostolate, therefore, was to carry a glow of hope and enthusiasm. Already "our citizenship [is] in heaven." We see as at a distance, the glory of the risen Christ. We feel the magnificent agony of such hopes. In this regard we remember Paul's words to the Romans:

> All creation groans and is in agony even until now. Not only that, but we ourselves, although we have the Spirit as first fruits, groan inwardly while we await the redemption of our bodies (Rom 8:22–23).

No matter the difficulties with the church at Philippi—Paul had already written those telling words earlier to the church at Thessalonica:

> Fresh from the humiliation we had suffered at Philippi . . . we drew courage from our God to preach his good tidings to you in the face of great opposition (1 Thess 2:2).

Paul remained an apostle of hope. We read in today's selection:

> Christ will give a new form to this lowly body of ours and remake it according to the pattern of his glorified body.

Another qualification for an apostle comes at the end of the reading from First Thessalonians: respect and hope for those to whom we preach or whom we serve. Paul says to the people:

> You whom I so love and long for, you who are my joy and my crown . . . my dear ones.

When we come finally to the gospel, the elevated spirituality of Christian ministry becomes the plain language of common sense. We are called upon to be "enterprising" and to act with "initiative." Most unfortunately, Jesus notes that "the worldly" possess these qualities more abundantly than "the other-worldly." As we make good use of our bodies and human talents, we are servants of God who created us "to the divine image and likeness" (Gen 1:26) and to offer spiritual sacrifice to God who dwells within us as the temple of divine glory (2 Cor 6:16).

Prayer:

Lord, we sing a new song. With each new action we can observe your kindness and faithfulness. Grant that we be your ministers, revealing you anew to everyone, even to the ends of the earth. Then in all that we say or do, we are journeying to your holy city Jerusalem, to worship before you.

Saturday, 31st Week

Rom 16 (selected verses). Greeting to Paul's co-workers. May glory be given to God who strengthens you in the gospel, the mystery hidden for many ages and made known to all the Gentiles.

Phil 4:10–19. In Jesus, the source of my strength, I have strength. It was kind of you to share my hardships and send something for my needs.

Luke 16:9–15. A series of maxims about worldly goods and the service of God.

God, the creator of the universe and the designer of our body and mind, does not want us to despise the earth or to reduce ourselves to passive automatons. Everything is to be put to the good service of God and of one another. Yesterday Jesus bemoaned that his ''other-worldly'' disciples do not manifest the enterprising initiative so visible in the ''worldly.'' Today, Paul greets and commends the faithful ''co-workers in the service of Christ Jesus'' (cycle I) and stresses how effectively he can ''cope with every circumstance—how to eat well or go hungry'' (cycle II). The gospel, again as in the case of yesterday's selection, lays it out clearly before us: ''Make friends for yourselves through your use of this world's goods.''

The list of co-workers in the final chapter of Romans is impulsively long. It witnesses to Paul's sensitivity and recognition of talents and enterprise in others. The tabulation begins with:

- ''Prisca and Aquila [who] risked their lives for the sake of mine . . . All the churches of the Gentiles are grateful to them . . . The congregation meets in their house.''

- ''My beloved Epaenetus . . . first offering that Asia made to Christ.''

- ''Mary who worked hard for you.''

- ''Adronicus and Junias . . . fellow prisoners, outstanding apostles . . . in Christ even before I was.''

Paul's secretary, ''Tertius, I who have written this letter,'' sends his greetings and those from ''Gaius, my host, . . . Erastus, city treasurer, and our brother Quartus.''

Paul did not run a one-person show nor was he a petty dictator. Paul believed in team ministry and endorsed the talents and divine call in others. Nor was Paul anti-woman. In this list women receive as much attention as they do in

Luke's gospel. In naming the Jewish couple, "Prisca and Aquila, my co-workers," Paul names the woman first; she too risked her "life for the sake of mine." We read also about "Mary who has worked hard for you" and "Junias," one of the "outstanding apostles." The mention and even the endorsement for these "co-workers" and "apostles" take on special significance. Here where Paul concludes his most elaborate, theological explanation of his gospel, he links with himself this large assembly of men and women.

Paul is asking us some serious questions. Do we conclude our important works, and therefore even our lesser undertakings, very conscious of the many people who cooperated with us? Do we call attention to our co-workers and give them proper recognition in the presence of others? Do we win for them the appreciation of all the church, the way that Paul writes: "Not only I but all the churches of the Gentiles are grateful to them."

Ultimately—and always—to God the Father "be the glory given through Jesus Christ unto endless ages." These final words in the long epistle to the Romans reunite all the apostles and co-workers, so that they and their accomplishments return to their source, gloriously and happily. Ultimately, we are all God's co-workers.

In Romans (cycle I) then Paul manifests a healthy and appreciative cooperation with other people in the apostolate. The selection from Philippians (cycle II) gives us another example of living maturely within one's environment and even of making a virtue out of necessity. Paul writes:

> Whatever the situation I find myself in I have learned to be self-sufficient. I am experienced in being brought low, yet I know what it is to have abundance—how to eat well and go hungry, to be well provided for and do without.

Most of us would cringe at admitting in public, in fact, in a public church document that "I know . . . how to eat well and . . . to be well provided for." We would confine our remarks to our heroic hardships for the gospel and for the neighbor!

We also might hesitate to state openly how others have helped us. Here again Paul shows a very healthy spontaneity in thanking "my dear Philippians," because "you sent something for my needs, not once but twice." Their gifts did more than make Paul's life pleasant. They comforted Paul "*in my hardships* . . . when . . . not a single congregation except yourselves shared with me . . . something *for my needs.*" In these words Paul shows how greatly indebted he was towards the Philippians.

Paul asks us to express our dependency upon one another. At the same time we are also instructed how to maintain our human dignity and self-respect. We have already seen how Paul can survive in hunger and serious need. He is not enslaved to others nor dependent in the wrong way. Paul, moreover, advises us to share our own selves, our time, our insights, our ability to work with hands and head, our sympathetic listening. Thereby, as each gives to the other, there is an "ever-growing balance" of each one's receiving. All have the dignity of knowing that they give what is helpful and even necessary to the other.

Paul also views the material world that is given and received as:

- from God "who is the source of my strength,"
- a fragrant offering, a sacrifice acceptable and pleasing to God,
- the "magnificent riches in Christ Jesus."

The gospel, once again as on the preceding two days, speaks in plain, unmistakable language. We are to make good "use of this world's goods." If we are faithful in these small matters, we can be trusted in greater things. Yet, do not be the slave of money. And in financial and other such matters, very often "what a human being thinks important, God holds in contempt."

Prayer:

I praise you, Lord. The wonderful world that you created for us speaks of your glorious majesty and calls upon us to respect and honor it, to make good use of it in the apostolate. Happy will I be, Lord, if I am generous with the poor.

Monday, 32nd Week

Wis 1:1–7. Think of the Lord in goodness, seek the Lord in integrity, for the spirit of the Lord fills the world and knows our thoughts.

Tit 1:1–9. Knowledge of the truth in the hope of eternal life. Qualities of a presbyter.

Luke 17:1–6. Instruction on scandal, forgiveness and faith.

Scripture urges us to reach outward and like God's spirit to be all-embracing. At the same time our attention turns inward and we "think of the Lord in goodness" and of others with forgiveness, self-control and compassionate understanding. As we meditate further upon the Bible texts for today, we are helped to form a delicate, healthy balance between interest and concern towards the world outside of us on the one hand and a silent, quest for inner peace on the other hand. The Bible also combines high ideals, even the faith to "transplant this tree," with care for the daily details of life like hospitality and the training of one's children.

In so many ways the Bible, particularly the Old Testament, strikes the new reader as a very earthy document. It is! Yet we need not apologize for that! This attitude of the Scriptures should impart the consoling realization that salvation is achieved in the midst of the real world, not in a fantasy world of plaster saints. God accepts us wherever and whoever we are, wherever we happen to live, whatever may be our family or neighborhood setting.

At once, however, we are expected to have an eye for details, even to be *heroically* practical! This attitude is evident in the first reading of cycle I for the final three weeks of ''ordinary time.'' This 32nd week draws upon the Book of Wisdom, the last of the sapiential books to be written; the 33rd and 34th weeks, upon the two Books of Maccabees and the Prophecy of Daniel where Jews suffer for their fidelity to the Mosaic law in its prescriptions for daily, family living. The Book of Daniel, like Maccabees, explodes in persecution; and particularly in Daniel we have a glimpse of the glorious coming of the Son of Man on the clouds of heaven. If we are faithful in small matters, God will entrust us with the greatest (see the gospel of last Saturday). Cycle II for weeks 33 and 34 reads from the New Testament counterpart to Daniel, the Book of Revelation.

We are to live with two feet firmly planted on earth. The Book of Wisdom already in its opening essay, introduces many practical pointers or warnings for this steady positioning of ourselves:

integrity of heart	avoid senseless counsel
do not test God	rebuke injustice
flee deceit	God listens to our tongue

We notice especially the close presence of God within this practical counsel: do not test God—God listens. The wise

Jewish person in Egypt who composed the book also gives us a larger setting, with heart and mind sensitive to God's presence within oneself and open to a God-filled universe:

- think of the Lord in goodness,
- God is the witness of one's inmost self, the sure ob-server of the heart and the listener to one's tongue,
- the spirit of the Lord fills the world, is all-embracing, and knows what each person says.

Whether we look inward or search outward, we find God always present. No place is too small, no question too trifling, nor is any place too immense nor any problem too complex, for God not to be immediately at hand, struggling and resting with us.

> Whether we eat or drink—
>   whatever you do—
>   you should do all for the glory of God
>   (I Cor 10:31).

The same, continuous interaction of ideals and dreams with homey advice and hard-nosed common sense is im-mediately evident in the Epistle of Titus (cycle II). This epistle must be a very late document. It lacks the enthusiasm of earlier documents and draws upon some painfully ac-quired wisdom.

Paul writes with paternal love, calling Titus, ''my own true child in our common faith.'' He also trusts the judgment of Titus:

> My purpose in leaving you in Crete was that you might accomplish what had been left undone, es-

pecially the appointment of presbyters in every
town.

Paul also surrounds his words with a vast sweep of God's
providence:

> promote the knowledge of the truth . . . in the
> hope of that eternal life which God . . . promised
> in endless ages past.

Within this setting of compassionate understanding, confidence and wide sweep of history, Paul inserts a serious, mature concern over the nitty-gritty. The "presbyter must be":

irreproachable	not self-willed
married only once	not arrogant
father of a respectable family	hospitable

Finally, the gospel for its part proposes a healthy spirituality. It tackles one of the most difficult phenomena
among people who are high-minded, trustful and idealistic.
Scandal is one of their most serious problems. Some will say
that such people are too easily scandalized; they need to be
more streetwise and hardened to life. Jesus, however, defends the innocent, those people often too good for the rest
of us. Paul wrote similarly, that if meat scandalizes his
brothers and sisters, he will never again eat it (I Cor 10:28).

These same idealistic people often find it difficult to
forgive. Because virtue comes second nature, they cannot
appreciate the force of temptation in others. Or they are so
obsessed with their own type of holiness and their own scale
of values, that they fail to see the goodness and the different
scale of values in the other. The inability of these pious folk

to forgive may turn out to be a still greater scandal to the less
pious, less religious person!

Pious people too can associate their religion too much
with their own holy activity and forget the force of God's
power, operative in their lives through faith and capable of
transplanting mountains into the sea. One's holy activity
needs to be balanced by faith in God's activity in the lives of
others.

Prayer:

Lord God, enable me to seek you in integrity of heart,
so that I can balance and unite all the parts and obligations
of my life along your everlasting way. Grant that I may always find you, even if I journey to the farthest end of the
heavens. In all that I do, I long to see your face and receive
your blessing.

Tuesday, 32nd Week

Wis 2:22–3:9. The souls of the just seemed in the view of
    the foolish to be dead, but they are in peace. God tried
    them and found them worthy of himself. Those who trust
    in God shall understand truth and abide with him in love.
Titus 2:1–8, 11–14. Practical instructions are given for dif-
    ferent groups, so that we may live temperately, justly and
    devoutly in this age as we await the appearance of our
    blessed hope, our Savior Christ Jesus.
Luke 17:7–10. Having done what is commanded, we ought
    to say that we are useless servants who have done no more
    than is our duty.

The tone or guiding principle for today's meditation is
provided for us most clearly in Wisdom (cycle I), that God

formed us to be imperishable and according to the image of the divine nature. Each of us, no matter our nationality or race, our sex or wealth, is equally created to image God's divine nature. Therefore, according to the Epistle to Titus (cycle II), nothing earthly and perishable can ultimately meet our needs and desires. We await a still greater "blessed hope, the appearance of the glory of the great God and of our Savior Christ Jesus." At that moment our reward will so marvelously surpass our expectations and our accumulated human endeavors, that we will exclaim: "We are useless servants. We have done no more than our duty."

We begin, created to the divine image; we end, discovering the full glory of that image in the appearance of our Savior Christ Jesus. In between, we pass along a human path of life. It was the same for Jesus. Jesus existed from all eternity "in the form of God [with] full equality" (Phil 2:6), "the image of the invisible God" (Col 1:15). Yet Jesus "emptied himself [of his divinity] and took the form of a slave, born in human likeness" (Phil 2:7). By the trials and hopes, even the persecution and martyrdom of his human existence, Jesus "learned obedience . . . and [was] perfected [and so] became the source of eternal salvation for all who obey him" (Hebr 5:8–9). Human life on planet earth, somehow or other in God's mysterious ways, helps to bring out the full glory of our divine image, even to "perfect" it, if our understanding of the passage from Hebrews is correct.

The reading from *Wisdom*, the last of the Old Testament books to be composed, reinforces this understanding. It picks up a common enough Old Testament phrase in the statement:

> As gold in the furnace, God proved them,
>   and as sacrificial offerings he took them
>   himself.

> [Therefore] in the time of their visitation they shall
>   shine, . . . and the Lord shall be their king forever.

Earthly existence provides the furnace that tries and embellishes our divine image, our "gold." And as mentioned already, the trials of human life cannot compare with the glory to be manifested through them. We also read in *Hebrews*: "Chastised a little, they shall be greatly blessed." At this point there follows a phrase difficult to accept: "*God* tried them and found them worthy of himself."

In the Book of Wisdom, the trials are inflicted on the just by wicked people. They are the normal jolts of life, faults of ignorance and impetuosity, the result of human frailty. Yet in the midst of these difficult experiences, we are told that *God* is trying us and making us worthy of himself. We can never adequately explain this situation; not even the cross of Jesus makes it clear to us. Yet there is strengthening consolation in realizing that God is actually writing straight with crooked lines and that our helplessness and suffering have a definite place in God's plans.

The Book of Wisdom is so certain of this that it adds:

> Those who trust in God shall understand truth,
>   and the faithful shall abide with him in love. . . .
> [for] his care is with his elect.

If we trust, we will learn great wisdom and true understanding. We need only to turn to many members of our family and ultimately to the saints to see how true this is. People who have suffered patiently can listen to us more sympathetically, can appreciate our words, and can give us the wisest advice.

In writing to his disciple Titus (cycle II), we find that

St. Paul respects the limits of our human existence, even of our human styles of culture, yet also encases this human life within a divine setting, what in the Book of Wisdom would be our divine image. The reading for today begins with a reminder that ''your speech be consistent with sound doctrine.'' At the end Paul becomes more specific about the nature of this sound doctrine: to ''await our blessed hope, the appearing of the glory of the great God and of our Savior Christ Jesus.'' What we do on earth is closely related to how we will be able to receive Christ Jesus in his glorious second coming.

In between, Paul writes very practically. Both his words here and the gospel accept cultural arrangements which are not acceptable today. Jesus refers to slavery and to what a master can expect from the slave. For work well done the master would not necessarily show any gratitude, because the slave ''was only carrying out his orders''! Jesus is not endorsing slavery, nor the inferior status of one class or race. Towards the end of his life, Jesus himself becomes the slave and cares for his disciples, washes their feet, and advises them to do the same:

> If I washed your feet—
> I who am Teacher and Lord—
> then you must wash each other's feet (John 13:14).

Jesus was preparing the way for the abolition of slavery. Yet during his lifetime he did not confront the institution head on. Another one of those mysteries of human existence where God is trying to find us worthy of himself.

At the end, if we trust, we will not only understand truth, as *Wisdom* promises us, but we will also be absorbed within a joy and glory far surpassing our human merits. Everything will seem useless by comparison.

Prayer:

I will bless you, Lord, at all times. You are close to the brokenhearted and to those crushed in spirit. Grant me always the faith to believe in you and in your mysterious way of trying and perfecting us, conforming us to our divine image by making us ever closer to Jesus. Then I will realize that salvation comes from you alone. I will dwell in the heavenly land and enjoy security forever.

Wednesday, 32nd Week

Wis 6:2–11. God makes the great as well as the small, and provides for all alike; but for those in power a rigorous scrutiny impends.

Titus 3:1–7. After urging us to responsible moral behavior, privately and publicly, St. Paul states that we are saved by the Spirit, lavished upon us through Jesus Christ, so that we are heirs in hope of eternal life.

Luke 17:11–19. Of the ten lepers who were healed by Jesus, only one, a Samaritan, returned to give thanks. "Your faith," Jesus says to him, "has been your salvation."

Jesus states the important fact very clearly: "Your faith has been your salvation." We stand in need of faith, a recognition of our total dependency upon God for life and for its good use, and especially for its direction towards kindly cooperation with others and towards eternal life. By faith we recognize and live within the good relationships by which God unites us in family and neighborhood, at work and in recreation, at church and in our works of mercy. By faith God enables us to put our *best* self to the service of one another, and so to give praise to God.

This injunction to go about the normal ways of life,

within our bonds of love and community, is expressed very simply by Jesus. To the Samaritan who "threw himself on his face at the feet of Jesus and spoke his praises," Jesus replied: "Stand up and go on your way." "Stand up" with dignity and joy, now that you are healed of the dreadful disease of leprosy. "Go your way," for you are no longer forbidden to live with others, no longer ostracized as "unclean." You can return to your home and family; you can resume life as it ought to be, now blessed with good health and gratitude to God.

Along with this final, encouraging remark of Jesus: "Stand up and go your way; your faith has been your salvation," the gospel contains a sad commentary on human life. "Jesus took the occasion to say,

> 'Were not all ten made whole? Where are the other nine? Was there no one to return and give thanks to God except this foreigner?' "

At that time Samaritans were worse than foreigners in the eyes of most people. They were scorned, feared and avoided. There was a long history of antagonism, mutual distrust and fighting between Jew and Samaritan. The Jews refused to allow the Samaritans to cooperate in rebuilding the temple (Ezra 4). The Samaritans retaliated by building their own temple on Mt. Gerizim and tended to side against the Jews in later wars. Jesus' words were not favoring this antagonism but were trying to break down the differences and show that even Samaritans could have true faith.

More to the point of our meditation, we note that good health distracted the other nine so that they forgot about Jesus and failed in the normal human courtesy of returning to thank Jesus for their cure. Strangely enough, God's finest gifts—life, strength, the ability to think imaginatively and to act creatively—easily become the means by which we not only forget God but also turn against God and against our neighbors and even our own family. With good reason then the first readings for today's liturgy warn us about the proper use of life and talents. The Book of Wisdom (cycle I) is actually addressing people with authority, but all of us possess power over others in the area of our giftedness or by reason of our position in family, society or church. We are parents or teachers or leaders, ordained or elected; we are well educated or eloquent speakers or physically strong and impressive or morally sure of ourselves. In these ways we can easily dominate others, take advantage of others for our own selfish advancement and display unusual forms of prejudice. The Book of Wisdom admonishes us:

> The Lord of all shows no partiality,
>   nor does God fear greatness,
> Because the Lord made the great as well as the small,
>   and provides for all alike;
>   but *for those in power* a rigorous scrutiny impends.

The Letter to Titus (cycle II) expresses the same conviction about faith in a somewhat different way. First, there is a list of practical instructions: to be loyally subject to the government; not to speak evil of anyone or be quarrelsome; be forbearing and display a perfect courtesy towards everyone. All these good actions seem within our normal ability. Yet Paul ends by stating: "God saved us, not because of any righteous deed we had done, but because of his mercy. He saved us [and] justified [us] by his grace." None of these good deeds are possible without God's "Spirit lavished on us through Jesus Christ our Savior."

Where we are at our best, we stand most in need of

God's Spirit. Our talents incline us to be malicious and envious, "slaves of our passions and of pleasures of various kinds." These vices were corrected by "the kindness and love of God our Savior [which] appeared to us" in Christ Jesus and were poured into our hearts at baptism and our renewal by the Holy Spirit.

Where we are at our best, we stand in particular need of instruction! The Book of Wisdom advises "that you may learn wisdom and that you may not sin." Where we stand in authority or power over others, we must be warned all the more seriously: "keep the holy precepts hallowed." We can too easily use them to our own advantage and unjustly dominate others.

Scripture and prayer, consequently, are all the more essential for us where we are healthy and talented. We easily forget about returning to the Lord and offering gratitude for our gift of life.

Prayer:

Lord, I am lowly and poor without you. Bless my life and the good gifts which you have bestowed upon me, so that I may always render justice to the afflicted and the destitute, as you do to me in my affliction and destitution. Shepherd me, Lord, so that I may be surrounded by your goodness and kindness and be your instrument in gathering others around your table.

Thursday, 32nd Week

Wis 7:22–8:1. Wisdom is a pure effusion of the glory of the Almighty. Wisdom produces friends of God, she reaches from end to end mightily and governs all things well.

Phlm 7–20. Paul asks Philemon to receive his run-away slave Onesimus as a beloved brother, so that he may be useful both to Paul and to Philemon.

Luke 17:20–25. The reign of God is not ''here'' nor ''there'' but already in your midst. Before coming, the Son of Man must suffer much and be rejected.

At the center of our personal life and that of the entire world, lies the wisdom of God or according to Luke's gospel, the reign of God. God's wisdom ''penetrates and pervades all things'' according to the reading for Cycle I. And according to Paul's letter to Philemon (cycle II) this bond of love includes a wide range of acquaintances. At the beginning of the epistle Paul calls Philemon ''our beloved friend and fellow worker,'' later in v. 4, ''my brother,'' and in the first sentence of today's reading Paul states that he experiences ''great joy and comfort in your love, because through you the hearts of God's people have been refreshed.''

Today we are called to unite and integrate, and to form this intimate bond of union so deeply within ourselves that we can reach out to find each man and woman our brother and our sister, our source of ''great joy and comfort.'' This other person may seem as distant from us as a runaway slave. Yet everyone is a brother and sister.

We note in passing that the New Testament does not make an issue out of slavery, at least not directly. But indirectly the Scriptures are supplying the data that will eventually make church and society realize the gross injustice of slavery. For instance, the New Testament speaks of Jesus as equal to God yet willing ''to empty himself and take the form of a slave'' (Phil 2:7). Furthermore,

> All of you who have been baptized into Christ
> have clothed yourselves with him. There does not
> exist among you Jew or Greek, slave or free, male

or female. All are one in Christ Jesus (Gal 3:27–
28).

Moreover, Paul writes of himself as "the slave of all" (I
Cor 9:19) and therefore each one of us "who has been called
is a slave of Christ" (I Cor 7:22). In this indirect, yet very
personal way of faith, the Bible was preparing for the eman-
cipation of slaves.

It is the interior bonding of faith and love, of respect
and honor that not only heals the social injustices of slavery
but also enables each of us, and all of us together, to unite all
loose ends in our lives and relationships, to integrate everything about ourselves and about our bonds with others.

The Book of Wisdom (cycle I) sees this done through
wisdom. As we meditate upon all the qualities of wisdom,
we realize ever more fully that this virtue is God's supreme
gift.

> In fact, it can come only from God, it is:
>   . . . and aura of the might of God
>   and a pure effusion of the glory of the Almighty.
>   . . . the refulgence of eternal light,
>   the spotless mirror of the power of God,
>   the image of his goodness.

According to the ancient, Vulgate translation of the final
verse in today's reading, wisdom "reaches from end to end
mightily and governs all things *sweetly*." Such is the way of
divine wisdom: mightily and sweetly. The bond which
unites is as mighty as God is strong and loyal, as sweet as
God is compassionate and good—always and everywhere.

We all become impatient when God's wisdom eludes
us. Like the questioners in today's gospel, we press Jesus
for an answer: "*When* will the reign of God come?" In replying, Jesus immediately puts aside one part of the ques-

tion, *when*. The kingdom of God is not to be identified with a point of time; this is an important statement for those of us who try to predict the end of the world on such and such a day. Jesus also refuses to locate the reign of God "here" or "there." There is no particular, all-holy place where the kingdom must appear, as though one country is better than another. Jesus' final answer is baffling but also consoling:

The reign of God is already *in your midst.*

Intimately, personally rooted within us, is the kingdom of God, Jesus who dwells within us. Here we already taste the sweetness of eternal life. Here we imbibe the strength to be strong and loyal, for God's wisdom lives in our heart. Jesus also advises us that when the Son of Man seems absent, we must remember that "he must suffer much and be rejected by the present age." We too will share the same suffering and rejection. Yet, the strength of God's wisdom will hold us together. We will remain conscious of the sweetness of God's ways, even in the midst of suffering.

Prayer:
   Your word, O Lord, is as firm as the heavens; keep us always united that firmly in you. Then I will experience how blessed are those whose help comes from you. Where I am blind, you will enable me to see. May your kingdom always extend over us, your kingdom of strength and sweetness.

Friday, 32nd Week

Wis 13:1–9. The greatness and beauty of created things can lead us to their maker, but this goodness can also distract us and become a substitute for God.

2 John 4–9. Love one another and acknowledge that Jesus
   Christ has come incarnate in the flesh.

Luke 17: 26–37. The Son of Man comes suddenly. Remember Lot's wife and the evil days before Noah's flood.

It happens very easily and very frequently: God's good
gifts distract us from God. This phenomenon is not difficult
to explain. Because God's gifts are so good, they can substitute for God, induce some kind of natural contemplation
and stifle any desire to think about life beyond this world or
the God who is invisibly present behind the good world. We
can bring the example close to home and within the home.
Once the good meal is on the table, we seldom remember to
thank the cook. Parents who lavish toys and gifts upon their
children are quickly taken for granted.

Yet, our normal way of finding God and appreciating
God's steadfast love and compassionate goodness, is by
being alert and enthusiastic, knowledgeable and curious
about the world and about the people inhabiting our world.
The Book of Wisdom (cycle I) put it very plainly:

> For from the greatness and the beauty of created
> things, their original author, by analogy, is seen.

The idea is the same, even though the expression is very different, in today's reading (cycle II) from the Second Letter
of John:

> It has given me great joy to find some of your chil-
> dren walking in the path of truth . . . Let us love
> one another.

The path of truth leads us through our home and family, our
religious communities and daily obligations. Here is where

we love one another patiently, compassionately, with forgiveness and forbearance, with joy and hope. From this interaction we learn the meaning of God's compassion and forgiveness towards us, about God's hopes and joy in us.

If we are always seeking God, the creator behind the beauty and greatness of our world, the lover who inspires our love and gentleness, then we will always be ready for the coming of the Son of Man. Even though the Son of Man comes without warning, we are ready.

The Book of Wisdom raises any number of important questions, not just for the agnostic and atheist, but also for the religious person. It states: ''They are distracted by what they see, because the things seen are fair.'' For religious people even the practice of prayer and worship can be an obstacle to knowing God. The *art* of prayer and the *rubrics* of worship become more important than the One to whom we pray and whom we worship. Parents can be so concerned about the impression that their children give to the neighbors, that fear of shame becomes more important than love for children. Also, when it comes to evil actions, there is more concern about not being seen or heard than about not doing what is wrong.

The ultimate reply is given to us in the gospel. The Son of Man will break through all of these face-saving devices and false concerns. First Jesus repeats the statement, difficult indeed, yet found several times in the Scriptures (Luke 9:24; Matt 10:39; Mark 8:35; John 12:25):

Whoever tries to spare their life, will lose it;
whoever seems to forfeit it, will keep it.

While living fully and enthusiastically, we must always be pulling aside the veil of goodness and greatness to see the Creator. While loving one another, we need to remember the love of Jesus, so that we will be always loyal and compassionate. If we forget Jesus, our love will become selfish; and selfish love does not last. Unselfish love often squanders or forfeits its life for the sake of others, yet finds it new in Jesus, the Son of Man.

The expression, Son of Man, might be translated, "child of earth." Or we can think of Adam (one of the Hebrew words for human-kind), formed from the dust of the earth to the divine likeness, who then becomes male and female to reflect God's love and God's bond of union with every creature. The sudden coming, then, of the Son of Man, may seem to snap the thread of life and whisk us off this earth, yet the very name, Son of Man, implies someone earthly, a child of earth. Jesus does not so much take away as transform.

Only, it seems, if we are willing to share with others, will God trust us to keep our life; and to keep it, we must find it with Jesus. We can never be in the company of Jesus, unless we love one another.

Prayer:

Lord, the heavens and the earth proclaim your glory, yet a glory so surpassing human speech that not a word is heard. Allow me to be silent and so hear that secret word of your presence in the world about me. In silence I will seek you with all my heart and follow your holy will each moment along the way. Then I can open my eyes and see ever greater wonders in your law and your earth.

Saturday, 32nd Week

Wis 18:14–16; 19:6–9. During the peaceful stillness of the night God's all-powerful word bounded from Heaven,

overcame Israel's enemies and led God's people to freedom and to the covenant on Mt. Sinai.
3 John 5–8. Exhortation to provide hospitality and other assistance for traveling missionaries.
Luke 18:1–8. God will act in response to persistent prayer.
He will provide swift justice. But will he find any faith on
the earth?

Most of us can be expected occasionally to be heroic,
occasionally to go the extra mile (Matt 5:41). Today's scripture readings ask for fidelity over the long haul, not necessarily for the single heroic act but rather for the heroism of
remaining *there* in the daily, monotonous routine of family
or work, of community or apostolate. What we are expected
to do may seem very ordinary, but others who see our daily,
monthly and yearly faithfulness know that God's extraordinary grace must be at work in our hearts.

We may seem to be getting nowhere and yet we are accomplishing very much, simply in keeping the family intact
or the business/work still functioning or the parish and religious community a place of prayer and patience. The gospel
addresses both of these reactions: getting nowhere and accomplishing very much! The latter idea of achieving our
goal by small, persistent action is exemplified in the widow
"who kept coming to the judge, saying, 'Give me my
rights.' " Finally the judge said to himself:

"I care little for God or any human person, but
this widow is wearing me out. I am going to settle
in her favor."

Jesus is admitting that God too can be worn down by inces-
sant prayer. St. Monica, the mother of Augustine, is of

course the patroness of persistent people. We can accomplish very much by daily fidelity in our routine.

Yet so often we think to get nowhere! We wonder if we can stay with it any longer. Here is where Jesus' final words speak to us:

> When the Son of Man comes, will he find any
> faith on earth?

It is a question—and a serious question. Can I remain a person of faith any longer? If Jesus came tomorrow, will the Son of Man still find me faithful? We wonder.

This final verse in the gospel is most probably a later addition to the original parable about the widow. No other parable in the gospels ends with a question. This fact makes the arrangement of the gospel all the more pertinent. The editor, possibly Luke himself, added this "floating" remark of Jesus that could fit into many different occasions, to voice our own question. Originally it probably referred to the long trial of the Roman persecution but it speaks to any number of situations.

When the Son of Man comes, like the all-powerful word in today's reading from the Book of Wisdom (cycle I), he will appear suddenly, with the dark night already in its swift course but only half spent. Jesus will act dramatically and definitively. The all-powerful word will leap forth like a fierce warrior against those who oppose God's people. It will lead them out of bondage, through every barrier and difficulty, even the mighty Red Sea. Already they prance about like horses, bound about like lambs, praising you, O Lord! their deliverer. The daily, monotonous, small-time routine has turned into "stupendous wonders."

Perhaps we hear ourselves repeating Jesus' question:

When the Son of Man comes, will he find any
faith on the earth?

Can I really believe and accept a challenge as stupendous as
this? Yet, little by little the wonders come true. It is interesting to note that this passage from the Book of Wisdom
about "peaceful stillness [when] your all-powerful word
from heaven's royal throne bounded," is used prominently
in the Christmas liturgy. From Mary's infant, helpless and
in need of continual care, day by day, in all the monotony of
caring for a baby's needs, salvation would come sooner or
later, but definitely, wondrously.

The Third Epistle of John (cycle II) is urging Christians
to do their small part in the work of evangelization. Again
the key word is *fidelity*:

Beloved, you demonstrate fidelity by all that you
do for the ministers of the gospel even though they
are strangers.

Such people can even become pests in their small requests
for time and lodging and money. John adds: "Help them to
continue their journey." One of the most effective ways to
be ready when the Son of Man returns, suddenly and even
fiercely, is to further the apostolate of the word, each of us
in our own way. Then when the all-powerful word bounds
from the heavenly royal throne, we will find ourselves ready
and waiting.

Prayer:
   Lord, may I always remember the marvels you have
done, so that I will not lose heart in the daily monotony of

my life. Day by day may I be faithful to your word and your commands. Let me even delight in them. Then I will welcome you at once when you come in glory.

Monday, 33rd Week

1 Macc 1 (selected verses). The great persecution of Antiochus Epiphanes, the abomination of desolation in the temple, terrible affliction upon Israel.

Rev 1:1–4; 2:1–5. The revelation to the seer John during the Roman persecution begins with letters to the seven churches, first of all to that at Ephesus that it repent and return to its former deeds.

Luke 18:35–43. At the entrance to Jericho Jesus cures the blind man who begins to follow him, giving God the glory.

During the last two weeks of the church year it is not surprising that the biblical readings focus upon the end—really the violent end—of one era and upon the heroic hope for a new, holier period of life. The two Books of Maccabees describe the historical background for the book of Daniel; the Book of Daniel along with important contributions from Ezekiel greatly influences the Book of Revelation in the New Testament. Luke's gospel brings us to the end of Jesus' public ministry, to the place where the narrative of his passion and death is told.

This liturgical arrangement of Scripture follows good contemporary scholarship, interpreting Daniel and Revelations not as a prediction of the end of the world, its exact date and circumstances, but as a dramatic challenge to put aside the past and to begin a new, consecrated life for Jesus. The focus, therefore, is not so much on the date when the world will end, but it is upon the necessity of strong hope in the midst of violent persecution and the need to accept serious changes in our lives.

The blind man at Jericho gate longed for the normal life that sight would give him. And so he begged Jesus, "Lord, I want to see." But to receive his sight meant a change, even a risk for him. His relationships to family and friends, his responsibilities, his whole way of life would be altered. He was willing and anxious to accept the change, to take the chance.

Once he received his sight, he "began to follow Jesus, giving God the glory." His new style was centered on Jesus. If he could now see his wife and children, he saw them as a gift from Jesus. The shining sun, the graceful palm trees clustered at the oasis, the birds that glided across the sky, even the bees that came out of the secret places in the desert between Jericho and Jerusalem, all this beautiful world was received in wonder as he followed Jesus up the road.

We may be so caught in the wonder of the miracle of Jesus' healing the blind person, that we overlook the drastic changes in life-style and the serious conversion if we are to remain a follower of Jesus in all the tasks, duties and spontaneous actions of life.

Our own conversion may not be as total nor as dramatic, but for each of us it is still very real and just as necessary. Perhaps we are like the people of Ephesus in the first reading of cycle I. We have never been bad people. In fact you may be commended for:

your deeds	your repudiation of false apostles
your labors	your patience and endurance
your patient endurance	your strength

If such is the case, we may wonder, what more can God ask of us? Nonetheless, God may be writing a letter to our conscience as once to the Ephesians:

> I hold this against you, though; you have turned aside from your early love. Keep firmly in mind the heights from which you have fallen. Repent and return to your former deeds.

Only we can know if these words are meant for ourselves. We alone hold the memory of our early love, the ideals from which we have fallen.

In cases like this, we do not besmear ourselves with scandalous sins; we maintain a veneer, maybe a token fervor, perhaps even a moderate degree of piety. But the enthusiasm of our early love, the zest of our first ideals—these have turned sour. We have become cynical and sarcastic. Our friends may wish to reason with us, but they hesitate, fearful of our ridicule or our invitation to mind their own business. We may really be better than many others. But joy in the Lord's service has gone. Strange as it may sound, it is often easier to live with honest sinful people than with cynical, mediocre religious people! At least the former are open to discussion, can admit their faults and seek conversion. But do we tell good people that they are not good enough in the very area of their goodness; they can be so much better, if only they return to their early love.

These words can be addressed to married people—to religious and priests—to lay apostolic ministers—to men and women in many secular or religious careers: "You have turned aside from your early love. . . . Repent, and return to your former deed."

As difficult as may be the conversion of "good" people to their early love and former ideals, there are other moments of still more heroic proportions. Each person, sooner or later, is faced with a decision so crucial that it is a matter of life or death, of loyalty or apostasy towards Jesus, of perseverance or repudiation towards our closest loved ones. At such times, we are tempted to cover up the marks or signs of our consecration to God and to one another and to abandon our covenant. At such times we must align ourselves with those in Israel who:

> were determined and resolved in their hearts . . .
> to die rather than to be defiled . . . and to profane
> the holy covenant.

The cost of such loyalty, as the text tells us, is ''terrible affliction.''

If we return now to our early love and former deeds, then we need not worry how we will respond when the time of the great trial hits us.

Prayer:

Give me true life that comes, O Lord, from following your commandments. Never allow me to be caught in those snares that pull me away from my early love and first ideals. Then I will know the joy of being planted like a tree near the running water of your grace and holy presence. You will be my delight, in the midst of severe trials.

Tuesday, 33rd Week

2 Macc 6:18–31. The elderly Eleazar refused to dissimulate in his loyalty to Yahweh and was put to death. In dying he found joy in his severe pain and provided an unforgettable example of virtue for the whole nation.

Rev 3:1–6, 14–22. A warning first to the church of Sardis
whose wealth enabled the people to hide their faults with
a sophisticated veneer. A warning to the church of Laodicea, neither hot nor cold, but lukewarm, and so vomited
out of the mouth.

Luke 19:1–10. Jesus accepts an invitation to dinner from the
tax collector, Zacchaeus, who promises to repay fourfold
to anyone he has defrauded. The Son of Man has come to
search out and save what was lost.

The final verse in today's reading from Luke provides
the key not only for our meditation but also for interpreting
other passages in the four gospels. It is interesting to note
that in some manuscripts it was added to Matthew's gospel
at Matt 18:11, a verse that is generally omitted in most translations as inauthentic. We found a similar case last Sunday
(Luke 18:8). These are always important verses—additions
or not to the original words of Jesus—because the early
church looked on them as ways to interpret and summarize
the great message of Jesus.

"The Son of Man has come to search out and to save
what was lost." This statement is exemplified variously, by
the gospel and by the other two readings, Second Maccabees
(cycle I) and Revelation (cycle II). Jesus' words can be
turned around and rephrased in a paradoxical way: we cannot be found unless we lose ourselves; unless we are found
by Jesus, we cannot be saved.

To be found by Jesus meant that Zacchaeus had to lose
very much. First of all, his dignity by climbing up a sycamore tree! Later, much of his wealth by paying back fourfold anyone that he may have defrauded. We cannot help
commenting that Jesus too had to lose his dignity as a "holy
person," by accepting a dinner engagement at the home of
the unclean sinner. Zacchaeus, after all, was even "chief tax

collector'' at the important city of Jericho, through which pilgrimages had to pass on their way to the festivals at Jerusalem. This city, moreover, funneled all the wealth of the East towards the capital city of Jerusalem. Zacchaeus certainly had a lucrative office and could gain much by an adroit use of pressure at the proper times.

Jesus must have seen a spirit of repentance in Zacchaeus' heart. It was Jesus who really found Zacchaeus:

> When Jesus came to the spot [where Zacchaeus had climbed the sycamore tree], he looked up and said, ''Zacchaeus, hurry down. I mean to stay at your house today.''

Jesus may have lost still more dignity, for he invited himself to Zacchaeus' house! Indeed, ''the Son of Man has come to search out and save what was lost.''

Jesus entered into the life of Zacchaeus. Jesus allowed this man to remain a tax collector—only to be honest at the job! While the external form of Zacchaeus' life did not change, the quality of his living was entirely new. In the long run, we lose very little, when we are found by Jesus. Rather we gain immeasurably in the quality of goodness and joy that permeates our actions.

In the story of Eleazar (cycle I) not only did the external style of life change for the old man, but it was ended dramatically by martyrdom. Again, by losing, he gained much. While dying, he confessed: ''I am not only enduring terrible pain in my body, but I am also suffering it *with joy in my soul* because of my devotion to him,'' the Lord our God. Eleazar gained not only for himself but also for the entire nation, in providing both the young and the entire nation ''a model of courage and an unforgettable example of virtue.''

Eleazar already was ninety years old with very little life

ahead of him. If he had dissimulated in eating the food (actually his own, but to all appearance the pork sacrificed to idols), he would have bartered for only a few years and would have been forgotten. If remembered, his name would be linked with the traitors to the covenant. In losing his life, he gained true dignity, even joy of heart in the midst of physical suffering. He left his memory as ''an unforgettable example.'' His name lives and inspires us today, because he lost his life for the sake of the covenant with God.

Sometimes we have no choice but to be heroic and suffer martyrdom like Eleazar. At other times our decision rests with something less dramatic and therefore more easily overlooked. It is easy to be lukewarm, like the church of Laodicea (cycle II). If we are lukewarm, we are not bad, not calloused. We help the poor—a little; we are sympathetic—sometimes; we are forgiving—towards a select few. In other words, we practice our token Christianity! Strangely enough, God wishes that we ''were one or the other, hot or cold!'' In the language of the gospel, God prefers that we would be great sinners, defrauding at every chance we have, like Zacchaeus. Then there is a possibility of conversion. But ''lukewarm, neither hot nor cold, I will spew you out of my mouth!''

The Church at Sardis seems to be in better condition: ''I know the reputation that you have of being alive.'' Both Sardis and Laodicea were among the wealthiest cities of Asia Minor. It will all end quickly, the way that a thief comes in the middle of the night. Jesus comes either to save what was lost, or to condemn what was left of a religion falsely supported by wealth, power, prestige. Jesus is not condemning wealth in itself. Otherwise he would never have invited himself to Zacchaeus' house. We must not consider wealth as the principal value of our lives. We must not depend on any human value for ultimate security.

Jesus stands at the door and is knocking. He is seeking what is lost, so that he can become the support of our lives. We must open and let Jesus come in and have supper with us. The words addressed once to the church of Laodicea are now spoken to us.

Prayer:

Lord, cleanse my heart, my eyes, my entire self so that I may sit beside you. Let me be present as you gather your faithful people together. Then I will never fear any difficulty. I can rise with renewed confidence from sleep to face each new day in your presence. You are my shield, my glory.

Wednesday, 33rd Week

2 Macc 7:1, 20–31. The mother of seven sons not only witnesses their martyrdom but even urges them to die out of loyalty to God and to the covenant.

Rev 4:1–11. Vision of God, seated majestically in heaven, surrounded by twenty-four elders and four living creatures and adored as eternal Creator.

Luke 19:11–38. Parable about a man who confided his goods to the care of servants till he returned as king. Upon his return he rewarded those who increased the investment and punished those who did not want him to become king.

While the reading from Second Maccabees (cycle I) portrays the most tragic moment of family life yet promises hope for the future, the reading from Revelation (cycle II) gives a passing glimpse or momentary vision of the final reward. The gospel takes a long view of one's entire life. We badly stand in need of those exceptional insights of faith, as in the Book of Revelation, so that when the serious trial strikes, we can call upon our faith to sustain us. The gospel supports us in a different way, not by a vision of heavenly glory nor a memory of a religious "high" in our life, but by practical advice on the normal sequence of life. If we do not live by bread alone (Deut 8:3; Luke 4:4), neither do we live by visions alone!

The reading from Second Maccabees presents one of the clearest statements in the entire Old Testament about the resurrection of the body and about the creation of the world out of nothing at the beginning of time. As such, Second Maccabees mirrors the popular piety of a lay group which eventually evolved into the Pharisees. These people chafed at the restrictions placed upon theological development by the Jerusalem priests and firmly believed in the resurrection of the dead. They expected a similar faith in their family and friends. This theological development did not evolve out of books or scholarly debate. It arose from the experience of daily living with strong faith in God's fidelity and compassion and also out of contact with pagan neighbors, many of whom possessed a much more advanced theology of the after-life than Israel.

The covenant presented Yahweh as:

The Lord, the Lord, a merciful and gracious God,
slow to anger and rich in kindness and fidelity,
continuing his kindness for a thousand generations, and forgiving wickedness and crime and sin
(Exod 34:6–7).

When Ps 136 retold the entire history of Israel, a refrain rang out after each line which explained each event and united all details:

For his mercy endures forever.

The word, ''mercy,'' in the Hebrew language signified the type of love and understanding felt between blood relatives. This word is not used for foreigners! God belonged to Israel's history as a member of the family of each generation.

The Maccabean mother rested her faith solidly upon this conviction of God's blood bond with her and her seven children. It must last through every trial, as Ps 136 proclaimed. Therefore, it shall endure through the barrier of death and the tomb. In this immediacy of faith and love, the mother also confessed faith in God's creation of the universe. Creation and pregnancy are linked together in her thinking. God loves his creation with the same concern that a mother has for a child in her womb. That concern and blood bond will surround a person through trials, death and the new resurrection.

The mother of the seven children acted from a firm faith in the blood bond of God's covenant with his people. The Book of Revelation draws upon Israel's tradition in another way. The framework of the vision is adapted from Ezechiel, chaps. 1–2. The words of praise, ''Holy, holy, holy, is the Lord God Almighty,'' come form Isaiah's inaugural vision in chap. 6. Other details are reminiscent of Moses' vision of Sinai in Exodus 19:18–20. The twenty-four elders might well symbolize the twelve tribes of ancient Israel and the twelve tribes (apostles) of the new Israel. The seven spirits of God may refer to Isaiah, chap. 11 (Greek version). Clearly, this style of writing is derivative, symbolical, theologically compressed, and deeply traditional.

In this vision the Book of Revelation is inviting us to let all of our religious experiences flood in upon us, in the roar of many waters, in the flashing of thunder and flaming torches! All of us treasure memories of peak religious experiences: our first communion, perhaps, decisions to be of service to others, moments when God seemed especially near, moments of peace after sorrow. At times God has been very close in intimate union. At times God has been lifted high in the wonder of his majesty and glory.

When our world seems to be falling apart through severe trial or poignant disappointment, we should recall those moments when the world fell apart in the joy or even the ecstasy of prayer. Those precious moments left us alone with God, and how happy we were. That happiness can sustain us in later difficulties and somehow add a touch of exquisite joy to the sorrow.

We cannot forget that life includes both religious "highs" and searing trials. But most of life is different. Here is where the gospel parable applies. Jesus is likely referring to a king all too well-known in Israel. Herod the Great had to flee for his life from enemies in Jerusalem. He made his way to Rome and charmed the emperor into naming him king of Israel. He then returned to Palestine to take over.

The parable warns us that the king will return. And so we must be prudent and loyal, industrious and honest. Otherwise what little we possess will be lost. There will be a strict accounting. We will one day be called to answer for our use of time and talents.

We cannot stand still, either in ecstasy or in laziness! We must work with our talents. Unless we give them to God and our neighbor, to our family and religious community, we will lose what little we possess. We can paraphrase Jesus' words: "Whoever has [talents put to the service of others] will be given more; but the one who has not [anything which he is willing to share] will lose the little that he has."

If the last sentence of Jesus, about the king's having his enemies slain in his presence, baffles us, the statement is here, first of all, because that is what Herod did, and secondly, because we can never understand everything that happens. Like the Maccabean mother, we must continue to believe in God's power and goodness. ''Belief'' always presumes lack of complete evidence outside of us, but it also presumes extraordinary evidence within our memory and blood bond with God.

Prayer:

Lord, when your glory appears, my joy will be full. This I firmly believe. I pray that you never allow me to wander from your path; keep me always in the shadow of your wings. At the end of this path I will sing with all the saints and angels: Holy, Holy, Holy Lord, mighty God.

Thursday, 33rd Week

1 Macc 2:15–29. Mattathias and his seven sons begin the great revolt against foreign oppression and stem the tide of apostasy.

Rev 5:1–10. The lamb who was slain opens the seals on the scroll and receives homage as savior who purchased a world kingdom by blood.

Luke 19:41–44. Jesus weeps over the forthcoming destruction of Jerusalem.

It is not surprising that tears and tragedy mark the readings for the final two weeks of the Church year. In the Books of Maccabees and Revelation, the source of our liturgical readings, no victory comes easily. Always there are tears— even in heaven. John, who ''was caught up in ecstasy'' ''on the island called Patmos,'' was conversing with heavenly beings, the twenty-four elders. One of them said to him: "Do not weep." Yet, how could a person not weep, even in heaven, not only because no one seemed able at that moment to open the scroll with the seven seals, but also because of the appearance of Jesus:

> See, he comes amid the clouds!
>> Every eye shall see him,
>> even of those *who pierced him*.
> All the peoples of the earth
>> shall lament him bitterly (Rev 1:7).

In heaven, Jesus bears the marks of the nails and the lance, his wounded hands and opened side. This is how the apostle Thomas saw the resurrected Jesus:

> Take your finger and examine my hands.
> Put your hand into my side (John 20:27).

Throughout the Book of Revelation Jesus is the "Lamb that had been slain." We will never forget that tragedy.

Yet, in the Bible blood is understood less as sign of suffering and violence, much more as a symbol of relationship and union. We are closely united in blood; therefore, we are more than willing to suffer and even to die in union with those we love. In this way we ought to understand the statement in today's reading from Revelation (cycle II):

> Worthy are you to receive the scroll . . .
>> for you were slain.
> With your blood you purchased for God
>> people of every race and tongue . . .
> You made of them a kingdom,
>> and priests to serve our God.

How were we purchased? Not in the crass sense of a price paid to God, much less to the devil. Rather, Jesus united himself so intimately with our flesh and blood that he became totally one with us. His love and obedience, his death and resurrection became our family treasure. All of God's children were forgiven for the Father saw them as one with their sinless brother, Jesus.

Little wonder then that only the "Lamb who had been slain" can open the scroll with the seven seals. Only Jesus has experienced to the fullest extent the trials and joys, the collapses and the triumphs of our human existence. Jesus alone knows their secret, can direct their development, and can lead them into the vision of heavenly joy. Through Jesus, we all become "priests to serve our God," that is, to turn each human experience into one of worship in God's presence.

When a bond of blood closely unites Jesus and ourselves through the mystery of the incarnation, God and Israel through the mystery of the Mosaic covenant, then we are always capable of dramatic action. These can be dangerous times; it is possible to be influenced by evil forces, as happens with some cults. These are also magnificent moments, when an unknown strength surges forth within us, when an unanticipated wisdom thrusts us forward. Such was the case of Mattathias and his seven sons. The old man would not succumb to bribery and gifts:

> I and my children and my kinsfolk will keep to the covenant of our ancestors. God forbid that we should forsake the law and the commandments. We will not . . . depart from our religion in the slightest degree.

It is not for us to judge the subsequent military violence of Mattathias; we have never been in such desperate circumstances. Yet, whatever be the severe trial that comes upon us, we must muster his courage and decisiveness.

Such moments are never simple and easy. Often enough they happen quickly and we must rely upon a hidden strength and secret wisdom. As we anticipate those moments and prepare ourselves, we should place ourselves with Jesus as the Lord wept over Jerusalem. If we spontaneously weep out of sorrow, even that deserved by ourselves or others because of sin and foolish mistakes, then we can trust our intuitions of faith.

Tears, we see, are not only a sign of great sorrow. They equally signify great love.

Prayer:

Lord, when severe trials come, let me see your saving power. Through your inspiration, guide me through such sorrows and distress, so that all of my actions will glorify you. Then I will be called to join the ranks of your saints and to praise you forever in glory. In heaven my tears at the sight of your sufferings will become my most exquisite joy.

Friday, 33rd Week

I Macc 4:36–37, 52–59. The temple is purified and rededicated; the feast of Hannukah is celebrated for the first time.

Rev 10:8–11. John is told to eat the small scroll, which was sweet to the palate but sour in the stomach.

Luke 19:45–48. Jesus cleanses the temple of traders and merchants. While the chief priests wanted to destroy him, the people hung on his words.

All three readings are preparing for the purification and reconsecration of God's temple: at Jerusalem after the desecration by Antiochus IV Epiphanes, in the First Book of Maccabees (cycle I); throughout the world after its desecration by sin, in the Book of Revelation (cycle II); again at Jerusalem after its profanation by trading (gospel). We begin to observe the many ways by which our lives, our world and our church become truly a house of prayer, a temple according to God's hopes and ideals.

The interaction between the world and temple is most evident. Most clearly of all the Book of Revelation is preparing for the final moment when John will see:

> new heavens and new earth . . . a new Jerusalem,
> coming down out of heaven from God, beautiful
> as a bride (Rev 21:1–2).

The transformation of the universe will mean that heaven and earth merge together, and in the midst of the new Jerusalem God will be enthroned. This insight helps us to understand better the stern action of Jesus in the gospel.

Jesus had just wept over Jerusalem (yesterday's gospel) for failing to recognize the time of its visitation. Today "Jesus entered the temple and began ejecting the traders." Jesus is casting merchants and traders out of the temple. He is not forbidding the mingling of business and religion but rather the abuse of religion for financial profit. The merchants, regrettably the religious leaders, were more concerned about their financial interests than about the worship of God.

Another abuse of religion shows up in First Maccabees. Here a foreign power attempted to manipulate religion to secure political loyalty. Once more, it is not that politics and religion cannot properly interact with one another, but rather God condemns subordinating religion to the interests of the state.

To purify the temple means to place God as supreme in our lives. That means that our business or financial dealings as also our politics are to be judged or moderated by God's law of justice and compassion. We should bring every aspect of our daily lives into the temple—our family and neighborhood, our work and recreation—so that these can be purified, sanctified and placed under God's protection.

At first, this program seems sweet and easy. We think of John in today's reading from the Book of Revelation (cycle II). When he ate the scroll, given to him by the angel, he was forewarned: "It will be sour in your stomach, but in your mouth it will taste as sweet as honey." At first, "sweet as honey." But later, as we begin to carry through on our program of personal and family dedication to God the words can become "sour." We begin to suffer. We feel unable to integrate God's desires with the secular part of our life. Our stomach becomes upset!

The second stage is not an easy one. Jesus' words and presence may be as stern as in today's gospel. We learn from the other gospels that Jesus made a whip of cord and lashed the money changers out of the temple, even knocking over their tables. Typical of his gospel, Luke omits these violent details, but he cannot entirely smooth out the violent confrontation between Jesus, the merchants and the religious leaders. These latter now looked for a way to destroy Jesus.

At times of conflict in our own lives, we must remember that there is another part of ourselves. One part, indeed, may want to give up on Jesus or on some aspect of God's will for us. But there is that other part, that much better part, which admires Jesus and is like the people in the gospel, "listening to him and hanging on his words." We should remember how there was a time when the words were indeed "sweet" to our palate, when we enthusiastically embraced them.

As we rededicate ourselves—especially those controversial and difficult parts of ourselves—to Jesus, God is saying over us: "My house is indeed a house of prayer." Every part of our lives, at home and in family life, at work and play, is contributing to the depth and sincerity of our prayer, as God is being enthroned everywhere in our being.

We return to the temple or church, like the Jewish people in the reading from First Maccabees:

> with songs, harps, flutes and cymbals. All the
> people prostrated themselves and adored and
> praised Heaven, who had given them success.

Now we are fully at prayer. No part of our life will be a distraction from God for it all belongs totally to God.

First Maccabees tells of the origin of the feast of Hannukah (= Dedication), generally celebrated in our month of December. It is marked with a great use of lights; there is a special Hanukkah candelabra. Rededication means that God's light illumines our entire life; nothing is anymore an embarrassment or distraction. The new heavens and the new earth have appeared. The new Jerusalem is in their midst, beautiful as a bride.

Prayer:

Lord, we praise your glorious name, your grandeur and your power, throughout the universe, for you are our God and sovereign, our compassionate parent and our all powerful ruler. You have loving dominion over our entire existence. How sweet is your law to have achieved such wonders in our lives.

Saturday, 33rd Week

1 Macc 6:1–13. Antiochus IV Epiphanes becomes mortally
sick. He sees his plans for empire and renown collapsing.
He attributes his failures to his unreasonable persecution
of the Jews.

Rev 11:4–12. The two prophets, powerful to control rain
and sunshine, are slain but after three and a half days they
are taken up to heaven in glory.

Luke 20:27–40. Jesus defends the resurrection of the dead
by stating that God is the God of the living, not of the
dead. Those judged worthy of a place in the age to come
will be like the angels, not liable any more to death.

The biblical readings seem to end with more questions
than answers! Yet all three passages rely upon a strong faith
which ultimately supports us better than rational answers. In
First Maccabees (cycle I) international political events seem
to justify fidelity to God. The tyrant, Antiochus IV Epiphanes, is defeated in his plans to unify an empire around
himself, even to the extent of demanding complete conform-
ity of the Jewish people to his pagan religion. Yet from the
Book of Revelation (cycle II) we find ourselves again in the
midst of persecution and the ascendancy of the Roman empire over Christianity. The question arises: does history
really vindicate the justice of God in the lives of God's faithful disciples? Another kind of question emerges from the
gospel: because God is the God of the living, does it necessarily follow that the just will rise from the grave? After all,
the Old Testament people for centuries did not include the
resurrection among their religious beliefs, yet they always
worshipped Yahweh, the God of the living! Somehow or
other, a link is missing in the argument, at least for our
method of reasoning!

The reading from First Maccabees, especially if we were to extend it beyond the liturgical selections which end today (next Monday we turn to the Book of Daniel), shows that the political solution is not the final, definitive conclusion. More sorrow and warfare lie ahead for the reader who continues into further chapters of First Maccabees. This Book, as a matter of fact, ends with the firm establishment of the Maccabeans, later to be called the Hasmoneans, as kings of Jerusalem. Yet this dynasty in time became corrupt, and by its infighting, intrigue, cruelty and dissolute members, led to the occupation of Palestine by the Romans in 63 B.C. The Second Book of Maccabees followed a much more religious viewpoint, delayed over the resurrection from the dead and absolute loyalty to the covenant, beliefs very popular with the people at large, as we saw in yesterday's feast of Hannukah, and so provided a better solution to our ultimate questions.

The fact that First Maccabees remains in our Bible affirms the biblical position that politics are necessary. We also learn that politics must be guided and sustained by deeper, more basic religious values, which reach beyond this life into the resurrection of the body.

The attitude stressed religiously is faith and perseverance, fidelity over the long haul. Such faith will not only provide intermediate solutions, as in today's selection from First Maccabees, but it will also lead us to ultimate victory and peace. The Book of Revelation (cycle II) provides a long-term view. It traces the history of the ''two witnesses.'' The passage is complicated, redolent of many Old Testament images and personages, reaching through the Books of Kings with the account of Elijah, the story of Moses in the Pentateuch, the account of the High priest Joshua and the Davidic governor of the postexilic age, Zerubbabel in the Prophecy of Zechariah. Ultimately God was true to his witnesses and brought them up to heaven in a cloud.

At the center of the account, moreover, is the reference to the place of their suffering, symbolically called "Sodom" and "Egypt," and here, we are told, is "where their Lord was crucified." They relived the passion and death of Jesus, so closely was Jesus united with them in their sorrows. Even the time between their death and resurrection, three and a half days, corresponds to the period of Jesus' sojourn in the grave. Here is one of the ultimate answers to our questions, as posed at the beginning of our meditation: we are united with Jesus and Jesus is one with us. Paul's words ring out in our mind:

> I have been crucified with Christ, and the life that
> I live now is not my own; Christ is living in me
> (Gal 2:19–20). Those who belong to Christ Jesus
> have crucified their flesh with its passions and de-
> sires (Gal 5:24).

The purification of our lives is more intense than we even imagine. Much time is necessary; history must take its full course, at times with seeming foolishness and weakness, as Paul admits in 1 Cor 1:21–25.

History takes its course in strange ways, as instanced in the Gospel. First the awkward story of the woman who was obliged to marry seven brothers, one after another, and then is further humiliated to become the enigmatic factor in the story. "At the resurrection, whose wife will she be?" It is only a story—and it is told by Jesus' enemies—yet it was told and repeated, to the chagrin of women. Jesus does not lower himself to the level of the questioners but picks up the question in a different way. Jesus reaches into the life after death and the mysterious form which our bodies will take at that time, mysterious, yet full of life, and by that life we testify to the God of the living.

The ultimate answer, for which we risk everything, our history and our human fate on earth, rests in God's hands and heart. It is a divine mystery. Yet we already live that mystery, we feel its attraction, we live off its strength, already we are part of life on earth and part of life in heaven.

Prayer:

Lord, I thank you and declare your wonderful love in my life. Each small gift of yours strengthens my faith in the ultimate gift of life eternal with you. Our hope, even in times of affliction, will never be lost; it will never be in vain. You are my refuge, my fortress, my stronghold, my deliverer.

Monday, 34th Week

Dan 1:1–6, 8–20. Through obedience to God's laws, Daniel and his three companions become more widely known and appreciated than all the magicians and counselors of the Babylonian empire.

Rev 14:1–3, 4–5. The hundred and forty-four thousand follow the lamb and sing a new hymn before the throne. They are the first fruits of humankind.

Luke 21:1–4. The widow drops two copper coins into the treasury, more than she could afford. Her mite is more than the biggest benefactions which come from a wealthy person's surplus.

We cannot compromise with God. We are asked to give ourselves totally and to follow God's will unconditionally. This ultimate commitment is repeatedly brought home to us during the last two weeks of the Church year as we read from Maccabees and Daniel (cycle I) and from the Book of Revelation (cycle II). At the roots of our existence, at the base of our reasoning, at the ultimate test of our loyalty, we must be unreservedly with God. The fact that one church year ends and another begins, shows that we are given another chance. We are allowed time to correct our previous mistakes. But at the rock bottom of it all, we come to a point of absolute loyalty, total commitment. We need to rest at this base of our existence, at least during these final weeks of the church year.

Like ourselves, at the end and at the beginning of our liturgical cycle, Daniel and the three companions in cycle I were at a turning point in their lives. Their former existence in the land of Judah had been disrupted and they must begin all over again in Babylon at the royal court. They are willing to adapt themselves, learn the new language and be instructed in Babylonian customs. They also drew the line where adaptation would be sinful and would actually amount to compromise with God's will. That line may seem strange to us: the refusal to eat unclean food, against the Law of Moses. Yet, this seemingly small matter was symbolical of their total loyalty to God. They were helped greatly by external signs of their interior dedication.

This sign of dedication led to extraordinary growth in wisdom and in graciousness. They came to be admired and loved. Loyalty to God somehow or other brought a peace and contentment, a unity about themselves, a strength to be calm and self-composed, a patience to wait and learn, a perception and intuition always on the right track.

We know from experience how we are at our best when we are peaceful. We make our mistakes when we are compulsive and nervous. Daniel, therefore, was able to make his way through the wily ways of a royal court, attractive and gentle, yet also no nonsense when it came to principles.

This last week of the church year gives us an opportunity, first to settle our loyalty with God, and then to allow ourselves the opportunity to be gentle and patient, as we grow in wisdom and attractiveness.

The Book of Revelation in cycle II allows us to see persons like Daniel at the end of their lives! They have suffered as everyone must; they have even endured martyrdom. They are numbered among the 144,000 elect who follow the Lamb that had been slain. The Greek text calls them "virgins," to be understood in the symbolical sense of people totally committed to the one whom they love, like a bride and groom on the day of their wedding. These are saints who enter the marriage feast of the lamb in heaven.

Our deeply interior dedication to God will sustain us through life, support us through severe sufferings, enable us to turn again to God after momentary lapses, keep us always on target. The trials of life do not destroy but purify. Even sins are an opportunity to trust ourselves less and to rely all the more fully upon God in the future. At the end, then, we are among the 144,000. All of us, no matter what may have been our way of life on earth, no matter how young or how old at the moment of our death, we will all be considered, symbolically, "virgins," total in our commitment to God, prepared for the marriage feast of the lamb and for the full espousals of love.

If then we never compromise our interior consecration to God, there will be a strength of wisdom and love within us that will carry us through to the end.

Like Daniel, we also need signs of this consecration during our lifetime. At times the sign may be ready at hand, like fasting during periods of sorrow, whether for the entire church during lent, or with a family during its time of death or sickness. Or small reminders of faith, prayers at mealtime, religious pictures, special times of silence and prayer manifest our dedication. At other times, Daniel was severely tried, even thrown into the fiery furnace or into the den of lions, again symbols of oppression and persecution. Or there may be an inspiration to go the extra mile and give our shirt as well as our outer cloak (Matt 5:40–42).

In the gospel we have the touching example of the widow who drops the two copper coins into the treasury. As Jesus declares: she has given what she could not afford, and that turns out to be more than the wealthiest benefaction. We too must be ready for the time when the spirit will inspire us to give in ways that hurt, ways that also unite us totally to Jesus who gave himself totally on the cross for our salvation. The widow dropped the two copper coins, never realizing that anyone saw what she was doing, never thinking that she would be remembered throughout the world. No wonder that she gave more than everyone else! When the time comes, each of us will secretly know what are the two copper coins by which we give everything to our neighbor and so to God.

Prayer:

Glory and praise to you, O Lord, God of our ancestors, that you have blessed us with such extraordinary examples of holiness, the young man Daniel and the aged widow. Allow me to enter their company and so to praise your blessed and holy name forever. Then my hands will be sinless, my heart clean, my desires worthy, as I seek you, my God.

Tuesday, 34th Week

Dan 2:31–54. The vision of the four kingdoms, eventually destroyed by a stone hewn from the mountain, which itself proceeded to fill the whole earth.

Rev 14:14–19. The earth is harvested, first the wheat by one coming on a cloud, then the grapes by one coming out of the temple in heaven. The ripe grapes are thrown into the winepress of God's wrath.

Luke 21:5–11. Take care not to be misled about the end of the world by self-proclaimed saviors. The end does not follow immediately.

We now meet some of the most controversial literature in the Bible. Because it deals with the "end of the world," it also ranks among the most popular chapters of the Bible! We must be careful because the language is highly symbolical. Indeed, Jesus declares: "Take care not to be misled." The liturgy, we think, provides the surest way to interpret and apply these passages in an effective way.

As we have noted, we are near the end of one church year and the beginning of another. The "end" means finality and responsibility. We must take responsibility for our actions, take stock where we are spiritually, and honestly face God. Yet, this "end" gives place to a new beginning. With the dawn of Advent and four weeks later with the birth of the Savior, we are given a new chance, a new life. The end and the beginning, responsibly taking stock and mercifully beginning over again, are both equally important.

As we look back, we may see so many efforts, badly inspired, buttressed with human strength alone, controlled by personal interests and pride. We see a statue, similar to the one which was presented to Nebuchadnezzar in a vision (cycle I). This statue with its four principal sections represented the four great kingdoms, as the Israelites remembered them: the Babylonians, the Medes, the Persians and the Greeks. No matter how colossal they were, and seemingly invincible, they collapsed. A stone hewn from the mountains struck the feet of the statue which were partly iron and partly tile and smashed them. This stone, in the symbolism of the Old Testament, stood for Israel. We read in one of the several passages:

> Look to the rock from which you were hewn,
> to the pit from which you were quarried;
> Look to Abraham, your father,
> and to Sarah, who gave you birth;
> When he was but one I called him,
> I blessed him and made him many (Isa 51:1–2).

Out of seeming, insignificant people, whose bodies seemed dead and hopeless according to St. Paul (Rom 4:19), God creates new life, comforts the ruins of Zion, and fills the holy city with "joy and gladness."

World empires, material wealth, political clout—none of these forces of themselves can last. Our faith will overcome each and every one. What God achieves in our lives through prayer and faith, through perseverance in the midst of trials and persecution, through obedience to his law and our conscience: that will become

> . . . a kingdom that shall never be destroyed or delivered up to another people. Rather, it shall break in pieces all these kingdoms and put an end to them.

The trials will be severe. We may pass through several great harvestings of the world. Eventually, as in the Book of Revelation (cycle II) the good deeds, like the wheat, will be harvested by the Son of Man who comes upon the cloud; evil deeds will be cut from the branches like ripe grapes and thrown "into the huge winepress of God's wrath." There will be times of accounting and taking stock. God does not let things just drift for ever and ever.

To examine our life, we must be at peace with ourselves and with God. We must be people of sincerity and honesty. We cannot be bluffing our way along. We have to attempt justice towards our neighbor—justice like God's that is characterized by sympathetic understanding of the human situation, especially when it is touched by poverty, sickness and difficulties.

At times like this, when we have been disappointed with others, perhaps cheated and lied to, it will be all the more difficult to deal with them in a kindly, compassionate and patient way. We will feel impelled to act quickly against others. This would be a wrong way of taking stock! We tend to summon the end of the world for these people—no second chance, forever out of our lives, totally condemned. We need to listen to Jesus' words in the gospel:

> Take care not to be misled. Many will come in my name, saying, 'I am he' and 'The time is at hand.' Do not follow them . . . .These things are bound to happen first, but the end does not follow immediately.

To translate this statement into the language of this final week of the church year: the end does not follow immediately—rather advent and the new birth of Jesus.

As we take account of our past year, it should be with patience and compassion towards others, with hope and honesty towards ourselves. We must learn where not to put our hopes and where not to seek our strength, for these will collapse like the statue in Nebuchadnezzar's dream. We, the stone hewn from the mountains, can become a new kingdom of God. We must extend this hope to others as well, as we look forward to a new year of grace, beginning in Advent.

Prayer:

Lord, we give you glory and praise for all that you have accomplished. We ask your pardon and compassion for many of the mistakes that we have been responsible for. Through faith, your kingdom comes. You will truly be our king. Heaven will be glad and earth rejoice. You rule with justice and constancy.

Wednesday, 34th Week

Dan 5 (selected verses). During King Belshazzar's banquet, while they were drinking from the vessels of the Jerusalem temple, a hand writes upon the wall and Daniel interprets its meaning: MENE, TEKEL and PERES.

Rev 15:1–4. In a single vision John sees the seven angels with the seven final plagues and hears the song of victory from the saints who overcame the beast.

Luke 21:12–19. The disciples of Jesus will be persecuted, even by their own family. Yet not a hair of your head will be harmed. By patient endurance you will save your lives.

The final sentence of the gospel, perhaps added to Jesus' words as a later commentary and application, directs our meditation today. "By patient endurance you will save your lives." The sentence is another one of those "floating" comments that can fit into many situations. It occurred earlier in Luke 8:15 in a somewhat adapted form: "The seed on the good ground are those who hear the word in a spirit of openness, retain it, and bear fruit through patient endurance." This last phrase became one of Paul's most insistent recommendations: i.e., "immortality by *patiently* doing right" (Rom 2:7). In still another passage of Romans, this same word, patience, becomes the key or major link:

> We know that affliction makes for *endurance*, and *endurance* for tested virtue, and tested virtue for hope. And this hope will not leave us disappointed, because the love of God has been poured into our hearts through the Holy Spirit who has been given to us (Rom 5:3–5).

The Greek word underlying these statements about patience and endurance (*upomone*) reflects a strong *interior* attitude of perseverance, consistency, dependability.

With this in mind, we re-read the scriptural passages of today's liturgy. First of all, the gospel. Persecution cannot break such a steady person, neither can it destroy the family relationships that seem to be strained beyond all limits. "You will be delivered up even by your parents, brothers, sisters, relatives and friends." In times such as this, we must continue in our own loyalty to God and to our family. We need the conviction that sooner or later God will justify us, and at that moment our family and community will reunite. We will be the center and the means of this reunion because of continued fidelity.

In the meanwhile, however, we seem at a loss for words and explanation. Jesus reminds us that "I will give you words and a wisdom which none of your adversaries can take exception to or contradict." For trials such as these, we cannot be prepared. It would be wrong to determine ahead of time what we will say if betrayed by a friend or family member. Our entire life would be embittered if we were to live with such suspicions. Yet, if we have prepared by patient endurance and constant loyalty, then as St. Paul wrote to the Romans: our "hope will not leave us disappointed, because the love of God has been poured into our hearts through the Holy Spirit." Our words will be prompted by true love and honest fidelity. Such words will have lasting power to be remembered, reflected upon and gradually bear their good fruit.

Such "patient endurance" will support us through persecution and long desolate periods. With good reason we can join, according to the Book of Revelation (cycle II), in the song of Moses, the servant of God. Moses sang his song of thanksgiving after leading the people through the Red Sea (Exodus, chap. 15) and he must have repeated it at crucial moments during the long period of wandering in the wilderness of Sinai and Kadesh.

Like the people under the leadership of Moses, we too face stretches of wilderness and desert. We can do nothing other than push onward and persevere. To stand still in the desert means self-destruction. It seems heroic, simply to survive another day in our circumstances; yet heroic we must be on this day by day basis. By "patient endurance" we will arrive at the promised land and join in the song of Moses:

Mighty and wonderful are your works,
  Lord God Almighty!
Righteous and true are your ways,
  O King of the nations!

Today's scriptures assure us that we will one day join in this song to God's "patient endurance." We will announce God's fidelity to us, as God blesses us for our patient, strong response to his grace at the heart of our lives.

Over our lives of patience and loyalty, God will write a consoling message. The words will be fearful to those who squandered God's graces and could never be relied upon—those who sit at the banquet table with the "King Belshazzar's" of this world, making merry with the sacred vessels. But to us, as to the prophet Daniel, the words are consolation and reward: **Mene, Tekel** and **Peres**:

Mene— God has *numbered* your kingdom. The sorrow will certainly come to an end;

Tekel— God has weighed on the scales and found your works worthy of eternal reward; nothing is wanting, for you trusted and believed;

Peres— God will *divide* the kingdom and bring into it those who persevered till the end.

Because we have continued in our loyalty to our family and community, to our vocation and obligations, we will open our eyes and see with us—because of us—those who persecuted us and ridiculed us. Now they have been united as our family once more, just as the Gospels will reach outward to the conversion of the nations and the triumph of the love of Jesus.

Truly, "By patient endurance you will save your lives" and the lives of all your loved ones. This line, which can settle into many different moments of our lives and enable us to carry onward towards the promised land, has a ring in the Latin translation that will echo forever: *in patientia vestra possidebitis animas vestras*, "In your patience you will possess your soul."

Prayer:

Lord, we call upon the universe to give praise and glory to you: the sun and moon, stars of heaven, shower and dew, all the winds, fire and heat—all these have participated in my life, accompanied me over many troubles and through persecution. Altogether we praise you, O Lord. We acclaim you for your kindness and faithfulness. You make your salvation known in the sight of everyone.

Thursday, 34th Week

Dan 6:12–28. Daniel is delivered from the lion's den; the king recognizes Yahweh as deliverer and savior, working signs and wonders in heaven and on earth.

Rev 18:1–2, 21–23; 19:1–3, 9. Babylon has fallen and Alleluia rings out from the heavenly assembly. Happy are they who have been invited to the wedding feast of the Lamb.

Luke 21:20–28. Jerusalem will be destroyed amid signs in the sun, the moon and the stars. The Son of Man will come on a cloud with great power. Your ransom is near at hand.

While Mark (chap. 13) combines the prophecy about the fall of Jerusalem with that of the end of the world, Luke separates the two events (21:20–24, the destruction of Jerusalem; 21:25–28, the final end). Writing after the collapse of the Holy City, Luke realized that its destruction did not usher in the final age of the world and the second coming of the Son of Man. This biblical data enables us to address a crucial moment in our own personal existence.

On a rare but very real occasion all of us face a crucial, dramatic encounter. It seems to be the end of our world. This terrifying moment is usually a severe trial, physical or emotional; a serious sickness; the death of a loved one; loss of finances and security; an episode very humiliating and discouraging. It is also possible that the event which seems to end our previous way of life may be a very happy episode, like a marriage or vocation to religious life, an unusual scholarship that revamps our plans for life, the birth of a new baby in a family. Whether stressful or joyful, the startling and decisive episode seems to turn our life around and we can never be the same again.

Nonetheless, after a few weeks or months, life is the same again! The old monotony is back, the same temptations are gnawing at us. We begin to question whether it makes any difference to have summoned one's total energy and to have dealt with the crisis heroically. We had steeled ourselves to accept whatever God wanted and were willing to accept the consequences of our decision, all this for so little results! As the classic poet wrote: a mountain was in labor and a mouse came forth!

Perhaps the most heroic part of life is not confined to the short moments of excruciating trial or exhilarating joy but rather is spread out over the plateau of one's middle years. This is the period of time when no more dramatic changes will come. We have to accept the consequences of our earlier decisions and live by them.

The Scriptures want us to remember the former days and the time of the great trial. In fact, biblical religion is based upon the remembrance of God's magnificent acts of redemption for the people Israel: from their exodus out of Egypt all the way to Jesus' exodus from earth to heaven by way of the cross, a pledge of our own glorification. These remembrances keep alive our faith that Jesus will certainly come *again*, dramatically, definitively, gloriously.

> The powers in the heavens will be shaken. After that, people will see the Son of Man coming on a cloud with great power and glory.

We were created to live on this earth, but only for a time of testing, whose glorious finale is not dictated by our merits or ability but by the strength of Jesus' love for us and Jesus' total union with us as Son of Man—Child of Earth. Jesus will ''ransom'' us; this word draws upon a long Old Testament tradition, by which the Messiah will be so intimately united with us that his life will be ours and his future our glory and reward.

The Book of Daniel (cycle I) draws upon many ancient traditions that reached back into the Babylonian exile and had become a classic part of Israel's heritage, again an indication how necessary are our memories of God's bountiful acts. Like Daniel, Israel had been preserved alive from the dangers of the lions' den of the exile. About four hundred years later, during the persecution of Antiochus IV Epiphanes (a general who fell heir to a part of the empire of Alexander the Great), Israel had to experience the same horrendous persecution and collapse of the holy city. The long years in-between—the silent, monotonous years—did not seem to go anywhere. Even though they were marked by intense interest in the law of Moses and an attempt to obey that law punctiliously, now this lowering cloud and whirlwind of destruction swept through the heart of their lives.

Daniel advises the people that God is preparing a letter to be written ''to the nations and peoples of every language.'' This letter will proclaim that Yahweh, the God of Israel's ancestors, is:

> . . . the living God, enduring forever; his kingdom shall not be destroyed, and his dominion shall be without end.

While the monotonous years provide the opportunity to appreciate and safeguard our prayer and fidelity with God, the tempestuous period of trial becomes a divinely appointed way of casting down those walls and sharing our God and our family with the world.

Such a moment, according to the Book of Revelation (cycle II), will avenge the blood of God's servants. False joys will be unmasked; futile waste of energy over flimsy securities will never again happen; all the buying and selling of world merchants will stop. Every attempt on our part to wrestle the future out of God's hands and to take control of it will end.

We cannot avoid the long monotonous period, but in the end God achieves the victory beyond all human endeavor. How necessary it is to persevere through each kind of trial: the heroically monotonous and the heroically intense.

Prayer:

Lord, we call upon our entire lives, the great moments and the low moments, to give praise to you: dew and rain, frost and chill, nights and days, light and darkness. Let all bless the Lord, praise and exalt him above all forever. Increase our faith so that we may never lose sight of the blessedness that will be ours when we are called to the wedding feast of the Lamb.

Friday, 34th Week

Dan 7:2–14. The terrifying vision of the four beasts coming out of the sea, of the little horn that spoke arrogantly, of the Ancient One enthroned in the glory, and the Son of Man coming on the clouds of heaven.

Rev 20:1–4, 11–15; 21:1–2. Satan is chained and the saints
  reign with Christ for a thousand years. All whose names
  are written in the book of life are summoned from the
  dead amid new heavens, a new earth and a new holy city.
Luke 21:29–33. When you see these things happen, know
  that the reign of God is near. My word will not pass away.

While the first readings, from Daniel (cycle I) and from
Revelation (cycle II), are typical of apocalyptic literature
and are replete with elaborate, even at times weird symbolism, the gospel addresses us plainly. From the example of
the budding fig tree—or ''any other tree,'' if you wish!—
''you know that summer is near. Likewise when you see all
the things happening of which I speak, know that the reign
of God is near.'' Perhaps we can smooth out enough of the
difference between the high symbolism of the first reading
and the earthly example of the gospel by stating: the signs
are there, like the nose on our face; but the meaning of these
life-signs, as we inhale and exhale, must be seriously and
sensitively intuited. Study and testing can take us only a limited way to solving the mystery. After that, our supernatural
instinct must guide us to what God is saying by the plain
signs around about us.

The symbolism in the Books of Daniel and Revelation
is drawn from a long, rich heritage that blends history and
religion, ritual and folklore, Israelite and non-Israelite images. Put as simply as possible, apocalyptic symbolism
comes from a school of thought convinced that God's mystery is so transcendent and yet so close to us, so overwhelming and yet so immediately at hand, so destructive and yet so
clearly creative of a new order, that only a whirling clash of
images with God's strong, steady presence in their midst can
properly communicate the message. Part of the history in-

corporated into the Book of Daniel comes from the four great empires of Israelite memory: Babylonian, Medes, Persian and Greek (see Tuesday of this 34th week). The little horn that displaced three other horns would be Antiochus IV Epiphanes. Of the four kingdoms into which Alexander's empire was divided, this one affected Israel most seriously. The fierce persecution, already described in the First and Second Books of Maccabees (last week), was unleashed upon Jerusalem by Antiochus IV Epiphanes. At this point, however, the Book of Daniel states that God is about to vindicate the persecuted saints and allow them to receive "dominion, glory and kingship; nations and peoples of every language." While past history can be extended through many symbols, contemporary and future history are compressed into a single great act of God.

A similar but different setting is found behind the Book of Revelation (cycle II). The Roman persecution is in full swing and the church feels hounded on all sides. The seer of Patmos, called John, announces the collapse of the cruel tyrant and an extraordinary period of peace for the church, the "thousand years" when Satan will be chained. After that will come the second appearance of Christ, the new heavens and the new earth, the new holy city Jerusalem, "coming down out of heaven from God, beautiful as a bride prepared to meet her husband."

Apocalyptic symbolism attracts attention and we can become totally preoccupied with computers in figuring out exact dates for the end of the world and in determining events in between now and then. Many attempts have been made through the centuries, and each masterplan had to be revised when the end did not come!

Yet there is a message, as clear, perhaps, as that of the blossoming fig tree. It is a statement for *each* of us *now*:

"the present generation will not pass away until all this takes place. The heavens and the earth will pass away, but my words will not pass."

If we live closely and lovingly within our family or religious community, within church and country, with our neighborhood and employment, many important signals will be given to us. Perhaps a spouse or child, a brother or sister in religious orders, a neighbor or another human being in a distant country, is silently shouting for our attention. Yet we are so selfishly concerned about our own interests, so stubbornly resolved to accept only our own judgment, that we do not see the blossoming fig tree which tells us that summer is near, that the time of judgment and final decision is at hand. The signs which others give may seem weird at times, so indirect that we excuse ourselves from seriously considering them. The sign is important for what it silently shouts about a mystery beyond words, even beyond rational speculation, like the signs of cancer and death, the signs of talents, hope and new life, the signs of the new heavens and the new earth. The signs can be positive and negative at one and the same time, as in the apocalyptic literature of Daniel and Revelation.

These signs, like the warning of Jesus, cannot be argued away. The fig tree is obviously in bloom; summer is that near! In our family and church, in our neighborhood and world, we have to be realists. A strange recommendation: to be realists in dealing with the weird symbols of apocalyptic seers! Realists in digging beneath the surface and silently, obediently and perceptively listening to the mysterious message. This message will not go away; it demands fulfillment. It is the word of God. It heralds the new presence of Jesus. It anticipates the new heavens and the new earth. Weird as it may seem right now, it will be transformed into the beautiful city of Jerusalem, the lovely bride prepared to meet her husband.

Prayer:

Lord, let everyone and everything offer you praise: mountains and hills, seas and rivers, dolphins and all water creatures, birds of the air, beasts wild and tame. You are about to transform our world into new heavens and new earth. You are about to appear in our midst. We yearn and pine for this holy presence. Our flesh and heart cry out for you, our living God.

Saturday, 34th Week

Dan 7:15–27. In terror Daniel asks for an explanation of the vision. The persecuted saints, loyal to God and the covenant, will eventually receive the kingdom and become part of the everlasting dominion of the Most High.

Rev 22:1–7. The river of life, flowing from the throne of God in the new Jerusalem, the vision of the Lamb, face to face, and the promise that I am coming soon.

Luke 21:34–36. The great day comes suddenly. Be on your guard. Pray constantly to stand secure before the Son of Man.

On this last day of the church year we are encouraged to be men and women both of practical realism and exalted hope. We need to see both sides of the heavy clouds; on one side, darkness and the sign of persecution, and on the other side, bright sunlight and the enjoyment of eternal peace. The readings affirm that the transition from darkness to light will be certain and sudden. In the meanwhile we must live with strong faith in God's eternal plan for us and for the entire world. Whether in darkness or light, we are not alone but are united with all of God's holy ones.

The three readings view this awesome change from sorrow to joy, darkness to light, in various ways. In the Book of Daniel (cycle I), the prophet writes that "I . . . found my spirit anguished within its sheath of flesh, and I was terrified by the visions of the mind." The great persecution of Antiochus IV Epiphanes still rages. He was the "little horn" on the beast, "greater than its fellows," who "made war against the holy ones and was victorious until the Ancient One arrived." Daniel was still awaiting that arrival. He is living in the midst of that period of time when "they shall be handed over to him for a year, two years, and a half-year." Three and a half years is a symbolical number for great distress which must extend its full course but must also end. The figure occurs in relation to the drought announced by the prophet Elijah (1 Kgs 17:1; Jas 5:17–18). Frequently in the Scriptures, sometime during the period of "three," whether it is days or years, the end of waiting will come and salvation be at hand (Josh 3:2, for the crossing of the River Jordan into the promised land; Hos 6:2, for the coming of rain; Exod 19:10–11, for the descent of God on Mount Sinai). Because three and one half is midway between the perfect number of seven, it is also a time of trial and imperfection; it always carries the note of coming to an end!

It may be a bit tedious to trace the symbolism of numbers through the Bible. Yet, it accentuates the faith of the Scriptures: a) we must persevere through the entire time of trial, no matter how tedious the waiting may become! b) we must be firm in our faith that this time will certainly end. And at the end we will see everything in proper perspective. Up till now, many details remain wrapped in darkness.

Luke's gospel was composed after one period of devestating trial, the destruction of the Holy City of Jerusalem by the Romans in A.D. 66. Luke generally bespeaks a breathing period of peace. Therefore, he warns:

> Be on guard lest your spirits become bloated with indulgence and drunkenness and worldly cares. The great day will suddenly close in on you like a trap.

It seems that we prosper more during adversity than during peace! Another day of trial lies ahead; it will come suddenly. Therefore, Luke also advises: "Pray constantly." Live in God's presence and then you will "stand secure before the Son of Man" when he comes in full glory.

The Book of Revelation (cycle II) views the momentous crises of earthly existence from the glory at the end. Here is the silver lining to the clouds, the end of the three and one half years of trial. The seer of Patmos, who wrote this book of symbols, is already standing with one foot within the heavenly Jerusalem and with one foot outside on planet earth! Therefore, he is told: "Remember, I am coming soon! Happy that one who heeds the prophetic message of this book!" Revelation here evokes from us those happy moments of our life; these are the pledge of eternal happiness. These moments of joy, if lived in God's presence on earth as Luke advises, will not decline into excessive play and sensuality. To use an image of this chapter of Revelation, they will provide a momentary, refreshing drink from "the river of life-giving water, clear as crystal, which issued from the throne of God and of the Lamb, and flowed down the middle of the streets." If we follow this river—that is, if we receive joy in God's presence—then we will come to the face to face vision of the Lamb of God in the new Jerusalem. These joys on earth then are our pledge of heaven.

The thirty-four weeks of the church year are about to end. They do so with an announcement that the Lord Jesus will come suddenly, soon and gloriously. We have been granted the long preparation of the church year. We will be graced with a special four weeks of intense, spiritual consecration during Advent. There is every reason that we will be ready to receive Jesus—rather, to be received by the Lord of glory:

> Therefore, since we for our part are surrounded by this cloud of witnesses, let us lay aside every encumberance of sin . . . and persevere in running the race which lies ahead; let us keep our eyes fixed on Jesus, who inspires and perfects our faith. For the sake of the joy which lay before him he endured the cross [and] had taken his seat at the right of the throne of God (Heb 12:1–2).

Prayer:

Lord, we give glory and eternal praise to you. We call upon the world to join in this hymn of praise as we draw near the throne of grace and the wondrous vision of our loving savior. Maranatha! Come, Lord Jesus! We kneel before the Lord who made us and shepherds us into the pasture of eternal joy.

PART TWO

Sundays of Ordinary Time
Weeks 23–34

Twenty-third Sunday, "A" Cycle

Ezek 33:7–9. The sentinel is obliged to warn the wicked person. If not, then both perish! If yes, then the sentinel is saved and may also save the wicked person, or else the wicked die in their own guilt.

Rom 13:8–10. The commandments are all summed up in the precept to love our neighbor as ourselves. Love is the fulfillment of the law.

Matt 18:15–20. Directions how to correct a brother or sister: at first, privately; eventually, before the church. The prayer of those who gather in Jesus' name will be heard.

The Bible this Sunday leads us in a most difficult venture, brotherly or sisterly correction. Attention here is not being focused upon the training of children nor upon the correct response towards adolescents. Here it is a matter of adults' dealing with adults! To make matters still more onerous, the adults are members of our family, relationship and neighborhood.

As with the twenty-second Sunday, "A" Cycle, the first and third readings dovetail nicely while the second reading which is not explicitly about correcting one's brother or sister still offers the basic attitude for approaching this difficult exercise: love for one's neighbor is the fulfillment of every law. While Ezekiel emphasizes the serious obligation of this law of correcting one's neighbor, Paul in writing to the Romans shows us how to go about it.

If we proceed with genuine love, then we are not setting out to win an argument and to prove the other person wrong. Love is a virtue of the will, not of the intellect. "Love," St. Paul insists, "never does any wrong to the neighbor." And it is wrong to humiliate the other, to shame the other person. It is wrong to shout down and to cleverly manipulate the language. Sarcasm is wrong; half-truths are wrong. In correcting the neighbor, therefore, "love never does any wrong" to them.

Because love unites, then in the difficult matter of correcting another person, love is as much concerned with how we are heard as with how we are speaking. According to the commandment to love we hear with the ears of the other person while admonishing them. What we speak must make sense to them and therefore be in contact with their values and hopes. We address what is authentically good in them that this goodness can become more visible and more effective in guiding their actions. If we correct others with love, then we are enhancing and affirming what is valuable in them.

To correct with love also means to share the *pain* of mistakes. Love, we all admit, unites, especially in the area of discussion and action. If we are discussing sins and failures, imprudence and impulsiveness, then we are bonded in suffering together. We weep with those who are weeping, we are shamed with those who are ashamed, we feel helpless with the helpless and impulsive. (*cf.*, Luke 7:32; 1 Cor 9:22).

Generally everyone agrees that wrong is wrong. Correction, therefore, is not an exercise in proving the wrong to be wrong, and the right to be right! It is understood by all of us in our better moments that adultery, murder, stealing and coveting are wrong. It is best to assume this good and healthy attitude in others. Correction, therefore, seeks to counteract what is working against the hidden yet real goodness in the other person. Correction seeks to motivate, to reveal unsuspected sources of strength, to revitalize ideals, to find and encourage what seems lost.

Even with the best of advice and the strongest motivation of love, all the world admits that correction is never easy. In fact, it is always difficult, certainly awkward, usually a risk of losing what little friendship is left. Despite all this—perhaps, because of it—Ezekiel's words are necessary. Correction of a brother or sister is at times not an optional matter like a menu in a restaurant. Correction can be so obligatory that our own salvation depends upon it:

> If . . . you do not speak out to dissuade the wicked from their way, they shall die for their guilt, but I will hold you responsible for their [spiritual] death.

To understand and accept this stern statement from Ezekiel, it is helpful to return to the commandment of love in the second reading. Love unites in family and community. Love means that we are all in it together. We sink or swim together. In this sense, consequently, we never save our own, private, individual soul. We live in heaven as we would in our home, with the entire family or community.

The responsibility is on both sides, with the one who corrects and with the one who is corrected. Ezekiel, therefore, also declares:

> If you warn the wicked . . . and they refuse to turn from their way, they shall die for their guilt, but you shall save yourself.

If the other party rejects our correction, what then? Again, the key to opening the door towards a solution comes from the second reading and from its basic law of love. Love, we have said very often, unites. If someone rejects correction, we appeal to a larger family of "two or three witnesses" or even to the total family of the "church." This appeal is not to be confused with dragging a culprit before a criminal court. It is an appeal from love and respect. It calls upon ancestral memories of right and wrong. It remembers family dreams. It receives the support of many prayers of intercession.

Jesus assures us: "Where two or three are gathered in my name, there am I in their midst." Love which unites includes the bonding love of Jesus.

Finally if every appeal of love fails to correct the wrong, then our action is validated in heaven, even if we must exclude the incorrigible person from the family where children and all of us adults in our weakness need support and good example. Like Jesus, however, we must continue to look for the lost sheep. Then each one of us, in that part of ourselves where we too are wrong, sinful and lost, will not be endangered of being lost for ever.

Prayer:

Lord, as we hear your voice of correction, do not let our hearts be hardened. Overcome our stubbornness, cure our blindness, soften our prejudice, so that together we may sing your praises and experience the joy of your shepherding hand.

Twenty-third Sunday, "B" Cycle

Isa 35:4–7. God comes to open our blind eyes, to clear our deaf ears, to strengthen our lame legs, to turn the thirsting ground into springs of water.

James 2:1–5. Your faith must not allow of favoritism. Did not God choose those who are poor in the eyes of the world to be rich in faith?

Mark 7:31–37. Jesus has done everything well! He makes the deaf hear and the mute speak.

We are being led into many enigmatic statements: we must lose to gain, die to live, be lost in order to be found, be in the last place to arrive at the first place, be sick in order to receive the attention of the divine physician. The readings for today infer something still more impossible: we must be blind in order to see, deaf in order to hear, lame in order to walk. All of these baffling conundrums unravel and become clear for us in the simple position of Scripture: life is God's gift. Unless we receive it from God, we do not possess it. Those really crippled person are the ones who pretend to see, hear and walk independent of God. They are actually blind, deaf and lame.

The Bible may be less poetic than we think when it insists that the blind, deaf and lame are the ones who walk in the kingdom of God, listen to its music and see its wonders. Again, it is summed up by the continually resonating statement: we must die with Christ in order to live with Christ:

> After all, you have died! Your life is hidden now
> with Christ in God. When Christ our life appears,
> then you shall appear with him in glory. . . .
> Christ is everything in all of you (Col 3:3–4, 11).

Christ becomes everything: our hearing and our speaking, our walking and our singing. At times, for this grace to be realized in us, our natural hearing must become deaf, our speaking must be silenced, our own songs muted, our walking paralyzed! Indeed, at times these disabilities (if that is the right word?) must strike us literally, either in our birthing or in our living as adults. Even on the natural level, when we are silent and immobile, perhaps lost in sleep, we dream our songs and dances. The words and movements are not artificially orchestrated; they come spontaneously from wellsprings of hidden life.

Our life is to be hidden with Christ in God, so that the life of Christ will be made manifest in our mortal flesh (2 Cor 4:10–11):

> I have been crucified with Christ, and the life I live now is not my own; Christ is living in me (Gal 2:19–20).

To be crucified with Christ means to lose the use of hands, feet and entire body, to be silent as Jesus was on the cross, even to be abandoned. Would it not be better to say that Jesus becomes like ourselves when we are muted, blinded and paralyzed? The bonding is complete.

It was complete for Jesus when Jesus was destroyed in the crucifixion and death. We are called to take up our cross and follow (Mark 8:34)—some of us literally in our physical condition. In darkness we see as Jesus did the blinding mysteries of human life; in deafness we hear as Jesus did the deafening sound of God's glory; in lameness we walk as Jesus did the glorious way of God's will, for our own and the world's salvation.

Other times come when we deliberately immobilize ourselves. As in the reading from James we show no favoritism. We are plainly dressed with the poor who have no resources for fashionable clothing and gold rings; we take our place at the footrest for the crippled who cannot choose to "sit right [wherever they] please," to paraphrase a statement in James' epistle. We deliberately take our place with those who are discriminated against, another of James' inspired words. Only in this company can we hear what the deaf alone hear and receive what only the poor possess:

> Did not God choose those who are poor in the eyes of the world to be rich in faith and heirs of the kingdom he promised to those who love him?

In the company of this elect—the blind, the lame and the crippled—Jesus will take us off by himself away from the crowd. He will put his fingers into our ears and, spitting, touch our tongue. This action of Jesus seems very uncouth, but only in the intimacy of the family, whimsically yet seriously, will we lick the spoon and say it's clean to use! Though we are still deaf, we hear Jesus emit a groan; though blind, we see Jesus looking up to heaven. The sound of Jesus' very own voice, "Ephphatha," is unscrambled from its foreign Aramaic accent to become the language that opens our ears and frees our tongue, and we begin to speak plainly.

Again, only in the intimacy of the family does the seeming contradiction at the end of the gospel become normal and consistent. We are strictly enjoined to tell no one, so we proclaim the wonder all the more openly! Families can mix a healthy modesty with spontaneous enthusiasm. Jesus acted out of love, not out of power; the deaf mute acted out of love, not out of exhibitionism. Love unravels the contradiction.

After such a marvelous moment in the ministry of Jesus, the prophet Isaiah declares to us:

Here is your God!
vindicating the most ancient promises,
giving recompense to those who waited
in faith and learned obediently.
God comes to save you and give you life.

Prayer:

Lord, let my entire self praise you. Give sight to my eyes to see as you see; hearing to my ears to hear what you hear; movement to my legs to follow your path, so that I may be your instrument to secure justice for the oppressed and food for the hungry.

Twenty-third Sunday, "C" Cycle

Wis 9:13–18. If we can scarcely guess about earthly things, how can we ever know heavenly secrets? God sends the holy spirit to make known our paths on earth.

Phlm 9–10, 12–17. In returning the runaway slave Onesimus to his owner Philemon, Paul asks the latter to receive the slave as a beloved brother.

Luke 14:25–33. We are to renounce all our possessions to be a disciple of Christ, even our father and mother, wife and children, brothers and sisters, yes our very self.

Jesus' words are radical, even incomprehensible at first reading. They can be easily misinterpreted and so become disruptive and destructive. There are times when Jesus' statement of turning one's back on father and mother, wife and children, is to be taken literally; and there are other times when it is *not* to be taken literally. Therefore, it is necessary to *interpret* the Bible. Interpretation adds another ingredient to the simple, bald statement in the Bible. In fact, Jesus himself reinterpreted his own words, even reversing them. To the Canaanite woman who asked the Lord to cure her daughter, Jesus first declared: "My mission is *only* to the lost sheep of the house of Israel," not to foreigners. Yet he relented when surprised by her "great faith" (Matt 15:21–28).

On another occasion Jesus advised his followers to take a difficult case "to two or three witnesses" and finally "to the church" (Matt 18:15–20). The Bible needed interpretation from the church to be applied adequately to a difficult problem.

We can question if Jesus' statement in today's gospel can be taken literally. True, we can physically turn our back on father and mother; a husband can desert wife and children. Yet when Jesus adds to turn one's back "indeed [on] ourselves," he is necessarily speaking metaphorically or figuratively: no one can literally or physically turn his back on his very self. How can we leave ourselves and so turn our back on "it"? At the very least this requires a schizophrenic personality!

Other statements of Jesus would contradict the literal sense of this present passage. The second greatest commandment after the love of God is to "love your neighbor as yourself" (Mark 12:39). How is this possible if we have left ourselves behind! Jesus, moreover, reaffirmed the basic demand of the fourth commandment to honor one's father and mother (Mark 7:10–13). We hardly honor them by leaving them behind!

Turning to the second reading, we see again the biblical respect for basic human relationships, at least as these were understood at the time. St. Paul would not break up the master-slave relationship. He sent Onesimus, a runaway slave, back to his owner!

Yet, Paul also summons Philemon, the master, to a new understanding of this relationship. Philemon is to look upon the slave "no longer as a slave but as more than a slave, a beloved brother [whom you know] as a man and in the Lord." If Paul's words are pondered prayerfully and obediently before the Lord, Onesimus will no longer be treated as a slave; sooner or later (unfortunately, it was so much later) slavery disappeared as morally wrong. Paul then is summoning Philemon spiritually to leave "himself" behind, i.e., his innate reaction as slave owner to punish the runaway; his selfish possession of another individual; his belittling another human being, beloved in the Lord, as a second class Christian.

For us who are a century or more distant from the world's condemnation of the cruel practice of slavery, this reinterpretation of the inspired words of Paul and of Jesus seems humdrum and a waste of energy. Yet there are many other, still unsolved mysteries, situations which we may not even consider a mystery for we have come to our own very clear, and let us add, very wrong conclusions. Vatican II should teach us to practice more humility and cross-questioning of our self-righteousness.

The first reading addresses these persistent mysteries within ourselves. The Book of Wisdom, very probably the last of the Old Testament books to be written, one with all the benefits of the long inspired tradition of the Bible, still admits:

> For what person knows God's counsel, or who
> can conceive what the Lord intends?

Even with the assistance of the Bible, we are left unsure of ourselves. The same Book of Wisdom offers advice to us as it addresses God:

> Or who ever knew your counsel, except you had
> given Wisdom and sent your holy spirit from on
> high?

We need to wait upon the Lord and upon the gift of the Holy Spirit. We will remain even for long periods of time without an answer. This disposition corrects impulsiveness and selfishness. It harmonizes well with Isaiah's advice:

> By waiting and by calm you shall be saved,
> in quiet and in trust your strength lies . . . .
> The Lord is waiting to show you favor,
> Blessed are all who wait for the Lord (Isa 30:15,18).

Lest we be misled, waiting is not always the answer, as Ecclesiastes advises: ''There is a time to be silent, and a time to speak'' (Eccles 3:7). To know the difference requires not only prayer, but also advice and experience. And if we are giving the advice, then we do not coerce or threaten, no matter how right we are, as Paul writes to Philemon:

> I did not want to do anything without your consent, that kindness might not be forced on you but freely bestowed.

Perhaps, we think to ourselves, Paul should have commanded in the name of the Lord, to free the runaway slave and to reject the whole institution of slavery. Paul did not compel acceptance, but neither was he above persuasion and diplomacy! Paul writes that the runaway slave is ''more than a slave, a beloved brother, *especially dear to me*.''

Prayer:
Lord, in every age and moment of our lives you have been our refuge. You teach us by our church's tradition and by our own experience. Yet we must continually turn to you. Teach us to number our days aright, that we may gain wisdom of heart.

Twenty-fourth Sunday, ''A'' Cycle

Sir 27:30—28:7. Forgive your neighbor's injustice; then when you pray, your own sins will be forgiven. Remember your last days and set enmity aside.

Rom 14:7–8. None of us lives as our own master. Both in
life and in death we are the Lord's.

Matt 18:21–35. We are to forgive brother and sister seventy
times seven. Unless we forgive from the heart, our Heavenly Father will treat us in exactly the same way.

Today is forgiveness Sunday. It should be easy to reach
out and reconcile oneself with family or neighbor. Everyone
has sinned and is in need of forgiveness. It ought to be second nature for us who have received much forgiveness, to
forgive others. Yet, we all realize how difficult and even
how risky it is to offer forgiveness. We may be taken advantage of again by new offenses from the other person, or our
open hand of reconciliation may be refused. Or we may say
honestly to ourselves: how can I forgive if I am unable to
forget the sting and pain of the wounds once inflicted upon
me?

Despite these valid difficulties, the Scriptures leave us
no alternative than to forgive our neighbor, or what is still
more demanding of us, to forgive the member of one's own
family. Sirach writes for us:

> Should a person nourish anger against another
> and expect healing from the Lord?
> Should a person refuse mercy to another,
> yet seek pardon for their own sins?

The answer in each case is obvious. Yet because of the inherent embarrassment, perplexity and pain, Sirach repeats
himself, this time in a clear statement:

> The Lord heals us only when we stop nourishing
> anger
> against another.

The Lord pardons the sins only of those who are
merciful
towards another.

The gospel is still more precise and forthright:

When we are wronged by a brother or sister,
we do not forgive seven times,
but seventy times seven times.
My heavenly Father will treat you in exactly
the same way unless each of you forgives
brother or sister from the heart.

The Scriptures not only place before us the clear expectation of forgiving one's brother and sister, but they also motivate and direct the process which is admittedly difficult. First of all, the Bible assists us by its clarity. Forgiveness is a matter of life or death, of peace or bitterness. Sirach's statement in today's selection begins very bluntly:

Wrath and anger are hateful things,
yet the sinner [who refuses to forgive] hugs them
tight.

The unforgiving person is self-consumed by ''wrath and anger'' and other ''hateful things.'' The failure to forgive brings much pain and a score of inhuman reactions. Not to forgive is like not breathing; it is that unnatural and inhuman.

Forgiveness then towards others enables us to be in control of ourselves, just as the inability to forgive delivers us over to a bitter slavery of wrath, anger and mistrust. Because we can forgive others, only through the example and grace of Jesus, forgiveness does not so much make us our own master or mistress, but rather as Paul writes to the Romans:

> While we live we are responsible to the Lord, and
> when we die we die as the Lord's servants. Both
> in life and in death we are the Lord's.

We become the Lord's, not just by forgiving others but by receiving the Lord's forgiveness in our own sinful lives. Consequently, Paul continues with these words:

> That is why Christ died and came to life again,
> that he might be Lord of both the dead and the living.

Christ himself has gone through the same cycle of death and new life, experiencing hatred that through forgiveness new life may ensue: "Father, forgive them; they do not know what they are doing" (Luke 23:34).

Another motivation from the Scriptures for our forgiving one another turns out to be less than the most inspiring and exalted form of pure spirituality, yet it is thoroughly practical and down-to-earth:

> Remember your last days, . . .
> remember death and decay.

This clear statement from Sirach puts the question bluntly before us: do we want to die with bitter and hateful memories?

Another honest piece of advice from Scripture helps us in deciding to forgive brother or sister. Forgiveness presumes that the offense against ourselves was wrong. We do not have to make an intellectual somersault and declare wrong to be right. Sirach speaks of:

> your neighbor's injustice [towards you],
> faults to be overlooked.

And in the parable of forgiveness by which Jesus explains the necessity to forgive seventy times seven times, we hear about the servant who refuses to forgive another, even after receiving for himself a still more generous retirement of all personal debts. In other words forgiveness covers a long period of ups and downs. Sirach for his part speaks of "healing." This too does not happen instantly. Even the healthiest of human bodies needs time to recover from sickness and be totally healed. While the act of forgiveness takes only a moment, the full effects cover a longer sweep of time and require careful attention.

Healing adjusts and blends the various parts of the human body, nervous system, blood, stomach, intestines, etc. Forgiveness too involves a process. We need to reestablish bonds of friendship across the family or parish or neighborhood or religious community. We need the help of many others in doing this, their concern and advice, their patience and their forgiveness. Forgiving one's neighbor is both simple and complicated; most of all, it is absolutely necessary: "Forgive your neighbor's injustice; then when you pray, your own sins will be forgiven." Without forgiving others, "the sinner hugs tight wrath and anger."

Prayer:
    Lord, you reveal yourself as slow to anger and rich in compassion. You pardon our iniquities; you heal all our ills.

Share your compassion with me that I may be your instrument of compassion and forgiveness towards others.

Twenty-fourth Sunday, "B" Cycle

Isa 50:5–9. The servant is not ashamed, even though smeared with spittle; the servant teaches others by first listening obediently to the Lord.

James 2:14–18. Faith that does nothing in practice is thoroughly lifeless.

Mark 8:27–35. After Peter confesses Jesus to be the Messiah, Jesus teaches the disciples the necessity to deny their very selves, take up their cross and follow in Jesus' footsteps.

While the first reading and the gospel seem to deal with contradiction or at least with mysterious aspects of human life, the in between reading from the Epistle of James levels with us in a matter-of-fact way. We need prose and poetry, mystery within reality, the invisible within the visible. We must respect ourselves as both body and soul, as natural and supernatural.

James is arguing with extremists, so spiritual that work (they think) will interfere with God's plans. At times like this we should go for the jugular vein of authentic spirituality: words alone, no matter how exalted nor how inspired, no matter how authoritative from the Bible, will not clothe the naked and feed the hungry. James concludes:

Faith that does nothing in practice is thoroughly useless.

Make no bones about it: it is *thoroughly* useless.

Food and clothing are essential for human existence and therefore for divine faith. We are already glimpsing, however, a mystery within this blunt, practical spirituality of James. We see a blending of the human and the divine. The human points the way to the divine: ''I will show you the faith that underlies my works!''

At times, and these are the heroic moments of human existence, we become preoccupied with the divine. It is not that we are spiritual extremists, pretending to be disembodied angels. We have no other choice. The facts declare that we are seriously sick, or that we are subjected to shame, ridicule and misunderstanding, or that discipleship leads us along a way of the cross after Jesus. The readings from the prophet Isaiah and from the gospel come to our assistance.

The selection from Isaiah is generally grouped with three other passages, called the songs of the suffering servant: Isa 42:1–4; 49:1–6; 50:4–9a; 52:13—53:12. In this third song, an autobiographical account of personal insults, the servant retains human dignity, interior strength and absolute trust in God. Interior faith shows up through confidence in God. This is in a different kind of work than was the case in the epistle of James.

In the opening verse of the servant song, omitted in the liturgy, we are told by the servant:

> The Lord God has given me
>   a well-trained tongue,
> That I might know how to speak to the weary
>   a word that will arouse them.

Literally, the phrase, ''a well-trained tongue,'' reads in the Hebrew, ''a tongue [within a person who has] listened.'' Because of the message heard from God through human experience, the servant speaks of "the Lord God [who] opens my ear that I may hear." Such a divine message brings its own obligation: the servant cannot rebel nor turn back, even though humiliated by blows, spittle and plucking of beard. God's word and the servant's reaction bring forth a message of strength and dignity: "I am not disgraced [not] put to shame." The final lines ring out strong and clear:

> See, the Lord God is my help
> who will prove me wrong?

If we read ahead into the fourth song (52:13—53:12), the servant does not seem to accomplish anything, only to be "spurned and avoided by people, . . . oppressed and condemned . . . smitten for the sin of his people" (Isa 53:3,8). Here is a startling example of accomplishing the most by doing nothing. Here is genuine mystical silence, like that of Jesus on the cross. Faith has led the servant along a journey, from preaching and other activities, to listening and humiliation for the sake of truth, to long perseverance as a loyal disciple, to a prophetic stance which will reach to the cross of Jesus. Viewed in this way, the encouragement to activity in James' epistle is a stage along the way.

The same development occurs in the gospel episode for today. First, Peter confesses his faith: "You are the Messiah!" and then the path plunges into suffering and rejection. Peter struggles against this and remonstrates with Jesus. Evidently, faith has not yet found the clear markers along its path. Jesus replied: "Get out of my sight, you tempter!" Jesus too was struggling and experiencing the pain of human weakness. Finally, as Jesus walks the path of the cross, the way becomes clear for the disciples: take up the cross and follow in my steps.

Faith, which began by urging a clear confession and

which later acted vigorously to preserve Jesus' life, now totally encloses the person in the silence of death. Yet, death is the most active moment of being alive, the most heroic decision for following the Messiah. In the humiliating moment of death, human dignity shines forth supremely, as for the suffering servant. Such faith is summarized by Jesus' words:

> Whoever would save their life will lose it, and whoever loses their life for my sake and the gospel's will save it.

We have passed through death to be one with Jesus in the resurrection. At this point faith gives way to full glory in the vision of God.

Prayer:
 Lord, I seek to walk always in your presence. As you guide me through the land of the living, you keep my feet from stumbling and you dry the tears from my eyes. In sorrow and death, I call upon your name in faith. Incline your ear and hear me.

Twenty-fourth Sunday, "C" Cycle

Exod 32:7–11, 13–14. The people revolt and worship a golden calf. God threatens to destroy them and raise up a new people through Moses. At Moses' entreaty, the Lord relented.

1 Tim 1:12–17. God forgives Paul, the former persecutor of the church, to show that Christ Jesus came into the world to save sinners and to display his patience.

Luke 15:1–32. Jesus tells three parables about God's joy in forgiving sinners: the man with the lost sheep; the woman with the lost silver pieces; the parent with the lost prodigal child.

This Sunday is for the lost-and-found department of our lives and home. Every family and enterprise have one. Before looking at the biblical readings more closely, it may be helpful to recall how personal items are lost: sometimes out of ignorance and forgetfulness; other times out of negligence and thoughtlessness; still again deliberately in order to collect the insurance, or selfishly to have a good time; or perhaps out of compulsion in gambling or once more from the spite or stupidity of others. The lost-and-found department contains an encyclopedia of life stories.

In the first reading from Exodus the Israelites almost lose their birthright as God's chosen people and Moses definitely loses his opportunity to become another Abraham and himself the father of "a great nation." At the center lies the incident of the golden calf. The people had induced Aaron the priest to make it because they had lost Moses and their God Yahweh. We are told that when Moses "delay[ed] in coming down from the mountain [of Sinai]:

> they gathered around Aaron and said to him,
> "Come, make us a god who will be our leader; as
> for the man Moses . . . , we do not know what has
> happened to him."

The ritual of the golden calf involved the people in religious excesses and even moral depravity. Here is an example of losing God and God's minister, Moses, because of sensuality and impulsiveness. The people could not wait; they could not live from the nourishment of their invisible faith.

The dialogue between God and Moses combines anger, sternness, compassion and even a divine change of mind! Pivotal in this discussion are Moses' common sense reasons and complete selflessness. The common sense shows up when Moses convinces God not to make a fool of his divine self, daring language but perhaps no more daring than Moses' willingness to argue with God:

> Why, O Lord, should the Egyptians say, "With evil intent he brought them out, that he might kill them on the [holy] mountain . . . ? Let your blazing wrath die down . . . Remember your servants Abraham, Isaac and Israel, and how you swore to them . . . 'I will make your descendants as numerous as the stars in the sky . . . ' "

Strange, isn't it, that Moses teaches God a lesson in compassion! Moses' words were accepted by God because Moses spoke out of complete selflessness. Moses passed up the opportunity to take the place of Abraham, so as to become, instead, a spiritual leader of compassion and generosity. What this incident does not tell us, but which remains true, is that Moses himself had learned the lesson of compassion from God (Exod 3:7–9; 34:6–7).

The first letter of Paul to Timothy records another way of losing what is most precious. Paul writes about himself:

> I was once a blasphemer, a persecutor, a man filled with arrogance, but . . . I did not know what I was doing in my unbelief.

We lose by ignorance and impulsiveness. We should note that many other people suffered because of Paul's ignorance:

After [the martyrdom of Stephen in which Saul concurred] Saul began to harass the church. He entered house after house, dragged men and women out, and threw them into jail (Acts 8:1,3).

We hear the early church asking in their anguish and bewilderment: ''Why does God allow this young man, as blindly ignorant as he was zealous, to inflict all this pain on us?'' It was for our sake, as Paul writes to Timothy:

I was dealt with mercifully, so that in me, as an extreme case, Jesus Christ might display all his patience, and that I might become an example to those who would later have faith.

The example is worth our consideration: ''I have been treated mercifully, and the grace of our Lord has been granted me in overflowing measure, along with the faith and love which are in Christ Jesus. . . . Christ Jesus came into the world to save sinners.'' We have not only an example of God's patience and abundant grace, but also of Paul's heroic humility and frank openness: ''Christ Jesus came into the world to save sinners, of these I myself am the worst.''

In the gospel there are still other examples of lost and found. The lost sheep and the lost silver coins were no one's fault. Sheep wander and are helpless in finding their way back; a silver piece can easily roll between the cracks and be lost. If again we ask: why does God allow this to happen? the answer is clearly provided by Jesus: to show the extent of heavenly joy ''over one repentant sinner.''

We will refrain from asking the other question: why more joy in heaven over one repentant sinner than over ninety-nine righteous people who have no need to repent? After all, that was the same self-righteous question put to the father who celebrated the return of the prodigal son. Jesus is informing us: we are all lost in some part of ourselves. Who has not squandered rich possibilities? Who does not possess within himself, yet lost to sight, the potential for goodness, helpfulness and pure joy? Each of us, somewhere in ourselves, is lost for any number of reasons. Jesus welcomes us, as he did tax collectors and prostitutes, that we find ourselves at our best. Then heaven rejoices.

Prayer:

Lord, in your goodness, have mercy on me. Open my lips that I might proclaim your praise as you find what was lost in myself and so create the clean heart and steadfast spirit within me.

Twenty-fifth Sunday, "A" Cycle

Isa 55:6–9. Seek the Lord while he may be found, call upon him while he is near. As high as the heavens are above the earth, so high are my ways and thoughts above yours.

Phil 1:20–24, 27. Christ will be exalted through me, whether I live or die. I long to be freed of this life and to be with Christ, yet it is more urgent that I remain alive for your sakes.

Matt 20:1–16. The parable of the owner of the vineyard who hires workers at different hours of the day. He pays the last the same as those who labored all day. Are you envious because I am generous? The last shall be first.

Typical of the entire Bible, the readings blend the heavenly and the earthly, but in such a way that we are left with more questions than answers. We are immediately reminded that the Scriptures are primarily intended to inspire prayer rather than to solve theological questions. The Bible presumes faith, that is, friendship with God and trust in God, and then sets out to deepen that faith. The Bible is more concerned with directing good people how to be still better rather than with condemning evil people for their sins.

The reading from Isaiah may seem to contradict this principle. It is addressed to "the scoundrel" and "the wicked person." Yet the prophet appeals to the nearness of God and to God's generous ways of forgiving people. Immediately, Isaiah soars aloft, "as high as the heavens are above the earth." At this point the prophet is speaking to us in our deepest moments of prayer.

We can express the prophet's position in this contradictory way: God is *so* close and near to us, *so* overwhelming in graciousness and forgiveness towards us, that we seem to be looking straight into the burning light of the sun. Or, to modulate the image, God is so close that it seems as though God's hands lie across our eyes and leave us in darkness. In any case, whatever the image, we are left in the dark because God is that close to us.

In darkness such as this, we are experiencing the mystic presence of God, outdistancing the scope of our words, blinding the eyes of our intellect. At times such as this we do not settle theological questions; we do not even address God with petitions and requests. We silently enjoy the peace and wonder. God says: "My thoughts are not your thoughts, nor are your ways my ways." It is not that our thoughts and ways are evil but rather that they collapse and disappear in the wonder of God. In these times of prayer we are not going to discuss our thoughts nor crossquestion our ways. Both are far beneath the glory surrounding us in God's presence.

Contemplative prayer like this is not reserved to the select few. It is in the Bible for everyone of us; the section is even introduced with reference to the scoundrel and the wicked one.

In a different way Paul moves back and forth between the mystical ways of heaven and the nitty gritty needs of earth. Whether Paul will "live or die," he declares that "Christ will be exalted through me." Because " 'life' means Christ, hence dying is so much gain." Through death Paul passes into still more abundant life. Therefore, "I long to be freed from this [earthly] life and to be with Christ, for that is the far better thing." If we connect Paul's statements with those of the prophet Isaiah (incidentally, Paul's favorite Old Testament writer), Paul advises us to extend the time of our contemplative prayer.

Yet, Paul is not a false spiritualist, ignoring or condemning the earth as evil. In his missionary work, and particularly in his letters to the Galatians and the Romans, Paul championed the acculturization process, so that the gospel would be understandable in the language and culture of new classes of people. Therefore, Paul adds at once:

> If I am to go on living in the flesh, that means productive toil for me. . . . I am strongly attracted by both [to die and be with Christ; to continue living and working on earth]. It is more urgent that I remain alive for your sakes.

This section continues with some *human* remarks of Paul, omitted from the liturgical selection: "My being with you once again should make you even prouder of me in Christ." Typically of Paul's letter to the Philippians, he speaks with disarming affection and easy simplicity—in this sense very different from the argumentative tone, even sarcastic inferences in writing to the Corinthians. In any case Paul the mystic remains a human, earthy person.

Finally, in the gospel Jesus uses a parable to speak a clear message to his audience: outcasts, long separated from the full religious life of Israel, receive the same full message of salvation as those other Jews who have been faithful observers of the law all their life, like their ancestors for centuries before them. People were continually taking offense at Jesus' hobnobbing with such ilk. Jesus' reply is both kind and stern at once: "Are you envious because I am generous?" Furthermore, if the workers want to argue the case with strict justice, their payment for the day's work is honest and even generous; it was agreed upon.

We are still left with our questions. Is Jesus really just? Labor unions will not adopt this parable as their charter statement. And children who undertake their assigned chores in the home will be very upset, even for days, if everyone receives the same, no matter how much longer some worked over others.

As we reread the final sentences, we see that Jesus directs our questioning and prayer in the way of generosity and humility: "Are you envious because I am generous? Thus the last shall be first and the first shall be last." Prayer that centers upon these virtues will turn out to be peaceful, serene, non-aggressive, open. We are being led far into the sacred domain of the heart of Jesus.

Prayer:

Lord, you are always near to us, yet your overwhelming graciousness and kindness seem to separate you from our selfishness and sternness. Yet, you are truly near to all who call upon you. Let me persevere in this truth.

Twenty-fifth Sunday, "B" Cycle

Wis 2:12,17–20. The just person, characterized by gentleness and patience, is tested, persecuted and even killed by the self-confident wicked.

James 3:16—4:3. Jealousy and strife beget inconstancy, conflicts and vile behavior. Wisdom is innocent, peaceable, impartial and sincere.

Mark 9:30–37. Jesus' announcement of his passion and death leaves the disciples speechless. In the meanwhile they argue who was the most important among themselves. Jesus' reply: whosoever welcomes a child for my sake, welcomes me.

Two main strands or threads are interwoven in today's biblical readings. The disciples of Jesus are called to be active and ingenius in serving others; they are also expected to be docile, gentle and patient as instruments of peace. Activity and passivity, the energy to direct events for achieving God's will as well as the surrender to accept what is already determined as God's will, these contrasting moments combine within the life of God's servants. If either one gets out of hand and is overemphasized, we are in trouble. Yet the tension of keeping them side by side, each one balancing the other, turns out to be one of the most challenging aspects of following Jesus.

The gospel exemplifies this tension with the example of the little child. We are told that

> [Jesus] took a little child, stood him in their midst, and putting his arms around him, said to them, "Whoever welcomes a child such as this for my sake welcomes me. And whoever welcomes me welcomes, not me, but him who sent me."

We are immediately conscious of the contrast: Jesus took *a little child* but said to *them*: "Whoever welcomes *a child* such as this for my sake welcomes *me*." The "me" of this declaration is Jesus, an adult, a teacher, one whose question had just silenced other adults. The child must live within the adult, for the adult to be a disciple of Jesus.

Jesus delineates the qualities of this child within us. First of all, directness and sincerity. While the disciples of Jesus had been secretly arguing "who was the most important," Jesus fearlessly goes to the heart of the matter. Returning home to Capernaum, he asked them, "What were you discussing on the way home?" Because these adults lacked the qualities of the child, they were afraid and embarrassed. Children rush where angels fear to tread; children are unembarrassed with any kind of question. Jesus, therefore, "took a little child, stood him in their midst, and putting his arms around him, said to them: 'Whoever welcomes a child such as this for my sake welcomes me [and] him who sent me.' "

Jesus' questioning of the disciples is neatly contrasted with their fear "to question him." Jesus had just announced persecution, his death and resurrection. We are then informed:

> Though they failed to understand his words, they
> were afraid to question him.

Jesus who possessed the child within himself (we recall the symbolic but real gesture of Jesus' "putting his arms around the child") would remain loyal and honest, even if it meant death.

We are beginning to perceive the childlike qualities expected of Jesus' disciples. The second reading from James' Epistle describes these qualities more theoretically and at greater length than the gospel. James calls these characteristics the good fruits of divine wisdom:

innocent	rich in sympathy
peaceable	kindly in deeds
lenient	impartial
docile	sincere

While these are the qualities of a child, James and the wisdom literature of the Bible are very conscious that they are possessed by the adult. Without them the adult turns into a monster guilty of conflicts, disputes, wars, murder, envy, quarreling and fights. Such people squander what they receive on their own pleasures. James sums it up in the phrase, "all kinds of vile behavior." He is not thinking of sexual aberrations but the hideous consequences of "jealousy and strife."

While the second reading, from the Epistle of James, is influenced by the sapiential literature of the Old Testament, the first reading actually consists of a selection from one of its books called *The Wisdom of Solomon*. Even though this book, written very late (perhaps around 25 B.C.) in Greece and in Egypt, was not accepted into the canon by rabbis of Palestine, nonetheless, it seems to have influenced New Testament writers. Today's reading, in fact, includes phrases which resonate again in the story of Jesus' passion and death. There is no doubt that the early Christian church revered this book.

"The wicked beset the just one, because he is obnoxious to us" (Wis 2:12). Later the wicked say, "If the just one be the son of God, God will defend him and deliver him from the hand of his foes." We find ourselves at the foot of the cross.

Wisdom does not reason at length how God can tolerate

the persecution of the just person. Neither do children who lack the sophisticated logic of educated adults. The child within the adult-disciple of Jesus will give a ''proof of gentleness and . . . patience.'' How badly we adults need to learn these childlike virtues especially when we are beset with trouble. We are given the opportunity to contemplate their beauty and attractiveness in the hideous but ever so lovely remembrance of Jesus on the cross.

When the reading from Wisdom concludes with, ''God will take care of that person,'' we are reminded of Jesus' action, taking a little child and standing him in the midst of the disciples, *putting his arms around him*. Lord, bestow on us this pledge of your love.

Prayer:

Lord, let me welcome you as a child welcomes you. Hear this prayer of mine. Then with patience and gentleness I will be assured that you will defend my cause and sustain my life for eternity.

Twenty-fifth Sunday, ''C'' Cycle

Amos 8:4–7. Condemnation of social injustices which trample upon the needy.

1 Tim 2:1–8. Prayers are requested for peace, peace with those in authority, between races and nations, among the disciples of Jesus, just as there is peace between God the Father, the mediator Jesus and the entire human family.

Luke 16:1–13. The parable of the wily steward, more ingenious about worldly goods than the other-worldly, is about spiritual concerns. A number of proverbs about wealth and stewardship are added.

The reading from Amos as well as the gospel take up the problem of wealth, for it can easily lead to greed, cruelty, social injustices and frustration. The in-between reading from Paul's First Letter to Timothy enables us to meditate upon the cure or the preventive medicine, namely, close bonds of prayer and concern.

Amos and the gospel approach the problem of wealth in two, very different ways. Amos is blunt and aggressive, the gospel is indirect and thought-provoking. Sometimes we need the direct speech which hits us between the eyes; at other times we require privacy and space to think and pray. In each instance we are startled, whether by the straight, unmistakable language which condemns injustice (''we fix our scales for cheating''), or by the baffling praise for the dishonest and ingenious steward and by the mystifying one-liners at the end of the gospel.

We tend to have problems with direct speech like Amos' because of its close interconnection with the immediate cultural and political situation. Today we do not speak about the new moon, shekel, ephah and pride of Jacob. To reel with the same stunned conscience as Amos' audience, we must become acquainted with the historical setting. However, if we do not get bogged down with details, Amos will continue to make us squirm at the nerve center of our conscience. How the wealthy can easily be guilty of:

> trampling upon the heads of the needy
> destroying the poor of the land
> fixing the scales for cheating
> selling rotten grain and food stuffs
> convicting the poor for debts as meagre as
>   the cost of sandals
> buying and selling people for money

This is a dreadful litany. God declares: "Never will I forget such a thing!"

The gospel is much less direct; it touches us where we react only a week later! At first it numbs and dazes us. After hearing the long parable about the devious and ingenious steward, we expect the owner to send the army against him. Instead, "the owner gave [him] credit for being enterprising!" Jesus then anticipates our question, "Why?"

In the answer, Jesus gives a general statement, absolutely true, yet with consequences which each one must work out on his own. Why is it, that on my unworldly or spiritual side, I am lazy and indifferent? On my worldly side with ambitions for money and prestige, I take all kinds of initiative. We almost reply to Jesus, "Why not?" except that we still possess that other spiritual side.

Jesus draws another conclusion from the parable of the wily steward:

> Make friends for yourselves through your use of
> this world's goods, so that when they fail you, a
> lasting reception will be yours.

Here we exclaim, "Really! Do you mean it that way, Jesus?" Maybe what Jesus really wants is our serious questioning. Then to our discomfort we will find that we are that wily and greedy. Now Jesus says to us, "Really, do *you* want to be that way?"

It is necessary to think over, not only these concluding statements of the parable, but also the series of one liners, added like an appendix right here to the gospel. The way to conversion is by way of serious self-questioning, interior illumination and final decision. While Amos puts us in a fighting mood, the gospel leaves us with ourselves and our questions.

It is too much to be left alone. The second reading draws us into a bond with others in prayer. Such prayer breaks down barriers and supports us within a family of genuine friends and authentically good people. Our trust in others is restored, even if we have been victimized like the poor in the time of Amos.

In writing to Timothy, his disciple and successor, Paul shows how prayer spirals outward to surround us with an ever growing number of encouraging and trustworthy friends:

- prayers for all men and women, especially for those in civil authority;

- civil peace leads to a new kind of peace: the salvation of all men and women whom God wants to "come to know the truth";

- universal salvation brings the recognition that God is one, and one also is the mediator between God and all people;

- this mediator, "the human being Christ Jesus gave himself as a ransom for all," suffering and dying for each and every person.

- such example leads people "in every place [to] offer prayers with blameless hands held aloft . . . free from anger and dissension."

As we reflect upon these spiraling and interlocking circles, we find ourselves: living within a large family of men and women across the universe; seeking and achieving social justice, so desired by Amos; acting with the ingenuity of the wily steward, only this time in the cause of honesty and justice; dealing with both money and divine matters, yet totally given to God; spiritually intent upon world salvation, yet closely in touch with politics. Prayer unites not only with God and with the human family, but it also induces the piety, dignity and tranquility which are the environment and the reward of social justice.

Prayer:

Lord, we praise you for lifting up the poor. We were once poor and you raised us up from our dunghill of sin and ignorance. As you cleanse our hearts and bring social peace, you are enthroned not only in the heavens but also upon our earth.

Twenty-sixth Sunday, "A" Cycle

Ezek 18:25–28. The Lord defends his ways as fair, condemning the virtuous person who turns to commit iniquity, forgiving the wicked person who turns to do what is right.

Phil 2:1–11. United in spirit and ideals, never acting out of rivalry or conceit, thinking of others as superior, we have the attitude of Christ who humbled himself even to death on the cross and so was highly exalted by God.

Matt 21:28–32. Tax collectors and prostitutes at first say "No!" to God but later regret it and do what God wants. These enter God's kingdom before the self-righteous who say "Yes!" but fail to comply with God's inspiration.

The Scripture for today comforts the sinful and the despised; it levels a strong condemnation against those who appear pious yet fail in good action or who cleverly manipulate religion to their own advantage. Today God speaks to those distant people who are afraid to walk into church, or if they do, they take the last and most inconspicuous place—like the publican (another name for tax collector) in the famous parable of Jesus (Luke 18:9–14).

First of all, God holds his ground against those good people who complain that God is too merciful and too soft towards sinners and therefore too unjust towards them and their piety. In the first reading from Ezekiel, people are bold enough to say, ''The Lord's way is not fair!''

The unethical practice for which God is being accused turns out to be the forgiveness of sinful people. It is not that God scatters pardons like leaflets from an airplane. God expects conversion, that is a change of heart from doing what is wrong to doing what is right. This fact becomes not only clear, but even clear to the point of boredom in the long chapter 18. It covers every possibility:

- the virtuous person who continues in doing what is right, shall live (vv. 5–9);
- the child of the virtuous person who turns into a thief and murderer, shall surely die; death is that one's own fault (vv. 10–13);
- the child of the wicked person, who converts from evil to goodness, ''shall not be charged with the guilt of the parent.'' ''That one shall surely live'' (vv. 14–20);
- the wicked person who ''turns away from all sin . . . shall surely live'' (vv. 21–23);
- ''the virtuous person who turns to do evil and . . . has broken faith . . . shall die'' (v. 24).

It is this point that today's first reading picks up the passage from Ezekiel. The people cry out: ''The Lord's way

is not fair.'' Yet, God does not reject out of hand these
haughty, proud, self-righteous and ''virtuous'' people.
Even they have a chance. Chapter 18 ends with the remarkable statement which allows us to eavesdrop upon the secret
thoughts of God:

> I have no pleasure in the death of anyone who
> dies, the Lord thinks to himself. Return and live!

When Jesus received tax collectors and prostitutes, Jesus was like John the Baptist who blended stern expectations
with abundant kindness. Jesus tells the sinful man or
woman, to sin no more. In saying this, Jesus is professing
divine confidence in the other person: you have ideals and
strength which can turn you from degradation and envelop
your life with innocence and kindliness towards others. In
fact, one of the most prominent themes or symbols in the
Old Testament, released in Israel's traditions by the prophet
Hosea, points out how the adulteress Israel (symbol for sin)
becomes the virgin daughter (symbol for grace)—in Hos
2:21–25 or Jer 31:4.

Like Ezekiel, the prophet Jesus avoids the theological
or theoretical question. He does get into the particularities of
the law regarding outsiders. Even though Jesus himself
never undertook a formal mission to outsiders—he simply
received them when they approached him with persistency
and hope—he was laying the ground-work for the Church's
later outreach to the gentiles. Several times Jesus stated that
he was sent only to the lost sheep of Israel (Matt 10:7;
15:24). Evidently it was more than enough, simply to announce the fulfillment of promises to Israel first. Yet Jesus
was giving flash insights into the future mission to the
world, to be undertaken by his disciples, especially Paul.

Such compassion and optimism towards others will extend our circle of friends in the faith; this attitude will enable us to glimpse possibilities of mission towards the needy and outsider. Our world will expand. Yet, like Jesus we should be ready for opposition and scandal from others. People will cry out against us that the Lord's way, which we follow and announce, is not fair!

Paul offers further, more explicit help in his letter to the Philippians. These were his favorites of all the communities to which he ministered. He speaks of those virtues or attitudes which strengthen our ever widening circle of friends in the faith:

encouragement	unanimity
solace	possessing one love
fellowship in spirit	united in spirit and ideals
compassion	never acting out of rivalry or conceit
pity	think of others as superior

Then your attitude will be that of Christ's. Here Paul introduces a hymn of the early church: the word eternal, equal with God the Father, emptied himself and took the form of a slave, a human likeness, humiliated and humbled to death on the cross and yet exalted at God's right hand, so that every knee in the heavens and on earth and under the earth proclaims: Jesus Christ is Lord! Through these unlikely means of compassion, forgiveness and hope towards outcasts, Jesus becomes the mediator of God's universal kingdom.

Prayer:

Lord, remember in our regard your ancient mercies, not the sins of our youth and weakness. Enable us to be just as forgiving towards one another, that we can be your instruments in extending your kingdom of love and fidelity.

Twenty-sixth Sunday, "B" Cycle

Num 11:25–29. Moses is pleased that the spirit of prophecy is shared with those not immediately present in the first ordination of elders. He reprimands his jealous aide Joshua.

James 5:1–6. Hard words against the wealthy who abused their workers and withheld wages.

Mark 9:38–43, 45, 47–48. Rejoice in everyone who expels demons or works miracles in Jesus' name, even if "not of our company." Scandal and bad leadership will be severely punished. We must adamantly cut away whatever stands in the way of the kingdom of God.

Both Moses in the first reading from Numbers and Jesus in today's gospel defend, in fact they rejoice over gifts of religious leadership in unexpected places. Such leadership is not to be taken lightly even by the one who possesses it more formally by ordination. Jesus utters stern, really harsh words against misusing leadership. Even though Jesus is speaking *metaphorically* about cutting off hands or feet, even gouging out one's eyes, nonetheless, the metaphor stands for something that is absolute and essential, never to be compromised.

While the second reading from the Epistle of James does not parallel the other two readings, especially in the matter of spiritual gifts' showing up outside the circle of immediate disciples, still it offers an insight into another type of abuse of power. James is speaking explicitly of the secular realm of employment, salaries and just recompense for work; Moses and especially Jesus are dealing more with religious leadership.

James is speaking out clearly and forcefully for just wages. If his words are extended to all types of leadership and power over others, that in the family and in the church, almost every adult must sit up and listen carefully. James addresses "you rich," but in this meditation we are thinking of people rich in spiritual authority, gifted in teaching, endowed with children in the family. All of you, James cries out, ought to "weep and wail over your impending miseries." What you have stored up for yourself at the expense of others will become moth-eaten, corroded and a witness against you. "It will devour your flesh like a fire." If students or parishioners, if family members or neighbors have suffered from our abuse of authority, then we ourselves shall weep and wail.

Spiritual authority especially can lead to serious abuses. If we have the reputation of being endowed with God's spirit, if we are the custodians of the laws of right and wrong, if we have been ordained with lifelong rights in mediating God's presence, then our authority is immense and the fear of us awesome. In a different but similar way, parents, teachers and civil leaders also sway their "subjects" with almost unbelievable power.

James writes:

> you lived in wanton luxury on the earth;
> you fattened yourselves for the day of slaughter.

With disdain James compares us leaders to the fattening of animals for slaughter!

Authority must be handled carefully, humbly, and justly. It must also be accepted wherever it shows up. In unexpected ways, God sent the spirit of prophecy upon others who took Moses and later Jesus by surprise. When Moses' aide, Joshua, wanted to squelch this so-called rebellion against authority, Moses replied:

> Are you jealous for my sake? Would that all the
> people were prophets! Would that the Lord might
> bestow his spirit on them all!

In Jesus' days, one of his favorite disciples, John, "tried to
stop" some whom they observed "using your name to expel
demons . . . because he is not of our company." Jesus' reply is as generous as Moses':

> Do not try to stop him. No one who performs a
> miracle using my name can at once speak ill of
> me. Anyone who is not against us is with us.

Jesus then reaches beyond the realm of expelling demons
and working miracles and gets down to the simple matter of
giving "a drink of water because you belong to Christ."
That too "will not go without its reward."

No matter what may be our privileged place of authority, we must always be ready to learn from others, to share
our work with them and so to unify the gifts of the Spirit.
Towards the end of his epistle to the Philippians, Paul puts
no restrictions upon our learning from outsiders:

> Your thoughts ought to be directed to *all* that is
> true, worthy of respect, honest, pure, admirable,
> decent, virtuous or worthy of praise (Phil 4:8).

Mark now adds other words of Jesus against scandal
and the misuse of one's hands, eyes and feet. We are
tempted to see here an abuse of authority, due to our inability to accept the giftedness of others. We make difficulties,
not thinking of others but blindly plunging ahead with feet,
hands and eyes. We ignore God's consecration of their

hands to work, of their eyes to perceive, and of their feet to walk God's special ways. We reject them as outsiders, foreign to our ranks as priests, teachers, parents and employers. Jesus declares it were better if we would cut off or gouge out the consecrated members of our own body! Then we would be forced to recognize the gifts of others and let them be put to good use for the sake of the church, the family, the neighborhood, or the place of employment.

Failure to cooperate is like living ''in wanton luxury on the earth'' and ''being fattened . . . for the day of slaughter.'' ''Better for you to enter the kingdom of God with only one eye, or one foot or one hand, than with both eyes, feet and hands to be thrown into Gehenna.''

Prayer:

Lord, your precepts give joy to the heart. Through the Scriptures enable me to follow you in recognizing the Spirit in others. This will give wisdom, joy and innocence.

Twenty-sixth Sunday, ''C'' Cycle

Amos 6:1, 4–7. A sarcastic condemnation of the men of Samaria, stretched comfortably upon ivory-inlaid couches, yet not heartsick for the moral collapse of the nation.

1 Tim 6:11–16. Seek after integrity, piety, faith, love, steadfastness and a gentle spirit . . . until our Lord Jesus Christ shall appear.

Luke 16:19–31. Parable of Dives and Lazarus. If they do not listen to Moses and the prophets, they will not be convinced if one should rise from the dead.

The Scriptures speak of several gaping chasms or divisions which somehow or other must be bridged to enjoy now and in the future the full glory of Jesus Christ. Very evident in the first and third reading is the dreadful split between the wealthy and the deprived. The destitute may appear close to the well-off and simultaneously light years away. Lazarus lay at the gate of Dives; this name traditionally given to the wealthy man comes from the Latin word for wealth. Interestingly enough, in the original Greek text Lazarus has a more pronounced personality than the non-distinguished wealthy person. The Latin Vulgate was kind enough to give this one a proper name "Dives," the personification of wealth! There is then a new chasm here, over and beyond that of wealth-poverty, the one that separates a striking personality from the sensuous blur of flesh in the other non-person.

This division between the wealthy and the destitute is concentrated particularly in the spirit or attitude. Physically, as just mentioned, Lazarus lay at the gate and in fact appeared along the edge of the dining room where he can catch the crumbs. People were inclined at table with their heads in the inner circle and legs and feet fanning outward. Lazarus and the dogs were situated still further outward.

The same physical closeness yet moral and attitudinal distance show up in the reading from Amos. The prophet condemns the ancient form of massage parlor or restricted country club where men "drink wine from bowls and are anointed with the finest oils," "stretched comfortably upon their ivory encrusted couches." The destitute are touching the wealthy with tender massage, yet also with disdain and anger!

If the real chasm is moral and spiritual within a context of earthly, physical proximity, then the solution comes from social justice, human sensitivity, and religious bonds. Religion, in fact, ought to be the leveling factor which not only bridges the chasm but fills it in, so that everyone lives with respect for others and in open communication.

Each group, the poor and the wealthy, stand in need of conversion. The anger and sarcasm, bursting the seams of Amos' sentences, are waiting to be healed by the forgiveness and concern voiced by the poor, sickly Lazarus and the calm, honest Abraham. From their heavenly home where both are reclined at banquet, they are willing to converse across the chasm with Dives. The final judgment has already taken place for Dives and cannot be reversed, yet there is hope for Dives' five brothers on earth, even if they are continuing the same sensuous lifestyle and the same supreme indifference towards the destitute. When Dives requested a messenger from heaven to warn them, Abraham replied: "They have Moses and the prophets. Let them listen to them."

Abraham shows a calm compassion, a willingness to forgive and cooperate. Yet the gospel also insists upon the prayerful reading of Moses and the prophets. The five books of Moses contain not only laws but also innumerable stories for understanding the laws. The prophetic books continue to judge and interpret, threaten or bless later periods of Israel's history from the ideals and expectations of the covenant and laws of Moses.

The prophet Amos supplies yet another ingredient for closing the gap, an element which is difficult to explain properly. Amos speaks with anger and sarcasm. From the example of Lazarus, such interior violence and disturbed speech are not the ultimate norm for action in the cause of the destitute. Sooner or later we must change from violence to what the First Letter to Timothy calls "a gentle spirit." Yet, there are too many prophetic books of outrage and blistering attack, for us to deny a place in God's plans for such turbulent and stern reaction. The Bible at least is advising us that such explosive situations are part of God's providence and must be dealt with. Only in this radical way at times can our elegant unconcern and deadened conscience be awakened. The prophet Isaiah calls these savage attacks, in God's name, ''my arm in anger, my staff in wrath'' (Isa 10:5). When the people of Jerusalem refuse to be disciplined and punished but rather continue in their violations of justice, Isaiah repeats the refrain over and over again:

> For all this God's wrath is not turned back, God's
> hand is still outstretched! (Isa 9:11, 16, 20).

The refrain also occurs after a series of ''Woes!'' (Isa 5:8–25).

From the continuous reading of Scripture still other norms are provided for filling in the gap between the insensitive wealthy and the angry destitute. Paul's words to Timothy read like a litany of biblical virtues to which we add a refrain of prayer and petition, ''Lord, grant them to us'':

integrity	love
piety	steadfastness
faith	gentle spirit

''Gentle spirit'' is the culmination of the other virtues. If there is integrity between one's own flesh and the suffering bodies of the destitute, integrity between one's prayer to God and one's response to the prayers of the needy, then faith is authentic and piety is genuine. These virtues lead to love and steadfastness. Such a person, integral, loving and steadfast, knows how to respond with the gentle spirit.

These virtues are to be practiced on earth and within the

earthly situation of social justice, family relationships, food and jobs. Yet at the end of the road we meet death, the door into eternity, the appearance of "our Lord Jesus Christ . . . at his chosen time." Here the chasm between earth and heaven, between time and eternity, is closed. An integral life on earth means a firm faith in heaven and the reunion at the heavenly banquet table. We possess a moment of this "unapproachable light" in our eucharist when God, "whom no human being has ever seen or can see," is already present with us in Jesus who lived, died and rose to glory.

Prayer:

Lord, let my heavenly joy and praise begin here on earth, as with you we secure justice for the oppressed, food for the hungry, freedom for captives, sight for the blind, protection for strangers. In such a kingdom you reign for ever.

Twenty-seventh Sunday, "A" Cycle

Isa 5:1–7. The song of a vineyard. It was lovingly cared for but severely punished when it yielded only wild grapes.

Phil 4:6–9. Direct your thoughts to all that is honest, admirable, decent and worthy of praise. Live according to what you have heard me say and have seen me do.

Matt 21:33–43. Because the caretakers of the vineyard reject the owner's emissaries and even kill his son, the tenants will be punished and the vineyard leased to others.

God has been generous and loving in confiding the finest gifts to us. These are to be protected, nourished and cared for, so that we can return the abundant harvest to God.

We are the vineyard! We can rejoice in our gifts, but we must also remember that the gifts are bestowed on loan and God expects good fruit from his vineyard. The responsibility is very serious.

We are the vineyard in Isaiah's prophecy. This chapter five of the prophecy rings with exquisite tones in the Hebrew; it is a song of delicate beauty. It begins with haunting sounds: *'ashirah na' lididi—shirath dodi lekarmo/kerem hayah lididi, beqeren benshamen.*

The charm of Isaiah's language—here the golden touch of the master Hebrew poet glistens beautifully—equals, if that were possible, the gracious and affectionate concern of God for the chosen people Israel:

> My friend [literally, my beloved] had a vineyard
>   on a fertile hillside;
> he spaded it, cleared it of stones,
>   and planted the choicest vines;
> Within it he built a watchtower,
>   and hewed out a wine press.

God has left nothing unimagined and undone in creating us and showering us with gifts—gifts of life, insight and inspiration; gifts of hope and ambition; gifts of loving others and being loved; gifts of sharing life and participating in the life of others; gifts of prayer and contemplative silence; gifts of strength and conviction to preserve goodness in others.

The prophet Isaiah portrays God thoroughly disappointed: "he looked for the crop of grapes, but what it yielded was wild grapes." Wild grapes multiply when the vineyard is not properly tended. God is disappointed in us when we lazily sit back and allow weeds to grow. In other words God expects us to recognize the dignity of our gifts, the beauty of our lives, the joy of our families and neighborhoods. The lazy indifferent person is properly condemned.

If we read the gospel at this point, we realize that Scripture is not so much denouncing our mistakes, our excesses, our misdirected energy. It seems that God can deal with these types of sins more sympathetically than the sins of sloth and stupor which let anything happen that happens. We recall the anger of another prophet, Amos, excoriating those "lying upon beds of ivory, stretched comfortably on their couches . . . yet not heartsick for the collapse of Joseph!" (Amos 6:4,6)—See the 26th Sunday, "C" Cycle.

According to the gospels, God sends a series of messengers or emissaries whom we know to be prophets. We are given many chances to turn and serve the Lord actively and obediently. The gospel parable states how these messengers were treated: "they beat one, killed another, and stoned a third." God even sends another series, "more than before, but they treated them the same way." At this point the Scripture listens closely to the heartbeat of God who says within that sacred silence: "They will respect my son." "Finally, he sent his son to them."

Yet God was mistaken! They did not respect God's own child, Jesus, the word incarnate. We are those people, "crucifying again for themselves the son of God" (Heb 6:6), when we ignore those most special times of grace. We all recognize those decisive moments, those particular appeals, those turns of our conscience, those insights of new beginnings in our lives, those gracious opportunities of reconciliation with God or with our neighbor. Those are the occasions when God allows us to place our ears close to God's heart and to listen in amazement as though to a divine soliloquy: "They will respect my child, Jesus."

Jesus may come to us in an unexpected way, in the advice of a friend or family-member, in a sermon, in silence, in the reading of Scripture, "out of the mouth of babes and sucklings" (Ps 8:3). In today's reading from Philippians, Paul outlines all the possibilities where God can speak to us through Jesus:

> . . . be wholly directed to all that is true, all that deserves respect, all that is honest, pure, admirable, decent, virtuous, or worthy of praise. Live according to what you have heard me say and seen me do.

"In fragmentary and varied ways [and finally] through his Son," God speaks (Heb 1:1–2). In this approach of God towards us, "There does not exist among you Jew or Greek, slave or freeperson, male or female [for] all are one in Christ Jesus." We must be alert to every facet of our own lives, our immediate family and neighborhood; we must be ready to hear Jesus speak through "Jew or Greek, slave or free, male or female." Paul also includes "what you have learned and accepted, what you have heard me say and seen me do." In this integral wholeness of our lives that includes ancient traditions and new expressions, God speaks to us, so that we can properly attend to our vineyard and produce good grapes, not wild grapes.

We must absorb and integrate within ourselves the word of God; "good grapes" grow from the vineyard which is nourished by the word of God.

Prayer:

Lord, we are your vineyard. Take care of us, protect us, give us always new life, send new messengers. Overcome our stubbornness so that we can listen, be converted and produce good fruit.

Twenty-seventh Sunday, ''B''Cycle

Gen 2:18–24. The creation of man and woman, their vocation to become two in one flesh and to be suitable partners
  for each other.

Heb 2:9–11. Jesus is perfected through suffering and tastes
  death for all. So, he is not ashamed to call them brothers
  and sisters.

Mark 10:2–16. Jesus prohibits divorce and remarriage and
  compares the kingdom of God to those who are like little
  children.

Today we celebrate hopes and ideals, particularly for
marriage. We can approach marriage in many different
ways: the equal responsibilities and rights of husbands and
wives; the obligations of responsible parenthood—to name
but two of the topics related to marriage. Hopes and ideals,
however, are always more appropriate matter for meditation
than difficulties and obligations!

The reading from Genesis, which is the second biblical
account about creation in the Book of Genesis, situates the
origin of sexuality and marriage in the first paradise. Jesus'
words in the Gospel of Mark for today explain our responsibility to seek through marriage the new paradise. Our second reading from the Epistle to the Hebrews admits the
difficulties along the way till we become truly and fully
God's children, gloriously consecrated as brothers and sisters of Jesus in the new paradise.

Along with the pain which accompanies every close
friendship and especially the bonds of marriage, other difficulties show up in today's readings. We mention them, not
so much to solve them in this single meditation but rather to
recognize their existence. Such honesty, we feel, is healthy

for authentic religious living. A not-so-subtle form of male favoritism pervades the reading from Genesis. Man, not woman, occupies the center of attention. Woman seems to be taken from man and created for man; therefore man leaves father and mother and clings to his wife. Nothing is said directly about woman's leaving her father and mother, nor is it stated that man is made for her sake. Part of the problem here lies in our English translations, and in our inability to absorb new scholarly studies into our translations. We leave these problems for another time of the day! Sufficient now to state that the first account of creation in chapter one of Genesis places woman and man co-equal in the timing and in the dignity of their creation:

> God created humankind to the divine image;
> in the divine image God created them;
> male and female God created them (Gen 1:27).

As we turn to the ideals of marriage in the first paradise, we discover that nothing on earth is to be preferred to one's spouse. Even after God showed the entire universe to the first human being and even stirred the remembrance of mother and father, a feeling of loneliness and separation swept over humankind. Nothing proved to be a suitable partner.

According to this ideal, spouses are to place their partner in marriage and their family before everything else—before their work and jobs and advancement, before their wealth, leisure and enjoyment. The bond of union between husband and wife makes them one person. Consequently, they are to approach problems and questions single-mindedly. Neither surrenders to the other; together in sharing ideas and judgments they arrive at what is best. The best, therefore, is not that which is theoretically best from a purely objective viewpoint. The best is the combination of what is subjectively helpful to the stability, respect, peace and (more spiritually) to the prayer, generosity and patience of the spouses.

In today's gospel Jesus reaffirms this ideal. He admits that the Mosaic law permitted the husband to divorce under careful restrictions. Jesus does not repudiate the Mosaic law at this point, but he decidedly states that such legal possibilities do not reflect the divine ideal for marriage. Jesus proceeds still more stringently and places husband and wife on an equal basis. *Neither one* can divorce and remarry.

Again, it is prudent and honest to mention that this divorce clause had a dramatic history already in New Testament times. Matthew and Paul (Matt 5:32; 19:9; 1 Cor 7:10 –16) already add the famous ''exception'' clauses. Here we are attending to the ideal, not to the exceptions for human weakness.

The second reading from Hebrews strengthens and protects the ideal still more resolutely. Marriage has been compared to Christ's incarnation when the eternal Word of God became ''one flesh'' with flesh and blood received from Mary. Together Word and flesh became the one person, Our Lord Jesus Christ. Biblically this union is considered in still another way, when Christ unites himself in the church with men and women of faith. St. Paul compares this union to a marriage bond (Eph 5:25–32).

So intimately is Jesus one with us, closer than in the happiest and most satisfying marriage, that we read in the Epistle to the Hebrews:

> through God's gracious will he tasted death for the sake of all men and women . . . through suffer-

ing God made perfect the leader in our work of salvation.

If the Greek text is studied carefully, we find a delicate nuance of meaning: Christ was being perfected through suffering. Christ was being ever more fully united with us and experiencing every aspect of our human existence, ''even temptation,'' the Epistle to the Hebrews adds in another place (Heb 4:15).

The return to paradise is through intimate union; this union includes the way of the cross. Through love we embrace the cross of Jesus. Suffering does not destroy and deaden; it brings us to new depths of mystery in our love for one another. Strange but true, this kind of suffering tempers our anger and impetuosity, it softens our sternness and argumentative nature. It gradually makes us ''like children,'' spontaneous in love, not counting the cost, risking everything, happiest when in the arms of another, dreaming with no restrictions on hopes. ''To such as these the kingdom of God belongs.''

This new paradise is wondrously attractive and terribly demanding. Little surprise then if the disciples scolded the parents who brought their children to Jesus. The disciples were not yet ready for this grand ideal of human love in the new paradise. Jesus was ready and he places the hope and ideal before us this day.

Prayer:

Lord, bless us in all the days of our lives. Then each moment, whether of joy or sorrow, will favor us with closer bonds of union. Our paradise appears in our children, like olive plants around our table.

Twenty-seventh Sunday, "C" Cycle

Hab 1:2–3; 2:2–4. To the prophet's questioning about the success of the wicked, God finally replies that the just person lives by faith.

2 Tim 1:6–8, 13–14. Stir into flame the grace given to you. It is no cowardly spirit. Guard the rich deposit of faith.

Luke 17:5–10. The apostles pray, "Lord, increase our faith." Faith, Jesus replies, can remove mountains. Yet when you have done all that is commanded, say, "We are useless servants."

We need all three readings to put the matter of faith in proper perspective. Faith places in us goals and hopes, even demands and expectations which reach far beyond our unaided human stamina. In this context we can begin to understand Jesus' enigmatic statement: "When you have done all you have been commanded to do, say, 'We are useless servants.' " Our efforts have hardly measured up to the final results of God's grace in us.

The goal is to be reached by ourselves, body and soul as we are; we are not whisked off planet earth and dropped into paradise. Therefore, Paul writes to the disciple Timothy: "Stir into flame the gift of God. [It is] no cowardly spirit, but rather one that makes us strong, loving and wise." *We* are parties to the achievement which God's spirit accomplishes in us and through us. Yet it is not easy, admittedly so, and many times we are hounded by questions. The prophet Habakkuk voices our questions, so that God eventually brings us back to the center: "The just person lives by faith."

We need to unpack this heavy but important biblical message about faith in these three readings. We need to delay over each reading, for the answer lies in between the words.

The apostles sense the extreme difficulty of the Christian vocation. It is not that each day ushers in a pain like martyrdom, even if this be the case for some people afflicted with physical ailments, imprisoned unjustly, or victimized by racial prejudice. At the halfway point of Luke's gospel, we see Jesus with his face resolutely set towards Jerusalem where he will be crucified. Still, the tone is one of peaceful instruction. If faith has become a serious problem, it is not so much by the pain which it inflicts but rather by the wondrous goals which it inspires. There are goals of patience, forgiveness, avoidance of scandal, humility, prudent use of financial resources, etc. These are the everyday topics of Luke's gospel in chapters 15 through 19.

Yet, each of these virtues is seen in an extraordinary light, in heroic proportions. We cry out, "Lord, increase our faith." Put another way, our words almost complain to God that it is too much for us and that we are willing to settle for less and be content at that.

Jesus' answer is right to the point: every dream will be fulfilled. God grants us no good desires which will not in one way or another reach a fulfillment beyond our best dreams. Jesus answered:

> If you had faith the size of a mustard seed, you could say to this sycamore, "Be uprooted and transplanted into the sea," and it would obey you.

Furthermore, "when you have done all you have been commanded to do, say, 'We are useless servants. We have done no more than our duty.' " At the end, when dreams come true, the results will far exceed our abilities and in amazement we will cry out, ''I have done nothing, except what it was only my duty to do!''

There is a bit of rhetoric in this language. At many moments along the way, we would have said it differently. We would have been feeling the cramp in our overworked muscles, the strain upon our patience, the worry about our pocketbook, the anxiety about children and family and community.

Paul addresses these earlier moments of distress. In writing to Timothy, Paul does not back down any more than Jesus did. In the larger setting of the opening chapter to Second Timothy, Paul speaks nostalgically:

- recalling your tears when we parted . . .
- thinking of your sincere faith . . .
- faith of your grandmother Lois and your mother Eunice, faith which I am confident you also have.

Within this lovely home setting, Paul can proceed to great expectations:

- stir into flame the gift of God
- no cowardly spirit, but rather one that makes us strong, loving and wise
- never be ashamed of your testimony to our Lord, nor of me.
- bear your share of the hardship which the gospel entails.

Paul verifies this demand from his own experience: ''In the service of the gospel . . . I undergo present hardships, but I am not ashamed. [Rather] I am confident.'' Paul then concludes:

- Guard the rich deposit of faith
- with the help of the Holy Spirit who dwells within us.

There must have been some faltering and stumbling on Timothy's part that Paul should write this eloquently. Just how Timothy was feeling may be found in the first reading from the prophet Habakkuk. If prophets ever had nicknames, Habakkuk's would have been like the apostle Thomas; the ''Doubter,'' or like ourselves, the ''Complainer''! Habakkuk announces the word of God; all prophets did that. Yet, he speaks in an unusual way. Instead of the word of God being a message or oracle from God to us, it is now our question put to God:

How long, O Lord? . . . you do not listen! . . .
Why do you let me see ruin?

When God answers that question, Habakkuk is not satisfied. Again the word of God to us in the Bible is identified with the prophet's second question put to God:

Why then do you gaze on the faithless in silence
while wicked persons devour
one more just than themselves?

If these questions, the prophet's and our own are in the inspired Bible, then they contain a message from God for us! Questioning helps us plummet the depths of faith. The second question remains unanswered. The prophet is left in silence. Yet in that awesome silence, a message is written on a billboard in letters so large (as the Hebrew text puts it) that one can read it on the run! "The Just person lives by faith." It will remove sycamore trees into the sea and bring us to a fulfillment beyond our best efforts. Joyfully, we feel like useless servants; the reward is far beyond our labors.

Prayer:

Lord, today I hear your voice. You speak in my questions and temptations. Do not let my heart be hardened. Through faith lead me to the promised land where I can find rest.

Twenty-eighth Sunday, "A" Cycle

Isa 25:6–10. The prophet announces the heavenly banquet for all peoples. Tears will be wiped away by the Lord God; death will be destroyed for ever.

Phil 4:12–14, 19–20. Paul appreciates the generous help of the Philippians who kindly shared in his hardships. God will supply their needs fully.

Matt 22:1–14. The invited guests refuse to attend the king's wedding banquet for his son, so guests are drawn from the byroads. One of these is punished for not having on the proper attire.

Feasting symbolizes heaven. The abundance of the food, the surprise of being invited, the gracious kindness shown to guests are among the colorful threads which are woven into the table cloth for the banquet table. The gospel adds some somber notes. First, we notice the sad lot of those who refuse the invitation, even to the point of murdering the king's servants. Then we are startled how one of those brought in from the byroads, almost at random, is severely punished for not being properly attired for the wedding.

While the gospel and another reading from Isaiah refer to the final, eschatological banquet, and Paul to his daily sustenance, all three biblical selections can be interpreted of the Holy Eucharist. The Eucharist is at once food for the daily journey, the prophets' reward in their quest for justice, a foretaste of heaven.

The reading from Isaiah climaxes a long prophetic career of several generations. It is quite likely that the passage in chapter 25 comes from the post-exilic period, somewhere around 350 B.C. The author was in the line of inheritance from First Isaiah who prophesized severe punishment upon Jerusalem and the Davidic dynasty for neglecting social justice and faith in God as savior. Second Isaiah, author of chapters 40–55, announced to the poor and needy a return to their promised land, once the exile is over. During the post-exilic age chapters 56–66 were added at the end and new sections were spliced here and there into the earlier parts. Chapters 24 to 27 is one of these latter.

Like the other parts of Isaiah, therefore in full continuity with tradition, yet also adapting and advancing the tradition, this ''new'' Isaiah speaks of God as:

> home for the poor,
> refuge for the needy in distress,
> shelter from the rain, shade from the heat (Isa 25:4).

If we, the poor and discouraged people of God, retain our faith-confidence in God, then by faith we will move mountains and sycamore trees which stand in the way (1 Cor 13:2; Luke 17:6). We will find ourselves at a ''feast of rich food and choice wines.''

At the Eucharist we are nourished with the word of God and with the body and blood of the Word Incarnate. Here we acquire the nourishment to share ourselves with others as Jesus does with us. Here we overcome all barriers of race and prestige, for we are *all* the "needy" looking for shelter. The Eucharist not only rewards social justice but is itself a new inducement to share still further with God's poor. Thus every tear is wiped away and death is overcome.

The reading from Philippians, in a somewhat humorous application, can be linked with the weekly collection, taken up at the Sunday Eucharist! In the larger context of the fourth and last chapter of this epistle, Paul even complains that "not a single congregation except yourselves shared with me by giving me something for what it had received" through my ministry. To his beloved Philippians he then says: "I am well supplied because of what I received from you through Epaphroditus . . . "

More seriously, Paul can live peacefully and "cope with every circumstance—now to eat well or go hungry, to be well provided for or do without" through Jesus "who is the source of my strength." This Jesus we receive and are intimately united with in the Eucharist. Jesus in the Eucharist gathers us with the wealthy and the poor, so that a natural confidence and healthy spontaneity accompany us in life. We live as one family in Christ Jesus. Like Paul, we are not ashamed to ask for what we truly need, and we are privileged to share what we possess. Thus we share in one another's hardships and we supply one another's needs "in a way worthy of God's magnificent riches in Christ Jesus."

The Eucharist is not only the pledge and reward of social justice; it is more than food for the journey of our life ministry. The Eucharist is also our pledge of heavenly joy. This symbolism was already present in the prophecy of Isaiah; it is all the more prominent in the gospel.

The gospel alludes to the long history of the chosen people and now by extension to our own history. God sends a series of prophets and emissaries to invite us repeatedly to the banquet. Refusal only prompts God to extend the invitation to people along the byroads. Human jealousy or pride will not stop God's generous outreach, only stir it to a still freer invitation.

Yet, when we are invited on such easy terms, we ought not to take advantage of our generous host. Throughout our lives God forgives us repeatedly. New prophets stir new ideals. Repeatedly we refuse, and God calls again. When we answer, God rightly expects us to wear the proper attire, that is, to be clothed with charity for others, with concern and politeness, with humble service to others. We are reminded of the importance of charity and humility to participate in the heavenly banquet of the Eucharist.

Prayer:

Lord, you have led me through dark valleys and now in your home you anoint my head with oil and spread a table of abundance before me. Lord, let me live in your house for ever, with all your family.

Twenty-eighth Sunday, ''B'' Cycle

Wis 7:7–11. I pleaded, and the spirit of wisdom came to me, and in her company all good things.

Heb 4:12–13. God's word is sharper than any two-edged sword. It judges the thoughts of the heart. Nothing is concealed. For everything we must render an account.

Mark 10:17–30. One thing more you must do. Go and sell what you have and give to the poor. Whatever we have given up to follow Jesus, will return to us a hundred more in this life, plus persecution, and in the age to come, everlasting life.

Today's biblical selections reduce voluminous pages of Scripture to the "one thing necessary" (Luke 10:42). This desire for simplicity and directness was shared with the rabbis. One of them, Rabbi Simlai in the third century of the Christian or common era, declares that the 613 commandments of the Torah are reduced to 11 in Psalm 15, while Isa 33:15 further refines them to 6, Mic 6:8 gets the number down to 3, and once again in Isaiah (56:1) a still smaller number of 2, and finally Amos and Habakkuk read only a single command: "Seek the Lord and live" (Amos 5:4) and "the just shall live by faith" (Hab 2:4).

In today's passage from Mark, Jesus begins with 10 commandments, but on further discussion with the man who ran up to Jesus, these are synthesized into the one demand: "Go and sell what you have and give it to the poor." At times we need all the direction that we can get, everyone of Moses' 613 commandments to keep on the right path. Each person, even those advanced in living the gospel and for a long time faithful to the Holy Spirit, is occasionally caught in a whirlwind of temptation and spiritual blindness. On such occasions we need to be told *exactly* what is right and what is wrong.

There are other moments when God is calling us to greater holiness: that is, to greater patience, to more generous sharing of time and resources, to a purer service of the poor. Jesus is saying to us:

One thing more you must do. Go and . . .

The completion of the sentence can vary. Maybe it is as simple as, "Go and forgive your brother or sister," or again "Go and undertake volunteer work at the county hospital or the local jail," or once more "Go and be more patient with your family or community."

At such moments of grace, as we are told in the second reading, "God's word is sharper than any two-edged sword, penetrating and dividing soul and spirit, judging the reflections and thoughts of the heart." We may not be able to explain why an inspiration of grace, long dormant within us, suddenly leaps up and declares to us: "Go and do this, at once." Perhaps the word of God comes to us in most unexpected ways. This eruption of the word seems to be implied by the passage in the epistle to the Hebrews. The preceding section was insisting upon "*Today* if you hear his voice." "God once more set a day [and it is this] 'Today.'" (Heb 3:7, 15; 4:7).

We cannot trifle nor put off. It is today, not yesterday nor tomorrow, when we must act upon the grace. This "today" may be sprung upon us by an occasional word from a friend, a sermon in church, a remark which triggers memory—all the many ways by which the two-edged sword penetrates and divides. God thus lays bare and we must render an account of this opportunity.

At other times we pray and plead with God for prudence and wisdom. For quite some time we seem to drift, not knowing what to do, when, or how. All that we can react upon is a vague desire, a sense that something must be done, but what? As we read further from the first selection, we begin to understand the conditions for wisdom and good judgment. What we are seeking must be preferred

> to scepter and throne,
> to riches which seem nothing in comparison,
> to health and comeliness.

We are back again to that special moment of grace. This is not any time of the day, but a crucial turning point in our life.

As we pray and plead with God, we begin to see that this new grace or inspiration will reorganize our lives with new vision and purpose. It is the two-edged sword reaching deeply and revealing the best within us. If we are willing to sacrifice everything for its sake, then God imparts true wisdom. We discover that we have lost nothing. It is only that we see and possess everything from a new slant. As the sage wrote at the end of the first selection in today's mass:

> All good things together come to me in wisdom's company, and countless riches at her hands.

Prayer:
Teach us, O Lord, to number our days aright that we may gain wisdom of heart. Then through this insight from you we are filled with your kindness, joy and gladness all our days. We are glad, Lord, for the times when you afflicted us, for our longing has come true.

Twenty-eighth Sunday, "C" Cycle

2 Kings 5:14–17. Naaman washes in the River Jordan and is cured of leprosy. He takes some of the earth of Israel home with him, in order to worship only the Lord as God.

2 Tim 2:8–13. Though Paul is in chains, the word of God cannot be chained. God will always remain faithful, for he cannot deny himself.

Luke 17:11–19. Of the ten lepers who were cured, only the Samaritan returned to give thanks. "Your faith has been your salvation."

Today we turn towards the foreigner or the outsider. Certainly the first and third reading about the Syrian general

Naaman and the Samaritan leper focus our attention upon the salvation and faith of the person on the fringe, the forgotten man or woman, the impossible one, the hopeless one, the no-person, the outcast. What can be worse than a Samaritan leper. While lepers were ostracized from normal society, this Samaritan would have been despised even by other lepers! This excessive isolation may have been his salvation, enabling him to think independently and then to break rank from the other nine to give thanks to God. Strangely, this Samaritan leper without a name eventually shows up with a more distinctive personality than the Syrian general named Naaman. The interaction with Jesus made the difference.

In meditating upon these scriptures and this topic, it is helpful to remember that some part of ourselves may be the outsider or the rejected outcast. This stranger within us may be an inspiration, wonderful in itself yet very difficult in its demands: for instance, to step forward and act for the sake of a defenseless person, or to undertake a difficult response to others, like forgiveness, or help, or concern, or just a listening ear. The ''foreign'' part in ourselves can be an inspiration to spend more time at prayer. Unfortunately, we can cast it aside with a shrug, ''Not me!''

The outsider may literally be a foreigner or stranger whom we habitually ignore or even reject. Or again this person may be our own self. The outsider can come forward from the woodwork or from the creaks in our bones! Since it involves a very special inspiration and belongs to our deepest personality, we need direction to recognize the stranger!

The first quality, strangely enough, is gratitude. A grateful person is usually that one who does not take anything for granted. Such people have an eye to see what is being done for them. They realize the long preparations before they sit down to eat! The careful planning before a family reunion or a parish bazaar makes them appreciate the unnamed workers behind the scenes. These grateful people, therefore, discover what most of us overlook, and they express their joy and appreciation.

Grateful people are usually optimistic people. They can anticipate the good which others are capable of doing. Not only the Samaritan but all ten lepers saw in Jesus the kindly person capable and willing to heal their disease. Similarly, some people have the wonderful insight to see and encourage great potential in others. They can turn the useless outcast into a ''miracle worker.'' They thus make it possible for others to find themselves. This kind of optimism, perhaps, is what Jesus meant by faith, faith in others as gifted by God. Jesus addressed the Samaritan, ''Stand up and go your way; your faith has been your salvation.''

In the first reading, Naaman also turns out to be a grateful individual. After he was cleansed of leprosy, ''he returned with his retinue . . . and declared: 'Now I know that there is no God in all the earth except in Israel. Please accept a gift from your servant.' ''

By gratitude then we are disposed to recognize talents and good dispositions in others, which they may have been overlooking and reducing to ''outsiders.'' Moreover, with all the more enthusiasm we honor this hidden part of them when we attribute the gift to *God's* generosity. The Samaritan ''came back praising God.'' Namaan declared that his cure shows ''that there is no God . . . except in Israel.'' Such praise of God not only enhances the hidden gift in the other person, but it also gives a note of urgency to act upon it. What God has graciously placed at the depth of our personality must not be overlooked nor squandered without paying the penalty of bypassing or suppressing one's truest and finest self, that trait by which our personality blossoms.

A good memory is also important to recognize the outsider and to allow this hidden aspect of ourselves or of others to reach full maturity. Memory is the ability to draw upon the best of one's life and one's tradition. Memory says: look what wonderful things you have already done; this proves you can do still more wonderful things, so don't give up. Memory is at the heart of biblical religion as we recall God's great redemptive acts and repeat them ''in remembrance of me.'' Naaman does not want ever to forget. When the prophet Elijah refused the gift,

> Naaman replied: ''If you will not accept, please let me, your servant, have two mule-loads of earth, for I will no longer offer holocaust or sacrifice to any other god except to the Lord.''

Naaman wanted this tangible remembrance of the promised land, so as to worship this God of many promises and hopes. Naaman would never again want to be the outsider but rather would continuously locate the stranger in himself or in others and bring them ''home'' to this little plot of promised earth.

Finally, as inferred at the beginning of our meditation, we are often afraid to locate the stranger for fear of the demands upon us. At the very least the outsider will upset our schedule; normally this castoff will require much attention. In some real way it imprisons us. It may even put upon us some of its ignominy and shame. We become contaminated by the leper and by the foreigner. Such too was the case of Paul in writing to Timothy:

> In preaching the gospel I suffer as a criminal, even to the point of being thrown into chains.

Paul immediately adds:

> But there is no chaining the word of God. There-
> fore, I bear with all of this for the sake of those
> whom God has chosen . . . to be found in Christ
> Jesus and . . . eternal glory.

Our suffering on earth enables the stranger and outsider
to find themselves, their true self, their hidden potential.
What was hidden is found for eternal glory. Paul also infers
the magnificent possibility that we who preach the gospel
will rediscover that gospel when by gratitude, by faith, and
by remembrance we bring to light God's wonderful gifts
hidden in ourselves and in others.

Prayer:
Lord, you reveal your saving power and wondrous
deeds when you enable us to recognize new goodness in ourselves and in others. At this remembrance of your kindness
and faithfulness, we sing to you a new song.

Twenty-ninth Sunday, "A" Cycle

Isa 45:1, 4–6. Cyrus the Persian conqueror is anointed by
the Lord, even without knowing it, to release Israel from
captivity and to bring the name of the Lord before the
world.

1 Thess 1:1–5. Paul thanks God for bestowing faith, love
and hope upon the Thessalonians, proving that his
preaching of the Gospel was done with power.

Matt 22:15–21. Give to Caesar what is Caesar's, give to
God what is God's.

The reading from Isaiah recognizes how the secular government, even without realizing it, advances the plans of God. Such at least was the case of the Persian Cyrus the Great who decreed the end of the exile, allowing the Israelites to return to their homeland. The gospel reading, on the contrary, seems to cut a clean line between the sacred and the secular. Once again the second reading mediates between the two positions.

The first reading is taken from the prophecy of the "Great Unknown," whose speeches of golden poetry were attached to the prophecies and traditions stemming from Isaiah of Jerusalem. Chapters 1–39 were thus extended into chaps. 40–55. From the very beginning and throughout the preaching of "Second Isaiah," the new exodus or return to the homeland remained the major motif. Thus this prophet, unnamed but inspired, fulfills God's opening commission to "comfort, oh give comfort to my people" (Isa 40:1), by crying out:

> In the desert prepare the way of the Lord! . . .
> every valley shall be filled in,
> every mountain and hill shall be made low (Isa
>   40:3–4).

This electrifying language, sweeping across the panorama of the universe so that the "glory of the Lord shall be revealed" (Isa 40:5), does not proceed, as one would expect, by continuous, colossal miracles. Excitement and grandeur are continuously enveloping each poem or sermon, yet the actual style of fulfillment turns out to be as human as can be! In today's passage Cyrus does not even know the Lord nor himself as the Lord's instrument. In verses 4 and 5 God parenthetically yet significantly remarks about Cyrus:

"though you knew me not." Cyrus acts as any military commander or governmental agent should act. The religious part of Cyrus attributed victory to his own gods rather than to Yahweh. Cyrus was a man of his own time, yet creative and innovative on the secular level so as to inaugurate an empire of almost three hundred years' duration.

For our purposes right now the secular, governmental actions of Cyrus were recognized by Second Isaiah as God's instrument for Israel's benefit. Through the darkness of war, exile and enslavement for Israel as well as through the light of new decrees and migrations homeward, through all these secular accomplishments of Cyrus, Second Isaiah announced the hand of God. Today's first reading actually concludes with a verse, omitted in the liturgy:

> I am the Lord, there is no other;
>   I form the light, and create the darkness,
> I make well-bring [literally, *shalom* or peace]
>   and create woe;
>   I, the Lord, do all these things (Isa 45:6–7).

The gospel seems to take a different approach towards politics and secular events. Jesus declares: "Give to Caesar what is Caesar's, but give to God what is God's." As a matter of fact, the translation of the *New American Bible* which we are quoting makes the cut between the two sections all the cleaner with the expression: "Give to Caesar . . . *but* give to God . . . " It almost read, "but on the contrary, give to God." The Greek text, while intending diversity, nonetheless reads with the simple "and."

To place the gospel statement in context we recall that Jesus' enemies are beginning "to plot how they might trip [him] in speech." Jesus quickly intuited this collusion among Pharisees and Herodians, once absolute enemies, and ''recognized their bad faith.'' On such occasions we detect less the hand of God and more accurately the presence of the devil. Rather than cooperate with evil or innocently accept it as God's will, we summon as much ingenuity as we possess, and silence or shame the opposition, as Jesus did.

Jesus' words still need to be interpreted, clear as they may seem to be. For instance, Jesus is not inferring that our giving to Caesar in taxation or in government employment is necessarily ungodly; nor is Jesus telling us that only what is purely spiritual can be considered godly. Giving to Caesar, then, is godly; giving to God benefits Caesar! To determine the proper interpretation and application of Jesus' statement, we too like Jesus need to take into consideration the immediate circumstances: are they plotting against us? or does it appear that they are cooperative or at least well-meaning?

Paul's letter to the Thessalonians, quoted in the second reading, offers us further help in applying Jesus' words to our everyday life. Whatever we do, Paul advises us, whether in the family or at work, whether in secular or spiritual moments of activity, we should be:

thanking God	laboring in love
remembering in prayer	strong in hope
proving our faith by constancy	acting out of complete conviction

These qualities integrate the secular and the spiritual; they enable us to accomplish the secular in a way best for the secular arena and without a doubt sanctifying us in a spiritual way.

As we reflect still further on this relation of the secular and the spiritual, upon what we give to Caesar and what we give to God, we find that the normal setting for the spiritual is provided by the secular. By secular we simply mean the world round about us, as we obviously see it and require no special revelation to know that it is there: our home and our neighbors, our streets and roads and what comes down them to meet us, our work and the products of our labor. Unless we begin with what our hands touch and our eyes see and our ears hear, we can never begin to know the spiritual and act with hope in our Lord Jesus Christ.

It is helpful to recall the main preoccupation in Paul's letters to the Thessalonians: one is the second coming of Jesus (as spiritual as anything can be) and the other is the necessity of manual work in 2:9 on Paul's part and in 4:11 on the part of the Thessalonians (as secular as anything can be). Authentic spirituality blends the two, does not separate them.

Prayer:

Lord, in all we do, say and think, we seek to give you glory and honor. By our faith we seek to bring a new fidelity and graciousness into our daily life and so to sing to you a new song.

Twenty-ninth Sunday, "B" Cycle

Isa 53:10–11. Through his suffering my servant shall justify many, and their guilt he shall bear.

Heb 4:14–16. We confidently approach the throne of God's grace where Jesus has entered, Jesus who is able to sympathize with our weakness as he was tempted in every way that we are, without sinning.

Mark 10:35–45. Anyone who aspires to greatness must serve the rest; whoever wants to rank first must serve the needs of all.

The Bible again demonstrates its uncanny (a better word would be its divine or inspired) way of blending the natural with the supernatural, leadership with others who are being led, humility and healthy aspirations. As happens often enough with the Sunday readings, the first and the third selection closely parallel one another, even to the point of the gospel's quoting from or alluding to the Old Testament passage. For this Sunday's liturgy of the word, Isaiah's remark about the suffering servant of the Lord is applied by Jesus to himself:

> He gives his life as an offering for sin (Isa 53:10).
> The Son of Man has come to give his life in ransom
> for the many (Mark 10:45).

While the first and third readings thus overlap, the second reading usually appears as a second-thought. Yet like an outsider who speaks from a healthy distance, the second reading frequently observes the inner truth and so unlocks for us the mystery of faith which binds the first and third readings together.

The Epistle to the Hebrews, the richly theological document from which the second reading is taken, insists in many different ways that the path of our human life has been trodden before us by a "cloud of witnesses," whose number includes not only the Old Testament heroes but also Jesus himself (Heb 12:1–4). Therefore, we can never argue, if we are honest and well-informed, that the saints and particularly Jesus do not understand. They also beckon us forward towards the heavenly sanctuary where Jesus has passed through the veil of his own flesh (Heb 9:24; 10:19). Jesus is at the head of a procession which includes ourselves.

Jesus does more than understand our human situation. He has endured every inch of our way of suffering. Again the Epistle to the Hebrews speaks of Jesus who "offered to God prayers and supplications *with loud cries and tears*" (5:7). Jesus, therefore, is:

> a high priest . . . able to sympathize with our weakness, . . . tempted in every way that we are, yet never sinned.

"Tempted in every way that we are"—this extraordinary statement makes us exclaim spontaneously: "Really?" and then with a sigh of relief, "How consoling!"

Temptations are often enough more shameful than our worst actions. We are baffled that such thoughts should ever have passed through our minds: unkind thoughts that would cut another down, impatient thoughts that would not tolerate our loved one any longer, vindictive thoughts that would get even in cruel ways, impulsive thoughts that would ride roughshod over the feelings of others. These temptations are far more shameful than any others, including those of a sexual nature. The first commandment towards our neighbor, also the second commandment of the entire Bible, concerns charity and justice towards our neighbor (Matt 22:37–38).

Jesus, tempted in every way as we are, "has passed through the heavens" "that he might appear before God now on our behalf" (Heb 9:24). Jesus speaks on our behalf from personal experience. Even though he never sinned, he realizes the pull of temptation and he has felt the lash and scourge of others' sins upon his own body. Jesus redeems us by being more than our eloquent representative. Jesus has thoroughly united himself with us, as the vine (1 Cor 12:12). Jesus is ourselves, and we are Jesus, even in the pores of our body where we sweat. Here Jesus sweat blood.

The reading from the prophet Isaiah belongs to the conclusion of what is frequently called the fourth Song of the

Suffering Servant. Earlier in the song we are told of the complete identification of the servant with the people Israel. The lines are very familiar to us:

> It was our infirmities that he bore,
>   our sufferings that he endured.
> He was pierced for our offenses
>   crushed for our sins (Isa 53:4).

The servant, we see, was no substitute for the people. Their infirmities and sufferings were his infirmities and sufferings. Because the servant bore an obedient, innocent heart in the midst of these offenses and sins, the servant's obedience and innocence belonged to the people. Therefore, we read in today's selection:

> Through his suffering, my servant shall justify many.

The servant justifies many, not by being their substitute but by being thoroughly one with them.

The same holds true for Jesus. As the Epistle to the Hebrews has already alerted us, Jesus is a high priest, able to sympathize with our weakness, even with our temptations. He too offered prayers with loud cries and tears, as we do. If Jesus is this completely one with us, then how obscene and ridiculous for any of us to claim superiority. Jesus refused to admit the power of allowing others to be seated ''at my right or my left'' in positions of glory above their neighbors, nor would Jesus tolerate the offense of the other ten apostles. They too needed to be corrected:

> Anyone among you who aspires to greatness must serve the rest; whoever wants to rank first among you must serve the needs of all.

As a convincing reason, Jesus points to himself:

> The Son of Man has not come to be served but to
> serve—to give his life in ransom for the many.

This spirituality is healthy for it does not short-circuit
any moment of earthly existence, even temptations; it is also
an honest spirituality, for it confesses sins and mistakes and
draws lessons from one's foibles; a loving spirituality, for it
keeps the first commandment of charity always first in its
bond of total union. It is also an effective spirituality, because all of us will be together with Jesus behind the veil in
the heavenly sanctuary.

Prayer:
      Lord, we feel the touch of your mercy upon us; so eas-
ily we place our trust in you. As we wait for you, we discover you already in our midst, you who are our shield, our
food in times of famine, our justice and righteousness even
in times of our sin and failure. The earth is full of your kindness.

Twenty-ninth Sunday, "C" Cycle

Exod 17:8–13. As long as Moses' arms are outstretched in
    prayer, Israel remains victorious against the army of
    Amalek. Aaron and Hur prop up Moses' arms!
2 Tim 3:14—4:2. All Scripture is inspired of God and is
    useful for teaching, correcting and training in holiness. I
    charge you to teach the word, never losing patience.
Luke 18:1–8. The parable of the widow, beseeching the
    judge continuously and never losing heart. God too will
    do justice to his chosen ones who call out incessantly.

The key, opening our door of prayer, comes from the second reading: "*constantly* teaching and never losing *patience*." Putting both words together we are able to beget the new one, "perseverance."

Each reading gives its own special insight into perseverance. In the Book of Exodus, unless Moses perseveres with his arms outstretched in prayer, Israel loses its crucial battle with the Amalekites. The Second Epistle to Timothy speaks of perseverance "from your infancy"; earlier Paul had referred to the "faith which belonged to your grandmother Lois and to your mother Eunice" (2 Tim 1:5). This perseverance includes docility towards "your teachers" and most of all towards "all Scripture." The gospel parable transfers these general statements into a pattern of action: "the widow in that city kept coming to the judge," who finally says to himself, "I care little for God or any human being, but this widow is wearing me out!" The judge is an example neither of patience nor constant teaching, our key words, but he proves that these qualities win the day in the person of the widow. Patiently and constantly she never gave up in teaching the judge a lesson in justice!

As we look more closely at each reading, unlocking its treasures old and new (Matt 13:52) through our key of perseverance, we first reflect upon the quality of prayer for winning God's favor. Perseverance is almost too bland a word in this circumstance. Many of us would question the cruelty of God, requiring us to keep on praying, even though God could stop the ravages of our troubles at once, really without our prayers. There is still another question: do we really want God to do everything God could do, and right now? Actually, we are fortunate that God is patient with us, allowing us to keep on praying and studying our Scriptures until we acquire more wisdom and certainly more restraint in what we ask of God.

Moses was praying for what was true and just, and the situation verged on total disaster. Amalek marched the army against Israel, either to annihilate this newcomer, encroaching on the small amount of water and grazing area in the Sinai desert and Negeb, or else to absorb Israel within his own ranks. Yet, God waited. And when Moses' arms drooped because they were understandably tired, the tide of battle turned in Amalek's favor.

We cannot enter into all the implications of biblical war during our meditation, but we ought to reflect upon the relation between prayer and fulfillment. Even in the case of Moses, God delayed fulfillment of what was true and just. This was one of those times, and we experience them as well, when we are helped more by waiting than by fulfillment. Isaiah put it succinctly and forcefully:

> By waiting and by calm you shall be saved,
>   in quiet and in trust your strength lies . . . .
> The Lord is waiting to show you favor, . . .
> For the Lord is a God of justice:
>   blessed are all who wait for God (Isa 30:15,18).

As we look back upon our lives, there are many times when it was to our advantage that God did not hear our prayer all at once. We too are not acting prudently if we give others what they want at once! Even in regard to sexuality and marriage, it is humanly prudent if God asks us to wait. By waiting we grow in proper understanding of the other person and in respect for what is sacred and good.

The Second Epistle to Timothy offers another insight into the importance of perseverance. Two sentences in particular can direct our meditation here:

From your infancy you have known the Sacred Scriptures.

All Scripture is inspired of God and useful.

We are being reminded to persevere a long time in studying the Bible, not only to season each day with God's words but also to extend our understanding to each book and even to each chapter of the Bible.

According to the rabbis every jot and tittle, "the smallest letter of the law . . . the smallest part of the smallest letter," "shall [not] be done away with, until it all comes true" (Matt 5:18). Thus spoke Rabbi Jesus! The longest psalm in the Bible dedicates the first eight lines of each stanza to the same letter of the alphabet and so proceeds one by one through each succeeding letter of the alphabet (Ps 119).

We need every sentence of the Bible, maybe not every sentence right this moment, but each sentence, the rabbis would insist each jot and tittle of each letter of each word of each sentence, sooner or later. Here is one of the byproducts of weekly and even daily mass. We store up biblical readings in our memory; we are thus prepared for the attack of our Amalekites.

"From your infancy" till old age we will always need to meditate upon the Scriptures. There are times when we need "reproof, correction and training in holiness," and there are other times when the Scriptures offers "hope . . . and the words of encouragement" (Rom 15:4). At times the Scriptures equip us for every good work on earth, but Paul immediately adds in this letter to Timothy: we prepare ourselves for that single, most important moment, when we stand "in the presence of God and of Christ Jesus, who is coming to judge the living and the dead."

Prayer:

Our help, Lord, is in you who made heaven and earth. You do not slumber nor sleep. Enable me to be always alert, persevering with the Bible in hand, from infancy with my grandparents and parents till death with my children and grandchildren.

Thirtieth Sunday, "A" Cycle

Exod 22:20–26. Israel's laws are conditioned by a compassionate concern for the defenseless person, the alien, the poor, the widow, the orphan, because I, the Lord, am compassionate.

1 Thess 1:5–10. You received the word of the gospel despite great trials, with the joy that comes from the Holy Spirit.

Matt 22:34–40. The first and second commandments, love of God and of neighbor, are the basis of the whole law and the prophets as well.

Upon initial reading the biblical selections for this Sunday seem simple enough. No one quarrels over Jesus' answer that love of God and of neighbor are the two greatest commandments or with the position taken in Covenant law code that all laws are to be administered with compassion, or with Paul's expectations of the Thessalonians that they imitate him and the Lord that the word of the gospel may take deep root in them.

Nonetheless, upon a second, more scrutinizing reading, questions begin to pop in our minds: if the Lord is a God of compassion, as he claims in the selection from Exodus, then why does he say that "my wrath will flare up and I will kill" those who violate the laws? Or in Thessalonians, if the people received Paul with joy and a sincere conversion, turning "to God from idols, to serve the living and true God," why then does it happen that the reception of the word was accompanied with "great trials"? Finally in the gospel, the Pharisees attempt to trip Jesus up and so they asked him to designate the greatest commandment (always a good way to get an argument under way—to name the greatest!). In response Jesus names *two* greatest commandments. Is this equivocation? Certainly, it was keenly diplomatic on Jesus' part!

Perhaps a quick solution to our problem lies in the simple rejoiner: we always argue with those whom we love! Strangers, even neighbors we can ignore, for what difference does it make? We seldom attempt to correct the manners of the friends the children bring home with them. Afterwards, we read the riot act to our own children if they do the same thing, dress the same way, act or speak in the same impolite style! Scriptures, therefore, which rely upon the basis of love and compassion, are bound to raise questions and arguments! Yet, it is always unsatisfactory to leave our family, friends or Scripture in a state of argumentation and questioning!

What Jesus calls "the greatest and first commandment" is enshrined in what may be the holiest lines of the most sacred part of the Hebrew Bible. The Torah or first five books of Moses are the most sacred. And in this sanctuary of God's presence as deliverer and director of Israel, the famous *shema* prayer occurs, the clarion call of Israel through the ages, spoken twice a day:

> *Shema Yisrael* —Listen, O Israel!
> The Lord is our God, the Lord alone!

There follows the formula of what Jesus called "the greatest and first commandment": to love God with all one's heart, soul and strength. The text of Deuteronomy then continues:

Take to heart these words . . . Drill them into
your children. Speak of them at home and abroad,
whether you are busy or at rest. Bind them at your
wrist as a sign, and let them be as a pendant on
your forehead. Write them on the doorposts of
your houses and on your gates (Deut 6:4–9).

Judaism follows these directions to the letter, fashioning little boxes with this and other sacred texts inside, to wear on
their forehead and left wrist when reciting the *Shema*, and to
be attached on their doorposts for reverencing on entry or
departure.

Surrounded on all sides with this commandment of
love, how can any Israelite not spontaneously love his
neighbor? This commandment, in the language of Jeremiah,
is ever new and can be renewed again and again with all the
fervor of a new convert. Jeremiah delcares:

No longer will they have need to teach their
friends and kinspersons how to know the Lord.
All, from the least to the greatest, shall know me,
says the Lord. (Jer 31:34).

When such love is violated and compassion is no
longer shown in the observance of the law, is there any wonder that questions, yes even anger and wrath will be stirred
up? Love, however, is always on hand to reassert itself with
forgiveness. Such love, nonetheless, is no soft, easy-going
maudlin type of affection which caves in with the first rain.
This love is strong, faithful, dependable and continuously
calling one to the covenant ideals.

As we read again the selection from Thessalonians for
this Sunday's mass, we realize that we should not be sur-

prised if the people's reception of the word of the gospel from Paul should be marked with ''great trials'' along ''with the joy that comes from the Holy Spirit.'' All of us willingly suffer for those whom we love. It is a natural part of life. We are proud to let it be known, and this pride, we rightly feel, is not punishable like other kinds of pride. If we suffer, then we also look forward to the final stage of the gospel, the second coming of the Lord Jesus. Paul writes about the Thessalonians:

> to serve him who is the living and true God and to await from heaven the Son he raised from the dead—Jesus, who delivers us from the wrath to come.

Instinctively we realize that our sorrows are a sharing in the cross of Jesus, and therefore our hope is strong in sharing in the ultimate victory of Jesus. Our suffering with and for one another is our surest guarantee to participate in the second coming of Jesus. Because charity is ''the greatest and the first commandment, and the second [of loving one's neighbor as oneself] is like it,'' then it is impossible to be present at the second coming selfishly alone!

If today's biblical readings about love and compassion raise questions and even angry disputes, they are following the normal way of love, and in this same way they find the solution and joyful outcome.

Prayer:

I love you, Lord, my strength, my rock of refuge, my stronghold. With love I confide myself to you; with love I trust my neighbor. Sustain this holy spirit always within me.

Thirtieth Sunday, "B" Cycle

Jer 31:7–9. Jeremiah announces the return of the northern tribes, exiled in their pitiable condition by the Assyrians.

Heb 5:1–6. Priests should deal patiently with erring sinners for they themselves are beset by weakness and must make sin offerings for themselves.

Mark 10:46–52. Jesus cures the blind man Bartimaeus, declaring "Your faith has healed you."

What Jeremiah announces, Jesus fulfills in the gospel. The spirit of the prophetic announcement as well as of the messianic fulfillment lies in humble compassion, the qualifying characteristic of the true high priest.

The distance between prophecy and fulfillment is spanned by a difficult, at times a frustrating road. Research into the words of Jeremiah, especially into chapters 30 and 31, brings to light the poignant disappointment, even the frustration close to despair that awaited Jeremiah. Jeremiah is here announcing the return of the exiled northern tribes, frequently called Ephraim in the Bible, from the name of one of their most powerful tribes. The north had been driven savagely into exile after two revolts against Assyria, in 736–32 and 724–22 B.C. Now, a century later in the days of the young man Jeremiah, Assyria is collapsing under the mighty blows of Babylonians, Medes and other lesser groups. The independent movement was lighting bonfires of revolt everywhere. Jeremiah joined in this chorus of excitement and jubilation. The north will return:

> carrying your festive tambourines,
> . . . dancing with the merrymakers,
> you shall plant vineyards
>   on the mountains of Samaria.

For the record, these northern tribes never returned. In fact, they are lost to history—and the subject of legend. What is not make-believe is the trauma of the prophet Jeremiah. The passage from chap. 31 read in today's mass, along with the other passage about Rachel's tears, was intended by Jeremiah in a way much different from the fulfillment announced by the New Testament in the life and ministry of Jesus. It may not be too outlandish to think that when the New Testament saw its fulfillment in Jesus, Jeremiah, now in the peace and charity of heaven, still shook his head in disbelief and mumbled to himself, ''No, that is really not what I meant!''

If prophecy is not fulfilled literally, nonetheless it is truly fulfilled, only with a new ''plus'' element that reaches beyond the horizon of the earlier prophet. Jesus' cure of the blind beggar Bartimaeus is turned into a sermon on faith. This type of application has a universal application which reaches us anywhere on the planet earth. Fulfillment then is not to be confined to a limited number of people within a circumscribed geographical location and time perameter.

In the gospel, moreover, fulfillment reaches beyond the purely historical or legal meaning of earlier words. Jesus acts, not to live up to verbal documents (he does that, yes, but he also does much more than that), but rather to find in Scripture a way to activate his interior compassion for outcasts. Kindliness and respect surround the healing of the blind Bartimaeus:

- Bartimaeus kept crying out all the louder, ''Son of David, have pity on me.''
- while bystanders were scolding the blind man, Jesus stopped and said, ''Call him over.''
- The bystanders now say, ''You have nothing to fear.

Get up! He is calling you!'' He threw aside his cloak, jumped up and came to Jesus.

- Jesus delicately asks, ''What do you want me to do?''
- ''Rabbi, I want to see.''
- ''Be on your way. Your faith has healed you.''
- ''Immediately he received his sight and [as though nothing unusual had happened, we are told simply that] he started to follow him up the road'' to Jerusalem.

This is not so much a Messiah and Savior, intent on fulfilling prophecy, but rather one anxiously compassionate. If no fuss is made over the miracle, the reason is the same. It is far more important that the blind person can see than that a miracle was performed. The single act of a miracle was but a stage on the way; the principal aspect of the way is the following of Jesus to Jerusalem.

The theme of compassion comes still more explicitly to our attention in the second reading from Hebrews. The epistle at this juncture is comparing the Jewish priesthood with that of Jesus. It is not so much that Jesus puts aside the old law and its ritual but that Jesus moves it a step further in reflecting God's design for true worship. Unlike the Jewish high priest in today's reading, Jesus did not have to ''make sin offerings for himself,'' as Jesus was sinless. Not to cloud the issue right here, we mention in passing how the Second Epistle to the Corinthians does say with a certain amount of exaggeration but also with a strong residue of truth:

> For our sakes God made him [namely, Jesus] who did not know sin, *to be sin* (2 Cor 5:21).

Other aspects of the high priest in the Epistle to the Hebrews are realized in Jesus:

- taken from among men and women and made their representative before God.
- able to deal patiently with erring sinners
- beset by weakness
- did not take this honor on his own initiative but only as called by God.

These marks of priesthood are mostly derived from compassion and understanding. These virtues then build the bridge between earth and heaven, between prophecy and fulfillment, between our blindness and sinfulness to the vision of God's glory.

Prayer:

Lord, you do wonderful things for us and fill our voice with laughter. We may have sowed in tears, long awaiting fulfillment, but now in abundant joy and good company, we reap rejoicing.

Thirtieth Sunday, "C" Cycle

Sir 35:12–14, 16–18. The Lord hears the cry of the oppressed. It pierces the clouds and does not rest till it reaches its goal.

2 Tim 4:6–8, 16–18. I have finished the race; I have kept the faith. I look for Christ's appearance with eager longing. The Lord will rescue me and bring me safe to his heavenly kingdom.

Luke 18:9–14. The parable of the publican and the Pharisee. Despite good behavior, the proud person is not justified; the humble person returns home justified.

We are urged today never to give up! In the short selection from Sirach, "the prayer of the lowly pierces the clouds [and] it does not rest till it reaches its goal, nor will it withdraw till the Most High responds." We are reminded of last Sunday's gospel about the persistent widow who wore down the unscrupulous judge (Luke 18:1–8). In the second reading it would seem that we are ready to give up for the good reason that "I have finished the race." Yet, Paul proceeds to give all sorts of instructions to Timothy: "Do your best to join me soon [along with] Mark [who] can be of great service to me . . . When you come, bring the cloak . . . and the books, especially the parchments" (2 Tim 4:9–13). If Paul sees the end, he intends to die in boots and saddle! Finally, in the gospel the word is: even if you are one of those dreadful publicans, one of those hated tax collectors, you too can go home justified. In fact, you seem to have a better running chance than the respectable Pharisee.

The first reading comes from Sirach, a master diplomat. He conducted a finishing school for noble youths in Jerusalem, as he states explicitly in 51:23, a subtle piece of free advertisement in the inspired word. Sirach covers his tracks rather well and cannot be accused of rhetorical excess. Although "the Lord is a God of justice . . . and hears the cry of the oppressed," Sirach, nonetheless, balances with a conditional rider: "God knows no favorites. He may be partial towards the weak, but not unduly so!" Sirach is advising us, never to give up, but also at the same time never to rush ahead impulsively.

Sirach may be prudent but he is no coward. In a line omitted from today's reading, a verse 15, Sirach warns the wealthy person about their harsh treatment of widows:

Do not the tears that stream down her cheek cry out against him that causes them to fall?

A beautiful line, indeed. God sees not only the tears on the face of the widow but also identifies the unjust person who brought on those tears.

As Sirach urges us to carry on, with prayers and hopes, he sees ultimate action on God's part for the indigent and mistreated people.

We must carry on energetically like the apostle Paul if we expect to repeat Paul's words:

> I have fought the good fight, I have finished the race, I have kept the faith. From now on a merited crown awaits me.

These lines could never have been written by someone who sat on his hands and waited for God to be the Savior. Justification by faith, proposed by Paul in Romans (Rom 1:17), is not to be pressed to the inhuman point of humanly doing nothing out of respect for God!

With Paul we reach towards horizons of hope beyond our human ability. Paul confesses that "the Lord . . . will bring me safe to his heavenly kingdom." Prayer was an important way by which Christ enabled Paul never to give up. At times Paul was so lost in prayer that he sensed "the Lord [who] stood by my side and gave me strength."

We can count on the Lord's consoling and strengthening presence. We also need the company of friends. In a series of verses, omitted from today's selection (vv.9–15) Paul refers to people like Demas who have deserted him and others like Crescens, Titus and Tychicus who were called elsewhere in the mission field. With a touch of pathos—and a tear which God would notice in Paul's eye as in that of the widow in the book of Sirach—Paul writes: "I have no one with me but Luke." Yes, to keep going we need friends; our friends need us. It is especially towards the end of one's life that loneliness can be dreadfully appalling. Even Paul felt its discouraging grip, the same Paul who had just written triumphantly:

> I have fought the good fight, I have finished the race, I have kept the faith. From now on a merited crown awaits me.

In order that the aged and the dying remain faithful to the end, we need to listen to Paul's appeal for them. We must never give up volunteering for such works of mercy.

Never to give up—that indeed is the theme of today's reading, vividly portrayed in the gospel parable. Some people felt that they could keep going for ever because of their conspicuous self-righteousness. True, as the Pharisee confessed publicly in the temple, he really was no grasping, crooked, adulterous person like many of the tax collectors or publicans. The Pharisee was blindly sinning by excess, inferring that every publican was evil. The publican is honest enough to admit his faults and to beg of God: "Be merciful to me, a sinner." And no doubt he was a sinner. Wasn't the Pharisee also a sinner, with the still worse sin of "holding everyone else in contempt"?

The gospel ends with a statement which appears elsewhere, again as a conclusion (Luke 14:11):

> Those who exalt themselves shall be humbled while those who humble themselves shall be exalted.

There are many ways of interpreting this floating "one-liner." For our purpose here, the humble person does not give up but keeps going, persevering so that the last can become first. The humble is always supported by a large company of friends. The person who sins is never alone! The proud, who are not like everyone else and hold everyone else in contempt, are isolated in their own homemade prison. The first have become last in dark isolation.

With prayer, with honest living, with continuous energy and strong hope, with humble company of others and with honest compunction before God, we shall never give up but carry on.

Prayer:

Lord, you hear the cry of the poor, our cry, for we are all poor and in need. We are at times brokenhearted and crushed in spirit, but you are always close by. You forgive the sins of the humble and redeem the lives of your servants. Let me never give up. Let me persevere till you come in glory.

Thirty-first Sunday, "A" Cycle

Mal 1:14—2:2, 8–10. God's good tidings, placed within our hearts and our community, will turn into a curse, if we break faith with God and with one another.

1 Thess 2:7–9, 13. Paul was among the Thessalonians, gentle as a nursing mother. He never imposed on them but supported himself by manual work, thanking God for the divine word within them.

Matt 23:1–12. Do not call anyone father or mother, teacher or rabbi. The greatest should be the one who serves the rest. Whoever humbles himself shall be exalted.

We approach the inner meaning, the secret message of the Spirit within all three biblical passages for this Sunday from the vantage point of the second reading. Paul's First

Letter to the Thessalonians (chronologically the beginning of the New Testament and its first section to be written) mentions his gentle attitude and describes the gospel as "God's good tidings." It is interiorly "at work within you who believe."

At this early point of his ministry, Paul is preoccupied with the second coming of the Lord Jesus. Even though "the day of the Lord is coming like a thief in the night," so that no one knows "specific times and moments," Paul writes as though it were imminent. An important section of chapter four is dedicated to this topic of the return of the Lord Jesus, with the conclusion: "Console one another with this message."

Yet, Paul is already highlighting the presence of Jesus within each disciple. This doctrine of the Body of the Lord will be developed in Paul's later epistles to the Corinthians. Writing in this letter to the Thessalonians, Paul refers to

> the message from us which you took, not as a human word, but as it truly is, the word of God at work within you who believed.

Almost each phrase of this sentence deserves our prolonged meditation. Paul's message was "not a human word [but] the word of God." Paul was not referring to any written word, because the New Testament was not yet composed. The word of God was received orally, audible sound structured within the pattern of the Greek language. Yet this blending of physical sound and rational sentence structure, the "human word" of Paul's message, contained at its heart a divine mystery. "It truly is the word of God." Paul's speech became a bridge between his own interior faith and the interior faith of the Thessalonians "who believed." After God's holy Spirit implanted this new life within Paul and within the Thessalonian converts, then the speech of the gospel message became, in Paul's lovely phrase, ''God's good tidings.''

Communication between Paul and the Thessalonians nourished God's presence. Clarity became a challenge in the spirit; it brought the Greek converts to the side of Jesus, interiorly present with them. As Paul's preaching was received within the heart of the Thessalonians and their implicit understanding of God's presence and holy will became clearer and ever more challenging, then ''the word of God [was] *at work within you* who believed.''

Communication such as this is delicate and gentle; the bridge between Paul and the Thessalonians rests its support ''in the spirit.'' What could be humanly so fragile, yet divinely strong and enduring? Because the span of communication is *cor ad cor*, spirit/heart to spirit/heart, Paul is enboldened to write

> that we wanted to share with you not only God's tidings but our very lives, you had become so dear to us.

Consequently, we take Paul's opening words in today's reading quite literally:

> We were among you . . . as gentle as any nursing mother fondling her little ones.

Interesting and intriguing! Paul portrays the secret moment of communicating faith with female imagery.

The selection from the prophet Malachi is stern, but we have grown accustomed to this attitude in prophecy. Malachi insists upon sincerity and upon a strong faith in God's directive word. The prophet's opening words are right to the

point: "You do not lay it to heart," a phrase to be repeated
again. Typical of prophecy, Malachi hones in upon the practical consequences of superficiality in religion, sterile for-
malism:

> you show partiality in your decisions [and] break
> faith with each other.

Faith should have led to that interior realization, which the
present situation forces the prophet to express in the form of
questions:

> Have we not all the one divine parent
>   [who is father and mother to us]?
> Has not the one God created [each and everyone of]
>   us?

From this background Malachi is always tilting towards the
salvation of the foreigners. This latter position is never developed by Malachi. It remained a germinal secret of life
within Old Testament religion, to be nourished and proclaimed by Paul.

Jesus follows in the tradition of Malachi. Jesus insists
upon the interior bonds of faith and its practical results in
daily life. Jesus excoriated those pious frauds whose religion is all show, "performed to be seen."

In the depth of faith, a life is engendered within each
person by "God's word . . . at work within you." Each person is called to reflect upon God's word and "lay [it] to
heart." Here in the most secret part of ourselves there is no
rabbi, teacher or even parent. God is creator, teacher, nurse,
protector, father, mother, brother, sister, our all.

If this language of Jesus were intended to be taken literally, "call no one parent, teacher or rabbi," then not even

Paul could compare himself to a "nursing mother fondling her little ones." Jesus is addressing the interior attitude of faith, the mysterious basis of life, where as Malachi explained, there is "the one God [who] created us" and the "one parent" of life. At this basis no one can exalt himself above the other. The greatest will be the one who serves the rest.

Prayer:

Lord, I have found my peace in you. Do not allow a proud heart nor haughty eyes to suppress the gentle life which you nourish within me. Like yourself, may each of us be instruments of peace, quieting the heart of others.

Thirty-first Sunday, "B" Cycle

Deut 6:2–6. The exhortation to obey all the statutes and commandments concludes with the first and greatest commandment to love the Lord, your God, with all your heart, soul and strength.

Heb 7:23–28. Jesus, the perfect high priest, remains for ever to save those who approach God through him. He lives to make intercession for them.

Mark 12:28b–34. The two greatest commandments center in love of God and love of neighbor. These are worth more than any burnt offering or sacrifice.

In meditating upon these biblical readings, we do not get very far, if we delay over the wrong or the negative interpretation. Neither the Old Testament nor the New Testament is rejecting religion with its ritual ceremonies and external, codified laws; nor for that matter was Jesus condemning our use of such titles as father, teacher or rabbi

(Matt 23:1–12). Jesus found unacceptable that parent, teacher or religious leader could function independently of God as the source of life and faith.

Jesus, in today's gospel, is quoting from Deuteronomy. This Old Testament book contains many rules for ritual ceremonies, sacrifices and other activities in the sanctuary. Jesus as high priest is not eliminating priesthood and ceremonies, no more than God as parent is removing parental acts of generating children, as well as teaching and disciplining them in the home.

Whatever is ritualized in church ceremonies as well as whatever is expressed with church authority began in the home and neighborhood. For that matter, whatever titles we give to God were first used in human society. Because we beget life, we call God father and mother; because we plant and care for vineyards, God is the parent stock or vine and we are the branches; because we are housekeepers, God is called builder and creator. The word which was originally used for a bedouin's tent and later for a stone or brick home becomes the word that is translated "temple" in another setting. The word for a king's palace turns into the name for the holy place of the temple area.

Religion, therefore, grows out of daily life, enables us to return to this secular existence with purer insights and more compassionate goals, so that we can again return to God with acceptable worship.

The gospel emphasizes this secular or worldly setting— "secular" and "worldly" being considered in the best sense of those words, the earthly home created by God and given to the human family as a home for their children, a setting for their labor and a place to meet God in the cool of the evening (Gen 3:8).

When we trace the original setting for the first and greatest of commandments in Jesus' estimation, we are back in the Book of Deuteronomy, in the first reading for today's liturgy. If we continue to read further in our Bible from where this selection is taken, we find these recommendations:

> Drill these words into your children. Speak of them at home and abroad, whether you are busy or at rest. Bind them at your wrist as a sign and let them be as a pendant on your forehead. Write them on the doorposts of your houses and on your gates.

The home and neighborhood provide the setting for this first and greatest commandment. The temple accentuates what is done at home and at the same time it focuses firmly upon God. Thus our home life is not smothered by business concerns or by arguments or selfishness. Our mind is to think and our arms are to reach out with this commandment of love for God inscribed upon them. Because this commandment can become blurred or even distorted by the unworthy ways at times of our minds and arms, we stand in need of ritual and ceremonies.

Yet, a warning is also needed. Unless we genuinely and effectively love God and our neighbor "at home and abroad, . . . busy or at rest," then our "burnt offering and sacrifice" become empty and even sacrilegious. Sacrilege and superstition are those erstwhile sacred actions which have lost their soul and their meaning, are actually a cover-up, pretending to be what they are not. Superstition is mere pretense of the sacred, sacrilege stains the sacred with its evil intent.

The Epistle to the Hebrews emphasizes the ways by which Jesus has exalted and purified ritual, not destroyed it. The death and resurrection of Jesus gathers into itself every moment of death and new life, every expression of love and heroic dedication, every nuance of law for loving God and one's neighbor with all one's heart, soul and strength. Jesus' earthly life imparts new meaning and dignity to its symbolic expression in liturgy. Again, we move from earth, to the sacred, so that we can return to our earthly activities and obligations with greater love and consecration.

Every human action, so easily scattered and diluted of its effectiveness and dignity, is now restored to its full unity in Jesus. The different types of temple sacrifices and the various categories of temple ministers are also seen to coalesce in Jesus, the one great high priest. The Epistle to the Hebrews urges us to recognize Jesus always and everywhere; to confess our faith in the continuous death and resurrection of Jesus ''at home and abroad, working or at rest.''

Prayer:

I love you, Lord, my life, my strength, my deliverer, my salvation. Your kindness anoints my daily life. And as I praise you at church, I perceive your presence everywhere about me. Lord, increase my faith.

Thirty-first Sunday, "C" Cycle

Wis 11:23—12:2. God loves all things that are and loathes nothing that he has made. God's imperishable spirit abides in all things.

2 Thess 1:11—2:2. May God make you worthy of his call and fulfill every honest intention and work of faith.

Luke 19:1–10. Jesus dines at the home of Zacchaeus, chief tax collector at Jericho, to the discontent of others. Zacchaeus promises fourfold restitution.

Today the Scriptures call us to graciousness and generosity, to respect for the world of nature and the society of human beings, to kindliness and forgiveness. The first reading from the Book of the Wisdom of Solomon (literature actually composed very late in Egypt and placed under Solomon's patronage) lays down the basis for this attitude in its address to God, "You love all things that . . . you have made." The second reading reassures us that the Lord does not come in an agitating and terrifying way but rather in "every honest intention and work of faith." The gospel episode about Zacchaeus exemplifies these principles within the first two readings.

One of the reasons for the composition of the Book of Wisdom in the Greek language and in the land of Egypt was to counteract current philosophies and pagan religions. The author also hoped to chart a way for the Jewish people in Egypt to appear reasonable to their non-Jewish neighbors and to realize a healthy integration within Egyptian society.

This encircling world, the author tells Jewish men and women in Egypt, has been fashioned by God, a simple statement from which important conclusions are reached in the form of a prayer to God:

> you love all things . . . and loathe nothing
> what you hated, you would not have fashioned
> nothing can remain unless you will it, nor
>   preserved unless you call it forth
> you spare all things, because they are yours,
>   O Lord and lover of souls
> your imperishable spirit is in all things.

This litany of earthly goodness excludes nothing: "You love all things." Sin, therefore, and evil are not to be found in what exists but rather in how they are used. Every sinful act, in a different set of circumstances, becomes a virtuous act, consecrated by the sacred anointing touch of the Creator.

The author, consequently, is combatting dualism, the philosophical or religious system which assigns some facets of reality to a good spirit and others to an evil spirit. Dualism claims that some things and for that matter some actions are by principle evil. This false spirituality can appear easy and simple. It draws a clear line separating good things from bad things. Saints and sinners are immediately identifiable. The authentic spirituality of the Bible, on the other hand, draws this line within the *intentions* of the human heart and within the *circumstances* of the action. People are simultaneously good as God's creatures and evil in some of their selfish actions. Things are created good but can be used badly. Moral judgments turn out to be complicated.

The Book of Wisdom, however, cannot be accused of materialism. What makes the earth a sacred place and the human body a temple of the holy spirit (to introduce some New Testament language) is the creative touch of God and God's imperishable spirit which guides human action and sustains earthly creatures. Otherwise,

> Before the Lord the whole universe is as a grain
> > from a balance
> or a drop of morning dew come down upon the earth.

Man and woman are given charge to till the earth and care for every living creature (Gen 1:28–30). In this way God's creative hand continues at work on earth to bless it; men and women, as instruments of God, keep in touch with God's imperishable spirit within themselves and across the planet earth.

In writing to the Thessalonians, Paul travels the delicate line between a good world and its bad use (or non-use). Paul is announcing the second coming of Jesus when the world will be remade into a new heaven and a new earth (Isa 65:17), yet he insists as well that the Thessalonians must not stop caring for the present world and making their livelihood from it for themselves and their family. Paul reminds them of his own efforts and toil:

> we worked day and night, all the while also preaching God's good tidings to you, in order not to impose on you in any way (1 Thess 2:9).

Therefore, Paul tells the Thessalonians:

> Work with your hands as we directed you to do (1 Thess 4:11). When we were with you we used to lay down the rule that anyone who would not work should not eat. . . . Earn the food you eat by working quietly (2 Thess 3:10,12).

From the background of the Book of Wisdom human labor which Paul endorses is not simply a punishment for sin. Rather it is a sacred way of cooperating with God's holy and imperishable spirit, creator and preserver of the universe.

The gospel exemplifies still further this same principle that everything and everyone are holy; it is only their evil use by reason of the selfish intention of the heart or the bad circumstances of the action which profane the holy and reduce people or objects to an unholy status.

Jesus invites himself to the home and dinner table of the wealthy tax collector of Jericho. Jesus is thereby consecrating food, deliciously prepared, and is declaring that the joy of participating in the banquet with the invited guests is a blessed happiness. Jesus is also seeing a sacred quality about the tax collector of Jericho, even though he was so small that he had to climb a tree to get a look at Jesus. Jesus is sanctifying quality, before quantity!

The crowds are right; "he had gone to a sinner's house as a guest." Zacchaeus confesses embezzlement and cheating in collecting taxes: "If I have defrauded anyone in the least, I pay that person back fourfold." But the crowds are not to be commended for murmuring and complaining that Jesus has gone to a sinner's house. Jesus saw an opportunity to change the circumstances and intentions in Zacchaeus' life. Zacchaeus remains a tax collector, but now an honest one. Zacchaeus was always a Jew, but now an observant one. Jesus enters into a new and good relationship with Zacchaeus, so that what was once evil is now sacred.

When Jesus finally declares that "the Son of Man has come to search out and save what was lost," we too are asked to help our neighbor, not by avoiding them as unholy and certainly not by destroying them, but rather by searching out the goodness already present within them and thus saving what had been lost.

Prayer:

Lord, you are gracious and merciful. Impart your kindness to me so that I too will always be slow to anger and compassionate towards all your works. You are faithful in your words and holy in all your works. Let me see your sanctifying and faithful hand in the words and works of my neighbor.

Thirty-Second Sunday, "A" Cycle

Wis 6:12–16. Wisdom is found by those who seek her and meets them with all solicitude.

1 Thess 4:13–18. We are consoled to know that the living and deceased will be reunited when the Lord comes again. Jesus who died and rose will bring to life all who have died believing in him.

Matt 25:1–13. From the parable of the ten bridesmaids, we learn to keep our eyes open, for we know not the day nor the hour.

We are being asked to develop a calm and believing attitude as we await the momentous coming of Jesus. Jesus will reappear, either to end our present earthly situation and inaugurate the eternal heavenly kingdom, or else to bring a dramatic, extraordinary grace into our earthly lives. The very prospect of either appearance is enough to accelerate our heartbeat and find us straining at the leash to break loose! Nonetheless, the Scriptures advise us to continue going about our normal way of life calmly (Book of Wisdom), strong in faith (Epistle to the Thessalonians), pursuing good works (Gospel of Matthew).

The Wisdom literature of the Old Testament, located in books like Proverbs, Ecclesiastes, Sirach and Wisdom of Solomon, lands with two feet squarely and calmly in a moderate or even conservative position. Prophetic challenge (Isa 1) and excitement (Jer 31) as well as the shouts and clapping in hymns of praise (Pss 47 & 150) do not properly belong in this literature. Wisdom literature makes very few demands upon us; many of the books can be read without any background in history, temple liturgy, etc. Job, another book in the sapiential tradition, is terribly upset because life is no longer moderate and peaceful!

The first reading for today from the Book of the Wisdom of Solomon typifies the finest and most ancient tradition of the sages. Although Wisdom includes a mysterious element at its heart, it can be found by anyone:

who loves her	who is prudent
who seeks her	who keeps vigil
who watches at dawn	who tries to be free of care.

We ask, who is this wise person today? First of all, he or she is that one who is a good listener, "watches at dawn" and "sits by the gate." They are people with wholesome desires and good hopes: "wisdom hastens to make herself known in anticipation of human desires." If we project good hopes and worthy desires upon others, people will tend to live up to our expectation. Greater wisdom and peace ensue. The wise person, moreover, will be sensitive and polite. Today's selection states that wisdom "*graciously* appears to them in the ways" of life. Finally, the wise person is solicitous about others, has an eye for their needs and weaknesses and "meets them" where they are.

If we follow these directions of the sage, we not only gain wisdom but we also welcome the Lord Jesus, who is "the way, the truth and the life" (John 14:6), the person wiser than Solomon (Matt 12:42).

The gospel describes another kind of preparation for the coming of the Lord Jesus. Parable is the medium of presentation, this time of the ten bridesmaids. This parable is one among others in a larger section of Matthew's gospel (Matt 24:36—25:30), insisting upon the need to be ready for the Lord Jesus. Vigilance is certainly one prerequisite. Another seems to be a concern for the daily needs in one's own family and among the wider family of neighbors even at a distance. "Oil" symbolizes good deeds in some Jewish traditions. In this case Matthew blends vigilance in prayer with a healthy cooperative spirit towards others. Matthew thus combines the two sides of the coin by which we win salvation: faith and good works. The foolish bridesmaids, therefore, did nothing in preparation for the wedding feast, or else were putting off their part of the work, or again were squandering their time. Suddenly, when all were awakened to the fact that the Bridegroom has arrived, the foolish ones hardly deserve any enjoyment in the festivities.

Similar to the first reading, we greet the Lord Jesus in non-exciting, non-dramatic situations. While the expectations are not heroic, not even threatening, still we take note of the fearful seriousness of this coming of the Lord. We may pass by a stranger in need; or we may be so lazy as to overlook the sick and the discouraged. We were not ready to greet the bridegroom and Jesus says to us, ''I do not know you.'' You were not there where I came to meet you.

The daily round of duties for oneself and for one's neighbor continues in Paul's Letters to the Thessalonians: ''Work with your hands as we directed you.'' This expectation appears only two verses before our present selection. And in the Second Letter to the Thessalonians, Paul becomes still more blunt and direct: ''Anyone who would not work should not eat'' (2 Thess 3:10).

Even though today's longer reading from Thessalonians calls upon apocalyptic language to announce the second coming of Christ the Lord (sound of the archangel; trumpet blast; caught up in the clouds; rising from the tombs), nonetheless Paul urges composure and strong faith:

Console one another with this message.
If we believe that Jesus died and rose,
God will bring forth with him from the dead
those also who have fallen asleep.

In many and varied ways then Jesus, our glorious, risen Messiah, comes to us. Sometimes we meet Jesus, even surprisingly in unsuspected moments, or amidst excitement and world transformation.

Prayer:

O God, my soul is thirsting for you, through night-watches and in the midst of tears, at church in the glory of the liturgy, in the everyday humdrum of family chores, in the hopes of my heart. I profess my faith that you will come and slake my thirst.

Thirty-second Sunday, "B" Cycle

1 Kings 17:10–16. A widow of Zarephath is willing to share her last food with Elijah and is rewarded with a continuous supply till the draught ended.

Heb 9:24–28. Christ has entered into the heavenly sanctuary to appear before God on our behalf. He will come to earth a second time to bring final salvation.

Mark 12:38–44. Unlike the ostentatious scribes and wealthy donors, the widow unobtrusively gives all that she possesses, two small copper coins.

When we give away the last of our possessions, we give ourselves away. There is nothing left, even of life. The words of the widow at Zarephath come to mind; "[I have left] only a handful of flour . . . and a little oil. . . . When we have eaten it, we shall die." While the widow in the gospel acts silently, her actions are interpreted for us by Jesus: "she gave . . . all that she had to live on."

We are looking at moments of profound, radical change. After such actions, which reach into the roots of our life, our life can never remain the same. Yet, such revolutionary moments may come in silent, insignificant ways; putting less than a cent into the collection or making a dinner out of a handful of flour and a little oil. Yet, this is the worship according to the Epistle to the Hebrews which Jesus offers in the heavenly sanctuary.

We must look more closely at the insignificant ways by which our entire life is changed. Some of these moments will be thrust upon us, others will be our own asking. Death is a moment over which we normally have little or no control, at least until its shadow falls upon us. Some deaths occur with drama, or at least the funeral attracts world attention, like the tragic assassination and momentous funeral of John F. Kennedy. At other times death hits suddenly but attracts no attention. A person is hit from behind by an automobile. Or someone slips on ice, breaks a hipbone and never recovers. Or the child falls from a tall tree. The litany is never ending. Each of these unexpected, insignificant but death dealing situations radically turn many lives around.

Religiously we must confess our faith that the hand of God was here, as Ps 139 confesses and Job admits: "We accept good things from God; and should we not accept evil?" (Job 2:10). Faith remains a mystery, for the forty some chapters of the Book of Job cannot explain why Job is being afflicted.

Or we can think of other situations when we must give everything, as little as it may be; and this "little" changes the course of our entire existence. For instance, at the time of marriage or of vows within a religious order or priesthood, there is no other way to happiness and life than to give everything. That everything may not amount to much on the stock market or glamour parade, but it's all we are. This insignificant gift of ourselves, however, takes on monumental proportions. Everything which we and a growing number of others (spouse and children and grandchildren; parishoners across a diocese; members of a religious community and its wide apostolate) are and will be for eternity is profoundly affected. Precisely because the gift is radical, inclusive of all that we are worth, it measures everything else in our lives in the scale of eternity.

The various ways, by which the poor put their two small copper coins into the temple treasury, become far more impressive and certainly more consequential than the elaborate robes, front seats, long prayers, places of honor at banquets and sizable donations of those who give from their abundance. In other words, God is more interested in receiving *ourselves* than in receiving our possessions. Whatever we give must symbolize the gift of ourselves.

The story about Elijah and the widow of Zarephath brings out another aspect of our total gift to God. We form a community of life with those in need, in this case the wandering prophet named Elijah. While we seem to be the benefactor giving to the other, the poor, needy person gives something more precious to us. Effectively, then, does the Scripture preserve the self-respect of each party, the one who receives and the one who gives. While the widow gives ''a little cake'' to the prophet, Elijah, who had nothing becomes the source of God's extraordinary blessing upon the home of the widow.

> the jar of flour shall not go empty, nor
> the jug of oil run dry until the day when
> the Lord sends rain upon the earth.

How many times, more often than we can count, the person whom we help turns out to be our lifesaver! Or to express this idea more carefully: the person to whom we give ourselves, is God's representative to save and enrich us. A spouse or a child in marriage, a new recruit in priesthood or religious life, a stranger whom we assist along the way, the litany again is endless, these bring exceptional joy and meaning into our existence. Each of these who first entered our life by surprise or by some kindly act on our part, turns out to be a source of marvelous, sometimes even of miraculous life.

Jesus, according to the Epistle to the Hebrews, has "entered heaven that he might appear before God now on our behalf." We who form one body with Jesus (1 Cor 12:12) and perform our good actions through the life of Jesus within us (Gal 2:20), are united with Jesus in this one, eternal offering of himself. Our small, insignificant deeds, even our silent daily prayers become part of the eternal service of Jesus in the heavenly Holy of Holies. How eagerly we await the glorious moment when our small copper coins become really and truly our very selves placed within the heavenly temple with all God's elect.

Prayer:

Lord, you keep faith forever, so that each small deed or moment of our lives is joined to yours as you reign in glory. As you enable us to protect strangers and care for the orphan and widow or widower, we find ourselves living with your compassion and you are transforming us into your likeness.

Thirty-second Sunday, "C" Cycle

2 Macc 7:1–2, 9–14. The martyrdom of the seven brothers and their mother, each encouraging the others to die for the sake of loyalty to God's law and of faith in the resurrection.

2 Thess 2:16—3,5. Pray that we may be delivered from confused and evil people. The Lord keeps faith and will guard you against the evil one.

Luke 20:27–38. The children of the resurrection do not
marry. They become like angels and are no longer liable
to death.

The Scriptures bring us face to face with one of the supreme mysteries of our faith, the resurrection of our body
from the dead. The fact of the resurrection lies beyond doubt
for the Christian. In his first epistle, the one written to the
Thessalonians, Paul was unflinching:

> If we believe that Jesus died and rose, God will
> bring forth with him from the dead those also who
> have fallen asleep believing in him (1 Thess 4:14).

In a key theological document, 1 Cor 15, where Paul is pro-
fessedly a man of tradition, the resurrection is central:

> I handed on to you first of all what I myself re-
> ceived. . . . If there is no resurrection of the dead,
> Christ has not been raised. And if Christ has not
> been raised, our preaching is void of content and
> your faith is empty too (1 Cor 15:3, 13–14).

While the *fact* is undeniable, the *mode* of the resurrection remains a theological disputation. Carefully comparing
the reading from Second Maccabees with the gospel, questions remain unsolved. The Maccabean family repeatedly
profess their faith in their bodily resurrection: ''The King of
the world will raise us up to live again for ever. . . . It was
from Heaven that I received these [hands and tongue]; . . .
from him I hope to receive them again.'' Yet, as the brothers
are dismembered (the liturgical text discreetly omits some of
the gory details) and piece by piece thrown upon ''the
heated pans and cauldrons,'' the theological question can be

raised: will these identical limbs, even the tongue, be restored in the resurrection? Most of us would reply in the negative, so long as the resurrected body has a tongue, two hands and feet, etc., and is suffused with the same immortal soul with which we live now and in which we possess our personality. But the answer, even if correct, remains theological speculation.

If we now compare the reading from Second Maccabees with the gospel, we are further confounded. If our body is restored exactly as it was during our lifetime, then what does it mean that the children of the resurrection "become like the angels"? Angels have no bodies. Jesus spoke this way in the context of a question from the Sadducees. These Jerusalem priests did not accept the relatively "new" doctrine of the resurrection. It surfaced clearly in the Old Testament only with the Book of Daniel, chap. 12, and the Second Book of Maccabees, our chap. 7. The Sadducees ask Jesus whose wife the woman will be, having been married while on earth to seven brothers, one after the other. She had done this to fulfill the law of the levirate (Deut 25:5–10). If marriage as it exists on earth is not to be found in heaven, then our resurrected body will have some notable differences in heaven. Again, theological speculation.

Returning to the mystery of the resurrection of our body, we risk everything for what remains unknown in details. Mystery remains with every doctrine: the Blessed Sacrament; the Incarnation of the eternal Word within the womb of Mary; etc. We do not know *how* it takes place. *That* it happens is professed even on threat of death, as in the case of the Maccabean brothers and mother.

As children of the resurrection, we will exist for all eternity in our earthly identity and personality: therefore, as husbands and wives, fathers and mothers, sons and daughters, priests and religious, martyrs and confessors. We will manifest all these bonds of love and faith in our resurrected body. The bonds, moreover, will be closer and more intimate than anything on earth. This *fact* we believe along with all its unresolved mystery. In Jesus' words the children of the resurrection will be fully and truly alive:

> God is not the God of the dead but of the living.
> All are alive for him.

In writing to the Thessalonians Paul presents the resurrection of the dead as a way to "console one another" (1 Thess 4:18). Paul returns to the same need of consolation in the Second Epistle to the Thessalonians:

> May God our Father who loved us and . . . gave us eternal consolation and hope console your hearts and strengthen them for every good work and word.

The resurrection of the body then should provide the needed momentum to keep going with good works, performed with our earthly body. Therefore Paul continues:

> In the Lord we are confident that you are doing and will continue to do whatever we enjoin.

We see here a careful line of continuity between our physical action now and the resurrection of our body.

Faith in the resurrection, finally, is not blind trust in mysterious, doctrinal fact. It is confident love in a person, our Lord Jesus Christ. Jesus never said that *it* is the resurrection but rather "*I am* the resurrection and the life" (John 11:25). And in today's gospel the resurrection is expressed in terms of persons: "as children of the resurrection, they are children of God.'' Prayer with, through and in Jesus who rose from the dead will always strengthen our faith in our own resurrection.

Prayer:

Lord, when your glory appears on the day of resurrection, we will be sharing in this wonder. Within our heavenly home we will realize how you have watched over us as the apple of your eye; in death you have hidden us in the shadow of your wings; in the full justice of your promises you will raise us to behold your face.

Thirty-third Sunday, "A" Cycle

Prov 31:10–13, 19–20, 30–31. The classic collection of Israel's wisdom is summarized and symbolized by this portrait of the ideal wife.

1 Thess 5:1–6. The day of the Lord's second coming will be like a thief in the night. We are children of the light . . . awake and sober.

Matt 25:14–30. Parable of the silver pieces. Ten, five and two thousand are given to three servants according to their ability. The last is severely punished for not making a good use of the silver pieces.

Today's readings offer excellent examples of service and work, of courage and ingenuity. The gospel blends well not only with the texture of faith and good work in the larger section here of Matthew's gospel (Matt 24:36–25:30), but also with one of Matthew's minor themes, the paralyzing effect of cowardice—i.e., when Jesus reprimands the disciples during the storm at sea, ''Where is your courage?'' (Matt 8:26). The portrait of the ideal wife is presented as a conclusion to the entire Book of Proverbs, an epitome of all the directions throughout the book for right behavior and prudent activity. Finally, the second reading from the First Letter to the Thessalonians indicates that along with industrious work we need to be "awake and sober" at all times, alert to sudden changes. Human life seems to consist of a creative molding of reality and a humble, obedient surrender to reality.

We of the twentieth century find problems within the parable of today's gospel. Lest we condemn the master for distributing his silver pieces unjustly, part of the difficulty, anyway, disappears in recalling that one thousand pieces of silver, given to the third person, was still an enormous wealth. Since there is only so much that anyone can prudently do in a lifetime, another million dollars will make little difference! Secondly, the silver pieces were distributed "according to each person's abilities." The intention from the start was to draw upon this ability to make the best use of the silver pieces. "According to each person's abilities" implies that each one had enough to use prudently, but not too much to squander or to be overwhelmed. Understood correctly, the parable is right on target with the themes of Matthew's gospel and the culture of the time.

The parable implies trust on the part of the master or employer, industriousness on the part of the servants and employees. After distributing the silver pieces, the master "then went away." This quick notice should not be overlooked. The master did not hang around, look over the shoulders of the servants, continually give advice and show displeasure at their doing things differently than himself. "He went away." There was now "a long absence," allowing the servants more than a fair chance to experiment and learn. Upon his return, he "settled accounts." His expectations were small, only that each one should have been "industrious and reliable.'' Upon receiving a good report, the master was overjoyed and put the servant ''in charge of larger affairs.''

In the parable, of course, Jesus is the master and we are the servants. Transposing its details, in the form of an allegory, the story leaves us pleased and amazed. Pleased that Jesus puts such trust and confidence in us; amazed that Jesus should take such pleasure in our insignificant accomplishments. We are also overwhelmed to be rewarded for doing only what was expected of us!

It is interesting to note that the first reading shifts from industrious *men* to the industrious *woman*. This conclusion, typical of Proverbs, goes into more detail than the gospel story. The passage is quite important sociologically for what it recognized about the public role of women in Old Testament times. For this aspect we ought to read the entire twenty-two verses. Incidently, twenty-two is the number of letters in the Hebrew alphabet, the perfect or complete number symbolically, in which every letter of the word of God takes on a special significance!

The ideal wife shows exceptional independence and ingenuity:

> she obtains wool and flax and makes cloth
> she secures provisions from afar
> she purchases a field and out of her earnings plants a
>   vineyard
> she reaches out her hands to the poor
> she makes garments and sells them
> she watches the conduct of her household

Most of all, she epitomizes the entire wealth of prudence and wisdom in the Book of Proverbs, certainly the classic collection from Israel's most famous sages.

Linking this section with the gospel, we see that God grants equal trust and equal ability to men and women.

A wise person, moreover, must know how to accept reality, work with reality, seek to improve it and to share it. The most difficult part of accepting reality lies in accepting the changes which come within the real world. Some changes repeat themselves over and over again. Most persons move through infancy, childhood, adolescence, adulthood, old age and death. Drawing upon the storehouse of human experience, each person ought to be ready for these stages of life. Some changes come suddenly and irreversibly: types of sickness, unexpected deaths in the family, serious changes in financial resources or employment, etc. Paul writes graphically:

> Just when people are saying, "Peace and security," ruin will fall on them with the suddenness of pain overtaking a woman in labor, and there will be no escape.

Even if the day of the Lord comes like a thief in the night, however, Paul advises us that "you are not in the dark that the day might catch you off guard."

If sudden changes belong to the real world, of which God is the creator and controller, then our faith prepares us to adapt and even to grow spiritually in these circumstances. It helps us to avoid bitter regrets; it engenders a mellow or warm spirit. Like the master in the gospel, we are enabled to give to others our silver pieces that the new generation can continue where we left off. We give to them confidently, trustingly. From a distance we rejoice in their accomplishments. Even when darkness closes in upon us, we remain, as Paul writes:

. . . children of light and of the day. We belong
neither to darkness nor to night

Our eyes are ever more accustomed to the coming of the
Lord Jesus in glory.

Prayer:
    Happy are we, O Lord, who are guided along the way
of wisdom. Our daily lives become our temple, preparing us
to be at home with you in church and eventually in the heavenly Jerusalem. As we eat the fruit of our handiwork, we
taste some of the sweetness of heaven.

Thirty-third Sunday, "B" Cycle

Dan 12:1–3. The splendid resurrection of the just is an-
    nounced.
Heb 10:11–14, 18. Jesus' offering of himself as a sacrifice
    for sin perfects those who are being sanctified. No further
    offering is needed.
Mark 13:24–32. Severe trials of every sort precede the com-
    ing of the Son of Man. As to the exact day or hour, no one
    knows, not even the Son, but only the Father.

    The church year is quickly coming to a close. Advent
will begin a new year, ecclesiastically and liturgically, as we
begin preparations for the new birth of Jesus. While next
Sunday, the final one of the "old" year, celebrates gloriously the Kingship of Jesus over our entire lives, in fact
over planet earth and all peoples, this Sunday's readings
provide a more tranquil setting for meditation.
    The references to the resurrection of the just in the

Book of Daniel, to Jesus' perfect offering of himself for sin
in the second reading from Hebrews, and finally to the second coming of Jesus in the gospel—all reminds us that we
become an entirely new, transformed person at the end. In
other words we enter heaven, innocent with all our sins forgiven, wrapped in the new flesh of the resurrection, linked
with the assembly of God's "chosen from the four winds,
from the farthest bounds of earth and sky."

This appreciation of ourselves and others at the end of
life expands or corrects our own small or warped hopes.
Most of the time we think of ourselves reaching heaven like
an old, beaten up automobile which squeaks into the parking
lot of the used car dealer. It made it in one piece, we sigh;
we'll get something after all in the trade-in. Heaven is not a
used car lot, nor Jesus the dealer. God tells us to look forward to "new heavens and a new earth [where] I create Jerusalem to be a joy and its people to be a delight" (Isa
65:17–18). Or in the vision of Ezekiel Israel becomes an entirely new creation:

> The Lord said to me: Prophesy over these [dry,
> scattered] bones . . . Dry bones, hear the word of
> the Lord! . . . See! I will put sinews upon you,
> make flesh grow over you, cover you with skin,
> and put spirit in you so that you may come to life
> (Ezek 37:4–6).

At the end of the church year, therefore, as at the end
of our life, our vision ought to be of new heavens and a new
earth, of new bodies and souls as innocent and as good as the
Spirit of God who indwells. As we turn to the second reading from Hebrews and read it in this context, we realize the
full scope and intense power of the sacrifice of Jesus upon
the cross:

> By one offering he has for ever perfected those
> who are being sanctified. Once sins have been for-
> given, there is no further offering for sin.

Because of the absolute perfection of Jesus' sacrifice on the
cross, the perfection and fulfillment of the ritual acts of the
old covenant, the end has come. Yet it is actually the beginning of an entirely new creation. The repeated acts of the old
covenant belong to the past. Because this final, perfect sacrifice of Jesus is commemorated in the Mass, each Eucharist
reminds us of the new heavens and new earth and our new
resurrected condition. There is no excuse for our not being
people of overwhelming hope.

The charity of the new heavens and new earth will enable us to look back upon the preceding church year, in fact
upon our entire life, and realize clearly how every part and
parcel of it fits together smoothly. Wisdom triumphs. Such
is the vision imparted to us by the Book of Daniel, from
which the second lesson is taken.

The young man Daniel is introduced to us as "hand-
some, intelligent and wise, quick to learn, and prudent in
judgment" (Dan 1:4), but most of all, as the archangel Ga-
briel addressed him, Daniel was "a man beloved" (Dan
9:23). With the insights of charity, we will be truly "wise"
and as such we "shall shine brightly like the splendor of the
firmament . . . like the stars forever." Everything about our
lives shall proclaim the compassionate and bonding love of
God; this love will be perceived in our own individual lives,
in all of our relationships with others, in the lives of every
other person. We are reminded of Ps 136, named "The
Great Hallel" and sung every sabbath when Israel rested
with God in paradise (cf., Gen 2:2–3). *Hallel* is the Hebrew
word for praise. Ps 136, in the first half of each verse,
moves through the entire history of Israel, actually from the

creation of the universe to Israel's settlement in the promised land. The second half of each line repeats the same refrain as in a litany:

> *ki   le'olam   ḥasdo*
> indeed, for ever [is] his bonding love.

We too will sing this same refrain, in the company of all the "wise," over each stage of our earthly life.

Meditating upon this grandiose moment, we become impatient, just as the early church longed and aspired for the second coming of Jesus, or as the disciples of Jesus during his early life strained at the bit to reach the glorious messianic moment. Jesus had two pieces of important advice:

> first, a period of "trials of every sort"
>   and the seeming collapse of our entire world;
> second, "as to the exact day or hour,
>   no one knows it, neither the angels in heaven
>   not even the Son, but only the Father."

No trials should frustrate or destroy us, even if "the sun will be darkened, the moon will not shed its light, [and] stars will fall out of the skies." We will discover at these moments a depth of consecration to God, an insight into reality and a bonding in love with others. Such we find in the stories about the prophet Daniel.

Even when taken by surprise with sudden sickness, financial loss, unemployment, death in the family, serious disappointment with children, probing questions about the church, we are prepared.

Prayer:
    Keep me safe, O God; you are my hope in the midst of trials and temptations. Through faith in your wisdom and

love I know that my heart will be glad, my soul rejoice and
my body too abide in confidence.

Thirty-third Sunday, "C" Cycle

Mal 3:19–20. The day is coming, blazing like an oven, but
for you who fear my name, there will arise the sun of justice with its healing rays.

2 Thess 3:7–12. Paul worked day and night, laboring to the
point of exhaustion. All Christians should earn the food
they eat by working quietly.

Luke 21:5–19. The temple will be destroyed . . . signs and
wonders in the heavens . . . persecution . . . yet do not
worry about your defense. It will be given you what to
say. By patient endurance you will save your lives.

The Scriptures weave honesty, realism and practicality
into the readings. We are about to end the church year (see
Thirty-third Sunday, "B" cycle); the liturgical readings
prepare the right attitude within us. The attitude of honesty
and realism admits "wars and insurrections, earthquakes,
plagues and famines, fearful omens and great signs"; and
the converse side of practicality warns everyone against
"not keeping busy but acting like busybodies" for they
should "earn the food they eat by working quietly." It is always difficult to keep on doing the practical thing when the
end seems near; we easily give up. Some people give up so
early that they are dying comfortably and without anxiety
over the last fifty years of their life!

Every so often, and for some people more severely than
usual, the world falls apart. For Judaism the cataclysm came
first with Jesus' radical preaching to the outcasts and his disciples' mission to the world, and then with the Roman de-

struction of Jerusalem and the burning of the temple. "Not one stone will be left on another." If any stones are left at the Western Wall of the former temple enclave (sometimes called by Christians the wailing wall), these are only a most poignant reminder of the once beautiful temple at this spot.

The gospels remind us, as Pope Pius XI once wrote, that "we are all spiritually semites" and must relive the experience of Judaism. Our temple, once "adorned with precious stones and votive offerings" will crash upon our heads. For reasons unexplainable to us, God will seem to disappear, Jesus will seem silently dead in the grave. Prayer becomes dry and barren. "Not one stone [of our former spirituality] will be left upon another, but it will all be torn down." Or it may be that the sacred place of our marriage, or our priesthood, or our vocation to religious life or single career seems desecrated and useless, devoid of God and of our previous sense of holiness.

At such times we badly need the advice of Jesus:

> Take care not to be misled. Many will come in my name, saying, "I am he [or she—or it—exactly what you are looking for]. The time is at hand." Do not follow them.

This is the dangerous time; it inevitably comes to every happy marriage, contented priest, peaceful religious or satisfied single person. It is usually associated with someone calling out to us and attracting us away from our committed loyalties to God and our loved ones.

Another way by which the heavens collapse with "fearful omens and great signs" comes with betrayal or compromise. We feel as though our former friends, even our blood relatives, are bringing us to public trial by their rumors and misunderstanding. Jesus goes so far as to say that "you will be delivered up even by your parents, brothers, sisters, relatives and friends."

Our response cannot be rehearsed ahead of time. Does any person prepare for such betrayals? If so, they live in continual suspicion towards their spouse, their family, their community in religious life. Jesus reassures us:

> I will give you words and a wisdom which none of your adversaries can take exception to or contradict. . . . By patient endurance you will save your lives.

The last statement indicates that our response at times will be silence, yet a silence with strength, loyalty and dignity. We are reminded of the Suffering Servant in Isaiah (Isa 50:4–9a) or of Jesus on the cross. The ancient Latin translation for the last line of the preceding quotation reads: *in patientia vestra possidebitis animas vestras*—"in your patience you will possess your souls."

The short reading from the prophet Malachi hits the nail on the head. On this "day . . . blazing like an oven" within our spiritual desert, at the seeming collapse of one's life, "there will arise the sun of justice with its healing rays." God will not forsake us always and for ever, only "one moment yet, a little while," according to the prophet Haggai (2:6).

Assuredly, then, "there will arise the sun of justice with its healing rays." These words of the prophet Malachi are helpful. Just as we are at the end of the ecclesiastical year, Malachi is the last book of the Twelve Minor Prophets, and in some editions of the Bible, like the *New American*, the final book of the Old Testament. Yet, Malachi, even at the end of the Bible, returns to most practical advice, particularly in chap. 2:

Priests, teachers and advisers: true doctrine
   should be in their mouth, no dishonesty,
   but instead, integrity and uprightness;
   a covenant of life and peace.
Friendship: have we not all the one Father . . .
   the one God who created us? Why then do
   we break faith?
Marriage: why have you broken faith with the
   spouse of your youth? I hate divorce.

This same down-to-earth, practical advice continues in
Paul's Letter to the Thessalonians. Even though Paul had
advised them to ''console one another with this message''
about the second coming of Jesus (1 Thess 4:18), nonetheless, he also insists:

We worked day and night, laboring to the point
   of exhaustion so as not to impose on any of you
   [and] present ourselves as an example for you
   to imitate;
We enjoin . . . urge strongly in the Lord Jesus Christ
   that you earn the food you eat by working quietly.

We remain on earth as we aspire for heaven. We need both
realism and idealism, or better, a faith in Jesus our glorious
savior as we walk faithfully the path of earth.

Prayer:
   Lord, you are coming to rule the earth with justice and
to fulfill all your promises. May we be your instruments of
justice and equity, and so bring melodious songs from the
hearts of all your faithful ones.

Thirty-fourth Sunday, Solemnity of Christ the King, "A" Cycle

Ezek 34:11–12, 15–17. Parable of the divine shepherd who rescues the scattered sheep, seeks out the lost, binds up the injured, heals the sick, judges between the wicked and the good.

1 Cor 15:20–26, 28. In his resurrection Christ represents the first fruits of all those who belong to him. He will hand over this kingdom to the Father.

Matt 25:31–46. The final judgment by the Son of Man, seated upon his royal throne, rewarding those who cared for him while caring for "my least brothers and sisters," punishing those who did not care for him in these "my least."

While the readings for the preceding Sunday, all three cycles, tilt the scale towards our human work and our mutual cooperation on earth, today's solemnity of Christ the King weights the scale in favor of God's action. From Ezekiel comes the firm statement that we have been *lost* sheep, sick and injured, and must *be found*. We do not find Jesus; Jesus seeks us out. From the important chap. 15 of First Corinthians, which is a classical statement or creed of the very early church, we have been dead and therefore lifeless, only in Christ do we come to life again. Finally, in the gospel, our misconceptions are corrected and we are judged, not by our human wisdom and experience but by the Son of Man, escorted by angels and seated on the royal throne.

It is reassuring that Jesus is our final judge, not ourselves nor any human law court. We are ultimately saved by our faith that the divine Shepherd will not permit us to die lost in the wilderness; and when called by death as is every child of Adam, we do not remain in the grave but will come to life again in Christ. Finally, what we at times judge worthless, as it was done only to "my least brothers and sisters," is seen by Jesus as done to himself and worthy of eternal life with him.

In the mystery of faith, it is not that our human wisdom and bodily actions are worthless. Rather, Jesus perceives more wisdom in our judgments, more goodness in our actions, than we ever gave ourselves and others credit for possessing:

> When, Lord, did we see you hungry and feed you, thirsty and give you drink, a stranger and welcome you, naked and clothe you?

Jesus' reply amazes us. You did it when you thought to be doing little or nothing for "the least."

This judgment scene in the overall context of Matthew's gospel maintains its healthy divine-human interchange. Words alone will not save us. Words do not give shelter to the stranger nor clothe those people shivering from the cold. Matthew consistently wants good deeds to accompany our faith. Matthew's gospel is also a document for church structure. The "little ones" or "the least" are seen by Matthew to be those disciples of Jesus who are sent as missionaries (Matt 10:40–42). At the judgment then Jesus is questioning our zeal, our church loyalty, our missionary spirit.

While we are judged ultimately by the small acts of the "corporal works of mercy," the prophecy of Ezekiel reverses the exchange. *We* are the lost sheep in need of shelter, food, clothing and healing. God seeks us out, finds us and so "I give them rest." Tenderly enough, a virtue somewhat unusual for the prophet Ezekiel, who is generally stern and unemotional, an excuse is found for our scattering "into every place." Ezekiel remarks, "it was cloudy and dark!"

We are able to do the kindly acts for "the least of my brothers and sisters," because we have already experienced such consolation from God in our own lives.

Beyond the painful condition of being lost, injured, hungry and thirsty lies the unknown terrain of death, which Paul calls "the last enemy to be destroyed." Here is the ultimate moment of God's tender, life-bestowing love for us.

We become even more completely a member of the flock of the Lord. We are given total rest, when the Lord finds us, heals us, binds up our broken limbs and brings us back—and finally when the Lord brings us back from death to eternal life. "In Christ all will come to life again." Every pore of our existence, every ounce of our blood, every beat of our heart belong to God in Christ Jesus.

Even though death resulted from sin, our own personal sin and the sin of our common human nature from Adam and Eve, nonetheless, what is caused by sin becomes the occasion for totally removing sin. Because we are rendered completely powerless in death, Jesus' life-giving touch reaches into the absolute depths of our existence. This extension of God's love touches us in our most sensitive area of personality, in our hopes, secrets and mystery. All that is opposed to God is overcome; this "all" must be taken literally.

This moment, when shared with the family of all God's elect, signals the moment for Jesus to say:

> Come! You have my Father's blessing!
> Inherit the kingdom prepared for you
> from the creation of the world.

"All has been subject to the Son," who in turn "will then subject himself to the Father who made all things subject to him." Thus "God may be all in all."

Christ appears then as king of the tired and weary, of the broken and lost, of "the least of the brothers and sisters." Christ is king because he became thoroughly one of them, even to the point of dying upon the cross. Christ is king as the first fruits of those who rise from the dead. Christ shares his resurrection with us, his total life in God the Father. "Thus God may be all in all."

Prayer:

Lord, you are my shepherd. Even when lost in the dark valley, I do not fear and there is nothing I shall want. You guide me along your path into the resurrection, anoint my head with fragrant oil and spread a table of goodness before me. To speak your goodness is to sing your praises in the kingdom of your Son Jesus.

Thirty-fourth Sunday, Solemnity of Christ the King, "B" Cycle

Dan 7:13–14. The Son of Man, coming on the clouds, receives an everlasting kingdom, with nations and peoples of every language serving him.

Rev 1:5–8. Jesus Christ comes amid the clouds. Every eye shall see him, even of those who pierced him. He loves us and has freed us from our sins by his blood.

John 18:33–37. My kingdom, says Jesus, does not belong to this world. Anyone committed to the truth hears my voice.

As mentioned last week, we are at the end of one church year, about to begin a new church year with Advent. The solemnity of Christ the King enables us, peacefully to confide our preceding year into the hands of God, hopefully and more wisely to look ahead. The biblical readings guide us in this process. The Book of Daniel locates us towards the end of a terrifying persecution (167–165 B.C.); the gospel reading from the Passion narrative, in the final moments of Jesus' earthly life. Once again the second or middle reading provides a different viewpoint and opens up a fresh insight for us. The Book of Revelation inaugurates a new, transforming moment for the Son of Man and for the world. In fact the book opens with the urgent announcement: " . . . the revelation [of] what must happen very soon."

This blend of the old and the new, of endings and beginnings, is characteristic of the New Testament message. The skillful scribe of the kingdom of God brings forth from the storehouse things old and new (Matt 13:52). By means of the motif of the "son of man" who comes with the clouds of heaven, the three readings are tied together; each looks backward and forward. While Daniel is recounting the end of a major oppression of Judaism, he also announces the final, eschatological kingdom. In John's gospel Jesus is in the final stage of his ministry, yet confidently alludes to "my subjects" who are "committed to the truth [and] hear my voice." This is not the statement of a beaten, frustrated person but of someone optimistically anticipating the future. The Book of Revelation, as mentioned already, is communicating "what must happen very soon," yet looks backward to the cross, in fact backward to all sinful acts on the part "of those who pierced" the Son of Man.

Who, we ask, is this mysterious Son of Man? Or perhaps the question should be reformulated: How is Jesus to be understood and appreciated as Son of Man? We are in the position of Pilate, pressing Jesus for answers: who are you? a king? where did you come from? (John 18:33; 19:9). Jesus was silent before Pilate. Humbly we pray that Jesus will speak with us.

Jesus appropriated the title "son of man." This phrase occurs frequently enough in the Old Testament. It always infers a special relation with God and actually has a more mysterious meaning than another title, "son of God," which was bestowed upon all Israel (Hos 11:1) and especially upon the kings at Jerusalem (Ps 2:7). The "son of man" is that one just a little less than the angels (the Hebrew text says "gods" in Ps 8:5–6), yet hounded by God and not "left alone long enough [even] to swallow my spittle" in Job 7:17–21, thrown to the ground by a fearful vision in Ezek 2:1. In chap. 7 of Daniel "son of man" is identified with "the holy ones of the Most High [who] shall receive the kingship" after being the victims of "war [waged] against them" (Dan 7:18, 21).

As "son of man," then, Jesus tastes the lowest stages of human existence (Heb 2:9) "with loud cries and tears" (Heb 5:7), and here in the depths of his person Jesus realizes that his entire existence is to be the Word spoken by the Father, the creature formed by the Creator, even the corpse brought back to life to become "Son of God" in full glory (Acts 13:28, 33).

The "Son of Man" who "comes amid the clouds [so that] every eye shall see him"—in today's second reading from Revelation—appears as one who has been "pierced." How this final, devastating proof of death was burnt into the memory of the Beloved Disciple in John's Gospel:

> One of the soldiers thrust a lance into his side. . . . This testimony has been given by an eyewitness, and his testimony is true. He tells what he knows is true, so that you may believe.

For John, it seems that the more baffling and difficult truth about Jesus is not the Lord's divinity but the bottom line of Jesus' total humanity.

The ''Son of Man'' becomes a parchment upon which our own sins are inscribed:

> He was pierced for our offenses,
>   crushed for our sins,
> Upon him was the chastisement that makes us
>   whole [literally, ''the disciplinary suf-
>   fering of our peace,'' in Hebrew *shalom*]
>   by his stripes we are healed (Isa 53:5).

This inscription of our sins has become our healing and our new life. The story of our infidelity is turned into a hymn to God's compassion. At the same time that

> they shall look on him whom they have thrust through, and mourn for him as one mourns for an only child (Zech 12:10),

we are also praising his ''dominion, glory and kingship [where] nations and peoples of every language serve him.''

As we look backward and look upon him who has been pierced by our sins of the preceding year, we are sorrowful. Yet as we and ''all the peoples of the earth lament him bitterly'' (Rev 1:7), we also look ahead peacefully to our future, healed of our weakness, wiser through our experiences. By our redemption through Jesus we belong to ''an everlasting dominion that shall not be taken away [nor ever] destroyed.''

As a wiser people, we resemble at least somewhat the prophet Daniel to whom ''God gave knowledge and proficiency in all literature and science . . . the understanding of all visions and dreams'' (Dan 1:17). We are ever more surely the disciples of Jesus ''committed to the truth,'' because as Jesus says to Pilate in today's gospel, this one ''hears my voice.'' Seeing our own sins and our healing in the dead body of Jesus, thrust through with a lance, we listen in the thunderous silence of such intimacy and love to the full truth about Jesus, our King.

Prayer:

Lord, upon the cross you are our king, robed in splendor. Your decrees of forgiveness, love and trust are forever inscribed upon your flesh. We confess you as our Savior and our God, yet truly one of us as ''son of man.''

Thirty-fourth Sunday, Solemnity of Christ the King, "C" Cycle

2 Sam 5:1–3. The northern tribes of Israel anoint David their king, declaring themselves to be ''your bone and your flesh.''

Col 1:12–20. God has brought us into the kingdom of his beloved Son and has reconciled everything in his person, making peace through the blood of his cross.

Luke 23:35–43. This is the king of the Jews. ''Lord remember me when you enter upon your reign.'' Jesus replied: ''This day you will be with me in paradise.''

This last Sunday of the church year, solemnizing the Kingship of Christ, enables us to acknowledge Jesus' dominion over the preceding year and to proceed onward into the new church year, reconciled through the blood of the cross. The biblical readings lead us across this threshold from the old year to the new year. The first reading from the Second Book of Samuel turns out to be mostly a political statement. The selection from Colossians is compressed with theological terminology. Finally, the gospel modulates into what is touchingly human, the conversation between the thieves crucified with Jesus and Jesus' reply to the ''good thief.'' Every part of ourselves belongs to the kingship of Christ, our politics, our theology, our humanity.

If we place the first reading within the sequence of events in the Books of Samuel, we find:

- Saul's persecution of David and the battle with the Philistines where Saul commits suicide (1 Sam 18–31);
- the anointing of David as king by the *southern* tribe of Judah (2 Sam 2:4);
- civil war between the forces of David and the forces of Saul's son Ishbaal (2 Sam 2:8—4:12);
- after the murder of Ishbaal the *northern* tribes come to David and anoint him as their king (2 Sam 5:1–3).

A series of tragic events, therefore, led up to a desperate struggle for survival. David remained the only political hope for a united north and south to overcome the Philistine domination and to emerge once again as an independent people.

When the liturgy chooses this reading from the Second Book of Samuel, it sanctifies and holds up for our example a political statement. On this feast of Christ the King, the liturgy urges us to discern in our own human way of life, with its tragedies and political moves, with its mistakes and successes, a path leading to the Kingship of Christ over us.

Coming to Jesus, we repeat and adapt the words of the
northern tribes:

> Here we are, your bone and your flesh . . .
> It was you who led us out and brought us back
> in the ways and byways of our existence.
> You are our shepherd. We solemnly agree
> to this and anoint you as our king.

A much more theological statement about the Kingship
of Christ is found in our second reading from the Epistle to
the Colossians. It recognizes that even our former way of sin
can contribute to our being absorbed within Christ's dominion:

> God the Father . . . rescued us from the power of
> darkness and brought us into the kingdom of his
> beloved Son. Through him we have redemption,
> the forgiveness of our sins.
> It pleased God to make absolute fullness re-
> side in him and, by means of him, to reconcile
> everything in his person; everything, I say, both
> on earth and in the heavens, making peace
> through the blood of his cross.

We should take the inspired word seriously: *everything* has
been reconciled *in his person*. We repeat to Jesus the words
of the northern Israelites: "Here we are, your bone and your
flesh." Wrestling with this mystery Paul wrote to the Corinthians:

> For our sakes God made him who did not know
> sin, *to be sin*, so that we might become the very
> holiness of God.

And as we reread further into the selection from Colossians for today, this sense of total solidarity with Jesus in his kingdom, that is, in his person, is repeatedly affirmed:

> In him everything continues in being.
> He is head of the body, the church,
> He is the beginning, the firstborn of the dead.
> God made absolute fullness reside in him.

This fullness embraces the presence of the godhead everywhere, as ''the heavens declare the glory of God and the firmament proclaims his handiwork'' (Ps 19:2).

While The Epistle to the Colossians leaves us somewhat breathless with its all-embracing theology of Christ's kingship, the gospel episode reasserts the human shape of it all. We need both expressions, just as Jesus as King is both divine and human. The gospel of Luke is here touching upon various human moments in the death scene of Jesus: the people's silent watch while the leaders keep jeering; the soldiers' self-entertainment; the seemingly ridiculous inscription above the cross, declaring Jesus to be a king; the sarcasm of one of the criminals and the tender response of the other criminal; finally the generous assurance of Jesus, ''this day . . . in paradise.''

The cross of Jesus enables us to refer in contradictory terms to the ''good criminal'' or ''the good thief.'' At various times and in different ways we have been the angry sarcastic person, the poker of fun at the defenseless, the offerer of sour wine to the person down and out, the selfish questioner who speaks without fear and deference. No matter where we have been, no matter what poise we have struck at the foot of the cross, we can still become the ''good criminal.'' All that God asks is an ounce of humanity and another ounce of humility; it should not be too difficult then to react with compassion and mercy. We pray in the Our Father, "Thy kingdom come . . . forgive us our trespasses as we forgive those who trespass against us." Jesus, who asks so little, promises us so much: "This day—on this solemnity, at this end of a church year—you will be with me in paradise."

Prayer:

Lord, we rejoice as we hear it sung round about us: let us go to the house of God, to the heavenly Jerusalem, to the place of your reign in paradise. In prayer and in faith your kingdom already reaches out to us on earth. We rejoice.

PART THREE

Feasts and Solemnities

September 14 - Feast of the Triumph of the Cross

Num 21:4–9. Those who had been bitten by the seraph ser-
    pents, were told to look at the bronze serpent which
    Moses had mounted on a pole, in order to be healed.

Phil 2:6–11. Christ Jesus, born in our human likeness, obe-
    diently accepted death on a cross and so was exalted by
    God and received a name above every other name.

John 3:13–17. Just as Moses lifted up the serpent in the de-
    sert, so must the Son of Man be lifted up, that all who be-
    lieve may have eternal life.

At first Moses' action may strike us as a bow to idolatry
or at least a surrender to popular superstition. How can people, who had been bitten by poisonous snakes be healed by
looking at one of those snakes, molded in bronze and
mounted on a pole?

The incident begins, typical of what was happening
among the Israelites in the wilderness. In fact, only three
days after they had been led through the Red Sea from slavery to freedom, they were grumbling about the foul-tasting
water. The place where this happened came to be called
Marah, the Hebrew word for "bitter"; another important
place name was *Meribah*, a Hebrew word for "dispute." Israel was constantly and bitterly disputing with God. Today's
first reading begins:

> With their patience worn out by the journey, the
> people complained against God and Moses: "We
> are disgusted with this wretched food."

Grumbling became a major theme in this biblical story of the
exodus. It provides the setting for such important theologi-

cal motifs as waiting upon the Lord, patience, faith, forgiveness, hope and self-discipline.

All of these religious themes seem to rest upon the bedrock of honesty and compassion. If we are not honest enough to admit reality, we begin to have false hopes, to make selfish demands and to live in a fantasy world. We easily give up when dream bubbles burst. We are never satisfied with even the best efforts of our family and friends. Expecting the impossible, we cannot forgive the possible human frailty in others. Patience runs thin, hopes explode, faith gives out, and we are bitter against God and our neighbor. Our rancor attacks and destroys ourselves most of all.

Moses went to the bottom or root of Israel's distress and demanded honesty. "Look," he seemed to say, "look at what you are and what you are doing. Look the evil straight in the face." He made an image of their sin and its punishment and mounted it on a pole. The serpent, for these people, symbolized sensuality and deceit, as we see in Genesis chap. 3, and it also pointed out the bitter effects of selfish grumbling.

When the people looked at the bronze serpent, they recovered. When they admitted honestly the reality of their bitter complaints and begged God to heal them, then they were far along the way to full recovery. That the people's actions were not simply superstition or idol-worship, we can tell from their words to Moses:

> We have sinned in complaining
> against the Lord and you.
> Pray the Lord to take the serpent from us.

Here is an excellent biblical example of the effective use of statues or images and of the prayer of intercession.

The incident of the bronze serpent typifies Jesus on the

cross and enables us to appreciate better the mystery of Jesus' crucifixion. Jesus becomes ourselves, even as Paul wrote to the Corinthians:

> For our sakes God made him [Jesus] who did not know sin, *to be sin*, so that in him we might become the very holiness of God (2 Cor 5:21).

Jesus "emptied himself [of his godhead] and took the form of a slave, being born in our human likeness, obediently accepting even death, death on a cross."

When we look at the cross, we see ourselves and confess the effects of our sins. Jesus was made "to be sin," our sins, our grumbling, our impatience, our complaints, our inability to forgive.

> Yes, God so loved the world! (John 3:16).

If on the cross we discover our honest self, sinful and ungrateful, we also find ourselves closely united with Jesus and Jesus with ourselves. If we look upon the cross with this kind of faith, we are healed and saved. "There is no other name in the whole world given to men and women by which we are to be saved" (Acts 4:12).

This recognition of ourselves, our evil and grumbling self, stamped upon the dying person of Jesus, is what John is writing about. To accept this union of our sinful self with Jesus' sinless self, to perceive such love on Jesus' part that he looks like ourselves and takes our burdens upon himself—all this requires unusual faith.

> Just as Moses lifted up the serpent in the desert, so must the Son of Man be lifted up, that all *who believe* may have eternal life in him.

We believe! Strangely enough, this kind of faith is not so much believing in Jesus' overwhelming divinity as in his total humanity, one ''able to sympathize with our weakness . . . tempted in every way that we are'' (Heb 4:15).

We have arrived at salvation, for we have reached most intimate union with Jesus, by honestly recognizing ourselves as we truly are and then by being drawn to look at the crucified Jesus.

Prayer:

Even when we lie to you, Lord, and seek to flatter you with false promises, you still provide a way of salvation. You turn back your anger and ask us to be honest, to confess our weakness and guilt, and to find our poor selves in your compassionate heart. Lord, we bend our knees before you, our God, our crucified Savior, ourselves in our sins and in our hope.

November 1 - Solemnity of All Saints

Rev 7:2–4, 9–14. The 144,000 from every tribe of Israel are the ones who have survived the period of great trial.

1 John 3:1–3. We shall see God as God is, for we are God's children. All who have this hope keep themselves pure as God is pure.

Matt 5:1–12. Jesus teaches the disciples the blessedness of following him as poor in spirit, sorrowing, single-hearted, peacemaker.

The Scriptures reaffirm and expand the blessing of this solemnity. We are honoring all the saints, not just those singled out for canonization. ''All saints'' designates men and women, girls and boys whose lives are so ordinary as to go unnoticed, who are not conspicuous for any heroic manifestation, who are not held up as noteworthy examples of martyrdom, confessing the faith, performing works of kindness. "All saints" have done all of these things, but in such a matter-of-fact, take-it-for-granted style, as though "this-is-my-life," that after a generation or two, they are forgotten. Their memory becomes absorbed within the next generation who without knowing it live the same normal, faithful way of discipleship. Yet, the new generation is alive with faith and goodness because of "all saints," their ancestors.

Even though not canonized by name, "all saints" have their name inscribed in the eternal book of life (Ps 139:16; Dan 12:1), never to be overlooked by God. Today we join with God in celebrating this wondrous "cloud of witnesses" (Heb 13:1).

"All saints" come from everywhere. This fact is emphasized in the selection from the Book of Revelation. The verses omitted from the liturgical reading call the twelve tribes of Israel each by name and ascribe to each the number of twelve thousand elect. Each person bears the "seal on the forehead of the servants of God." Twelve thousand symbolizes completeness, a thousand times over: the number twelve stands for the complete embrace of the twelve tribes of Israel; the number thousand for abundance. No one is missing; everyone bears "a seal on the forehead of the servants of God." Some of these tribes like Reuben and Simeon disappeared quickly from the history of Israel when their tribal portions were overrun by foreigners; other tribes like Benjamin and Gad were small; still another tribe like Levi possessed no property; the tribe of Dan is not even mentioned while Joseph gets double citation, himself and his son Manasseh; the royal tribe of Judah gets no more attention than any other. On this feast of "all saints" no one is missing and there are no favorites. No one has a head start on the others. Everyone is called to holiness.

The gospel continues this same general call to sanctity but it also provides more detailed instruction. Matthew's gospel, as compared with Luke's, portrays Jesus as the new Moses. In true rabbinical manner, Jesus is *seated* while giving instructions. Even though the teaching is imparted directly to the disciples who accompanied Jesus "up on the mountainside," not to the crowds on the plain below, nonetheless these disciples are to spread out across the countryside and to teach all the people.

The general application appears ever more clearly in comparing Matthew's beatitudes or blessedness with Luke 6:17–23. While in Luke Jesus addresses "you poor," seemingly those materially hard up, in Matthew the audience becomes "the poor in spirit." This third person, "the poor," and this category of "poor in spirit," is all-embracing. Everyone, no matter what may be his financial situation, is included.

The beatitudes, moreover, make few demands, except that we interact realistically with our lives. At one time or another everyone feels:

poor in spirit	thirsting for holiness
sorrowing	single-hearted in goals
lowly	peaceful

On second thought, however, reality can be very demanding. God endows us with faith to recognize the divine presence in our sorrow and goals, in our thirsting and lowliness. This perception of faith becomes ever more clear, provided, first of all, that we do not isolate ourselves in self-commiseration, but live openly and trustingly within our family and community; and secondly, that we see in our lowliness and sorrow an effective way to reach out to others in their pain and poverty.

In this bond of faith within the extended family of the church or within our immediate family or neighborhood and community, we realize how our being poor in spirit has settled the reign of God in our midst; how consoling others in their sorrow brings the blessedness of forgetting one's own sorrow; how sharing one's goods with others soothes the hunger and thirst within ourselves. With such blessed single-heartedness in reaching outward, we become "children of God" and even "see God." "Where two or three are gathered in my name, there am I in their midst" (Matt 18:20).

In the Beatitudes Jesus draws us together in the realism of our daily lives and shows us the opportunities of sanctity right here. The promise of the beatitudes comes true when we live as a family of faith. This is the condition where the second reading from the First Epistle of John meets us:

> See what love the Father has bestowed on us
> in letting us be called children of God!
> Yet that in fact is what we are.

As children of one and the same Parent, we are one family in receiving and sharing life. The Epistle of John repeats the promise of the beatitudes:

> We shall be like God,
> for *we shall see God* as he is.

In this context we understand the prescription to keep oneself pure "as God is pure." Purity refers primarily to the spontaneous openness to God's presence in our church and family. Without shame or inhibition, we share ourselves and we share others, in sorrow and hope, in rejoicing and reward. Purity in the language of the beatitudes is "single-heartedness." "They shall see God."

All saints, then, are our family and relatives, our neighbors and parishioners, our community members, our ancestors, that "cloud of witnesses" who accepted the godly realism of their lives, shared it with others and so already on earth, as now before the throne of the Lamb in heaven, are truly "Blessed!"

Prayer:

Lord, this is the people that longs to see your face. And you allow us to seek and find you in the pathway of our daily lives. May we always desire this humble, ordinary way of life, for it is your way of holiness for us.

November 2 - Commemoration of All Souls (*)

Job 19:1, 23–27. I know that my Vindicator lives; my inmost being is consumed with longing.

1 Cor 15:51–57. Death is swallowed up in victory. Thanks be to God who has given us the victory through our Lord Jesus Christ.

John 6:37–40. Everyone who looks upon the Son Jesus and believes shall have eternal life. I will raise up that one on the last day.

Today we commemorate gratefully and lovingly the faithful departed. They are on the final lap between death and eternal happiness in heaven. With consolation the scrip-

(*) The reflections are based upon the first of the three masses for this day.

tures remind us that the bonds of earthly love and dependence are still maintained. In a very unique way they and ourselves reach towards each other with inspiration and help. The reading from Job rests on the faith that our bonds of love and life are rooted in God. In First Corinthians the paralyzing sting of death is removed; death's apparent victory is swallowed up in Jesus' resurrection from the dead. Therefore, all of us together share in the resurrection. Finally, the gospel assures us the certainty of eternal life, enjoyed already by the souls in purgatory, pledged to us by Jesus.

The faithful departed are on the final stage before reaching heaven. They have died and been judged faithful. They have already glimpsed the presence of Jesus in a way far more intense and intimate than ever upon earth. Their desire and thirst for God both tantalizes and strengthens them. They are joyful with their desires, for they *already* possess what they seek; they are *sorrowful* with their desires, for they do *not completely* possess what they seek. Their pain, consequently, is evoked by the intensity of their desire. This pain is purifying, for it springs from love and partial possession. The more it purifies, the greater the love, the closer the full possession, and mysteriously enough the greater the pain. Loving ever more passionately yet separated ever more slightly, how much more painful is the longing for the loved one.

This unifying and separating love is present in the word "Vindicator." A line from the Book of Job refers to God in the Hebrew form of *go'el*, our "vindicator." The word *go'el* basically means bonded by blood and consequently to be obligated to help and protect one's relatives. Blood calls out this strongly, as each member of the human body immediately and instinctively goes to the rescue of the other members (1 Cor 12:26). Chapters 25 of Leviticus, 35 of

Numbers and 25 of Deuteronomy discuss some of these obligations of the *go'el.*

Job calls upon God as ''my *go'el.*'' Job is using a word that was applied to God repeatedly in Isaiah 40–55, where God undertakes the demands of blood by bringing his people back from slavery and by repeopling the city of Jerusalem (Isa 43:1–7; chap. 54). Once the word is applied to God, it is usually translated ''redeemer.''

If such is the intimate bond of blood between ourselves and God, then little wonder that Job speaks as daringly and as boldly as he does. His words, with a clash of images typical of the Semitic person, are inscribed . . . with an iron chisel and with lead . . . cut in rock forever,'' that is, inscribed and cut unforgettably in the flesh and blood of the *go'el* relationship. Because Job lives, he knows that ''my *go'el* lives, my bonded or blood relative, God!'' Because of this intimate bond:

> my own eyes, not another's shall see him,
> from my flesh I shall see God
> my inmost being is consumed with longing.

The same *go'el* relationship binds us together with the faithful departed and with God. As we pray for God's mercy upon them, they share their longing for God with us. We intercede that God increase the love which will purify their hearts and hurry the moment of vision; they reach out to us and impart within us this longing of their blood, really our mutual blood, for God. The purification of purgatory begins already with us.

Our *go'el* bond of life has truly overcome death and its sting. Now we can better appreciate Paul's words to the Corinthians. In the important chapter 15, a mini-creed or formula of faith he writes: ''I handed on to you first of all what

I myself received . . . in accordance with the Scriptures" (1 Cor 15:3). While Paul deliberately writes "in accordance with the Scriptures," he knowingly reverses one of the biblical texts that he quotes! His reference in today's mass is to the prophecy of Hosea:

> Where are your plagues, O death!
> where is your sting, O nether world!
> My eyes are closed to compassion. (Hos 13:14).

Typical of New Testament fulfillment, prophecy reaches a completion that equals the Old Testament *plus* the new revelation in Jesus. And as a matter of fact, if we reread the entire prophecy of Hosea, other intuitions of this "plus" factor can be detected, as in the outburst of divine passion:

> I will not give vent to my blazing anger.
> I will not destroy Ephraim again;
> For I am God, no human person (Hos 11:9).

The holy souls in purgatory see ever more clearly what we intuit from afar. They are already within reach of eternal life, the loving arms of Jesus; but they are not yet closely within the embrace. The sting of death has been removed, but they are still sensing the pain of love which only complete union with Jesus can heal. The healing process is accomplished by the same love which makes the separation momentarily very painful.

In our bond of life with the faithful departed, we too, with them, give "thanks to God who has given us the victory through our Lord Jesus Christ."

This bond is as close as blood. Therefore Jesus admits in the gospel:

I do not do my own will . . . but the will of him who sent me that I should lose nothing of what he has given me.

We, who look upon the Son with faith, have eternal life. Our prayers for the faithful departed increase that faith and love within us; they draw us to look upon the Son with ever greater longing. Jesus, therefore, states clearly, ''I will raise [you] up on the last day.''

Prayer:

Lord, our shepherd, you are leading us through dark valleys of faith, ourselves on earth, our beloved ones in purgatory. We gladly endure the pain of loss for it purifies our love and quickens the day when we will dwell together in your house.

November 9 - Feast of the Dedication of St. John Lateran

2 Chron 5:6–10, 13—6:2. Solomon dedicates the temple with elaborate ceremony. The ark is placed within the Holy of Holies. The Lord's glory filled the temple.

1 Cor 3:9–13, 16–17. You are the temple of God, a structure that is holy, a temple where the Spirit of God indwells. The foundation can be none other than Jesus Christ.

Luke 19:1–10. Jesus invites himself to dine at the home of Zacchaeus, the tax-collector, who returns stolen goods fourfold. The Son of Man has come to search out and save what was lost.

This feast honors the cathedral church of Rome and its bishop, the successor of St. Peter. This is a day then for celebrating the unity and holiness of the entire, worldwide body of Christians. Although the cathedral church of St. John Lateran is a material structure of stone, marble, wood and other substances, the biblical readings enable us to detect a deeper symbolism and a rich spiritual value for ourselves.

The first reading from the Second Book of Chronicles brings the long history of Israel to a magnificent climax. Actually in the Jewish arrangement of the Holy Scriptures, this is the final book. And its last verses, which inspired Jesus' farewell instruction to the disciples as world missionaries in Matthew's gospel (Matt 28:16–20), center "all the kingdoms of the earth" around God's "house in Jerusalem." The scope of Solomon's dedication becomes still more comprehensive in the simple act of bringing the ark of the covenant into the temple and enshrining it within the Holy of Holies. This ark had led the people Israel through all their history. From Moses to this day the ark embodied all of God's marvelous deeds for his chosen people.

Every church, but particularly St. John Lateran, is heir to the temple traditions. The walls of this cathedral church have heard the story of world conversion and world unity, of persecution and new life, of triumphs and defeats, of saints and sinners. Likewise the walls of our parish churches and community chapels have ears for other thousands of prayers. Here God's people have been baptized with parental hopes and joys, here they have married with hopes for their own family, here they have been buried with a promise of eternal peace. The parish church has listened to prayers of agony and prayers of thanksgiving. It has witnessed the salvation history of its family of faith, just as the Jerusalem temple had done.

This salvation history has been awesome and overwhelming, beyond our understanding yet within our experience. With this in mind, the reading from First Chronicles tells how ''the building of the Lord's temple was filled with a cloud . . . since the Lord's glory filled the house of God.'' The church's memories also envelop us in a blinding cloud of glory and like ''the priests,'' we too can ''not continue to minister.'' We are stunned with wonder and excitement. St. John Lateran's church is filled with such a cloud, both because of what it has seen in the past and because of what its hope indicates for the future.

The wonder of the church comes from its people. It is what the walls hear of their prayers and hymns that consecrates the walls with sacred oil. Therefore, St. Paul wrote to us, in the person of the Corinthians:

> *You* are God's building . . . the temple of God.
> The Spirit of God dwells in you.

The foundation is none ''other than the one that has been laid, namely Jesus Christ.'' Many have cooperated in the building. Paul claims:

> Thanks to the favor God showed me, I laid a foundation as a wise masterbuilder might do, and now someone else is building upon it.

Again we see how the temple, composed of the living stones of our lives, contains a wondrous history. The preaching of the gospel through the centuries has contributed to who we are as the temple of God.

When we transpose the image of the temple to ourselves and our living bodies, then the masterbuilder Paul requires obedient faith as the foundation. By this faith we believe in Jesus as our savior; by this same faith we are directed in healthy moral living. Paul, however, had to admit that not everyone builds with the same quality of work and material:

> different ones build on this foundation with gold,
> silver, precious stones, wood, hay or straw. . . .
> Fire will test the quality of each one's work.

This feast, therefore, is a day of triumph and glory, of memories and graces, but also of challenge and the need to build well and to submit to purification.

The gospel meets us at this point. Zacchaeus is not a saint. In fact, the people who murmur that Jesus eats "at a sinner's house" may be wrong in their murmuring but they are dead right in their estimate of Zacchaeus. Zacchaeus admits his sinfulness by declaring: "If I have defrauded anyone in the least, I pay that person back fourfold." The Mosaic law required only 20% restitution (Num 5:5–10)!

The temple of Zacchaeus' person and dwelling is reconsecrated not simply by the presence of Jesus but also by Zacchaeus' strong and practical reformation of morals. Zacchaeus typifies the entire history of Israel and the ministry of Jesus. The history is frequently called "salvation history." Therefore, Jesus declares about Zacchaeus: "This is what it means to be an offspring of Abraham and Sarah." Such is the long experience of their children. Such is the history of Jesus:

> The Son of Man has come to search out
> and save what was lost.

This feast of St. John Lateran confirms the long salvation history behind us. By this memory it revives our faith and desire for holiness and repentance. It leads us forward into the cloud of glory whereby we are the living stones of the eternal temple of God.

Prayer:

Lord, how lovely is your dwelling-place. How beautiful are the living stones of your saints. Let me dwell in this your holy temple and become a lasting member of its edifice. Invite me beyond the threshold into your heavenly Holy of Holies.

Biblical Index

(Asterisk indicates a more extended reflection)

Topical Index

ALSO BY CARROLL STUHLMUELLER: